Israeli Society in the Twenty-First Century

Publication of this book is supported by

Michael Liberman (Brandeis '85) and Polina Liberman

in honor of Professor Jacob Cohen, beloved mentor of

generations of Brandeis University students

The Schusterman Series
in Israel Studies

EDITORS

S. Ilan Troen

Jehuda Reinharz

Sylvia Fuks Fried

The Schusterman Series in Israel Studies publishes original scholarship of exceptional significance on the history of Zionism and the State of Israel. It draws on disciplines across the academy, from anthropology, sociology, political science and international relations to the arts, history and literature. It seeks to further an understanding of Israel within the context of the modern Middle East and the modern Jewish experience. There is special interest in developing publications that enrich the university curriculum and enlighten the public at large. The series is published under the auspices of the Schusterman Center for Israel Studies at Brandeis University.

FOR A COMPLETE LIST OF BOOKS IN THIS SERIES,

PLEASE SEE WWW.UPNE.COM

Calvin Goldscheider, *Israeli Society in the Twenty-First Century: Immigration, Inequality, and Religious Conflict*

Yigal Schwartz, *The Zionist Paradox: Hebrew Literature and Israeli Identity*

Anat Helman, *Becoming Israeli: National Ideals and Everyday Life in the 1950s*

Tuvia Friling, *A Jewish Kapo in Auschwitz: History, Memory, and the Politics of Survival*

Motti Golani, *Palestine between Politics and Terror, 1945–1947*

Ilana Szobel, *A Poetics of Trauma: The Work of Dahlia Ravikovitch*

Anita Shapira, *Israel: A History*

Orit Rozin, *The Rise of the Individual in 1950s Israel: A Challenge to Collectivism*

Boaz Neumann, *Land and Desire in Early Zionism*

Anat Helman, *Young Tel Aviv: A Tale of Two Cities*

Nili Scharf Gold, *Yehuda Amichai: The Making of Israel's National Poet*

Itamar Rabinovich and Jehuda Reinharz, editors, *Israel in the Middle East: Documents and Readings on Society, Politics, and Foreign Relations, Pre-1948 to the Present*

Israeli Society in the Twenty-First Century

Calvin Goldscheider

Immigration, Inequality, and Religious Conflict

BRANDEIS UNIVERSITY PRESS

WALTHAM, MASSACHUSETTS

Brandeis University Press

An imprint of University Press of New England

www.upne.com

© 2015 Brandeis University

All rights reserved

Manufactured in the United States of America

Designed by Eric M. Brooks

Typeset in Arnhem and Akko by Passumpsic Publishing

For permission to reproduce any of the material in this book, contact Permissions, University Press of New England, One Court Street, Suite 250, Lebanon NH 03766; or visit www.upne.com

Library of Congress Cataloging-in-Publication Data
Goldscheider, Calvin, author.
Israeli society in the twenty-first century: immigration, inequality, and religious conflict / Calvin Goldscheider.
    pages cm.—(The Schusterman series in Israel studies)
Includes bibliographical references and index.
ISBN 978-1-61168-746-0 (cloth: alk. paper)—
ISBN 978-1-61168-747-7 (pbk.: alk. paper)—
ISBN 978-1-61168-748-4 (ebook)
1. Israel—Social conditions. 2. Israel—Population.
3. Israel—Emigration and immigration. 4. Israel—
Ethnic relations. 5. National characteristics, Israeli.
6. Palestinian Arabs—Israel. I. Title.
HN660.A8G66   2015
306.095694—dc23   2014045489

5 4 3 2 1

For
my children and
grandchildren

Contents

List of Tables and Figure xi
Preface xiii
Acknowledgments xix

1 Nation-Building, Population, and Development 1
2 Ethnic Diversity
   Jewish and Arab Populations of Israel 17
3 Immigration, Nation-Building, and Ethnic-Group Formation 38
4 Arab Israelis
   Demography, Dependency, and Distinctiveness 62
5 Urbanization, Residential Integration, and Communities 82
6 Religiosity, Religious Institutions, and Israeli Culture 111
7 Inequality and Changing Gender Roles 134
8 Education, Stratification, and Inequality 154
9 Inequality and Mortality Decline 177
10 Family Formation and Generational Continuities 194
11 Emergent Israeli Society
    Nation-Building, Inequalities, and Continuities 227

Appendix: *Data Sources and Reliability* 255
Bibliography 257
Index 273

Tables and Figure

Tables

2.1 Ethnic and Religious Composition of Israel, 1948–2012 27

4.1 Arab Population of Israel by Religion, 1948–2012 65

5.1 Population of Israel by District and Region 86

6.1 Religious Self-Identity, Adult Jewish Population of Israel, 2009 118

6.2 Religious Self-Identify, Adult Moslem Population of Israel, 2009 129

8.1 Transition of Males in Israel to Higher Levels of Education 159

8.2 Employed Men in High-Level Occupations, Israel, 1972–2011 166

Figure

3.1 Israel Migrations, 1947–2013 44

Preface

This is book is about the emerging society of the state of Israel in the second decade of the twenty-first century. The goal is to provide a comprehensive and systematic understanding of the major contours and trends of social life against a background of its history. I have been struck by how important books on Israel have tended to focus primarily on the history of Zionism and on the Arab-Israeli conflict and often how they have not sufficiently emphasized the major themes that characterize the development of Israeli society. Few have provided a framework for understanding what currently characterizes the dynamics of Israeli society, how social changes have unfolded over time, and what continues to be the basis for assessing the trajectory of Israel's future.

Most have been written by journalists or historians. I am neither, even as I incorporate history and pay serious attention to observers of daily and yearly events in Israel. My approach is that of a social scientist with a strong bias toward studying structural factors that influence and sustain social life and emphasizing the powerful role of demographic and ethnic factors shaping social change. I have made these arguments over the last half century in books and articles on ethnic and religious groups in Europe, Israel, and the United States.

The themes that help us identify changes and continuities in Israeli society remain salient in the twenty-first century. Issues of population change including immigration and family processes continue to shape the emergent Israel society. Inequalities among Jews and between Jewish and Arab Israelis have also changed over time but remain at the forefront of the daily life of Israelis. And questions about the role of Judaism and Jewish culture in the Jewish state of Israel have plagued Zionist thinkers and analysts for well over a century.

Three conspicuous changes have unfolded in the state of Israel over the last decades. In their interconnections, these changes have profoundly transformed Israeli society. First, a large number of immigrants from the former Soviet Union have immigrated to Israel, adding well over a million persons to the population, altering the demographic profile of Israeli Jews, and changing the society's social and cultural configuration. How have they and their children been integrated into Israeli society? How have they altered the ethnic balance among Jews and shaped the emerging political structure in Israel?

Second, the economy has shifted into high tech, and temporary workers from a variety of countries have entered Israel to take unskilled jobs, mainly to replace Palestinians. Immigrants from the former Soviet Union have disproportionately contributed to new developments in the Israeli economy and have enhanced the concentration of expanding opportunities in technological industries and occupations. What impact have these economic changes had on the social and ethnic inequalities that have emerged and on the integration of Israel's newest immigrants? How have economic inequalities been influenced by this new economic growth?

The newest immigration to Israel and emerging socioeconomic inequalities confront the third challenge of religious conflict. Israel has endured considerable internal clashes, cultural and political, among Jews of different religious beliefs and practices. The increases in the ultraorthodox and the religiously defined Jewish population have again raised questions about the role of religious authorities in the secular society and the relationship between state and religion. The immigrant population has brought new forms of Israeli nationalism without religion as significant numbers of secular Russians have declared themselves Israelis of no religion (i.e., they are not Jewish); the large number of Israelis who have settled on the West Bank have brought about new forms of Zionism often with religious fervor and in the guise of traditional Judaic values. The political and social clashes between secular and religious Israeli Jews are among the most conspicuous changes emergent in the last decades in Israel. Many of these tensions are not new but are rooted deeply in the experience of nineteenth-century European Jewry and earlier Zionist debates.

The three transformations have taken on new forms in twenty-first century Israel and have wider ramifications for Jewish communities throughout the world. Immigration, inequality, and religious conflict within Israel are often exacerbated by the continuing conflicts between Israelis and Palestinians inside and outside Israel. Continuities in social and cultural processes as well as the continuous unfolding of changes characterize the transformation of Israeli society. An understanding of these processes includes analyses of families as well as communities, for they are the locus of change and reflective of transformation.

In my studies of Israeli society over the last several decades, I have grounded my explanations and descriptions of changes in detailed empirical materials. The evidence presented in this book is primarily based on the official statistics of Israel located in the *Statistical Abstract of Israel* of 2013 and 2014 as well as other sources from the Central Bureau of Statistics of Israel, conveniently located on the bureau's website (cbs.gov.il).* As I noted in the preface to my previous books on Israel, starting with the publication in 1979 of the *Population of Israel* with Dov Friedlander, my goal is not simply to describe the latest statistics on Israel by using the reports of the statistical bureau but to analyze the data to identify processes and trends. This volume focuses on the contemporary Israeli scene but allows us to identify the continuities as well as the changes and place in context the major contours of developments.

The fundamental analyses of population/immigration, social inequality, and religious conflict draw as well on several pathbreaking research studies on Israel. My colleague and friend Dov Friedlander has organized a complex and innovative project linking individuals in various Israeli censuses. These longitudinal files are a gold mine of data, and he has generously shared some of the major findings with me. These matching files link information in a manner that allows for the analysis of inequalities among Jews and between Jewish and Arab Israelis in education and have important policy implications for redressing the ethnic gap. I am again grateful to him for permission to cite some of these findings. He has worked together with another demographer, Barbara Okun of the Hebrew University, to identify issues of family changes and inequality. I have readily incorporated the major findings from their research. However, there is no substitute for a detailed and in-depth examination of their original publications.

As I prepared this volume in the spring of 2014, Israelis and Palestinians were locked in a continuing battle over territorial control and the future of their communities. The various stages of the intifada had been raging for the last several years, and the peace process had been on again

---

*In the appendix, I have outlined the statistical sources that are the basis of the analysis.

and off again. I have reflected on that conflict and examined the roots and voices associated with that conflict in other publications. Now, in this book, I have included some notes in the last chapter to reflect on this new/ old crisis but have not in any way focused on it. I am committed to the principle that a focus on the contours of a society allows you to understand its problems better than a focus on the contours of an external conflict. The Israeli-Palestinian conflict continues to have a major impact on population processes, on development, and on ethnic relationships in Israel. I have no special insight into the resolution of the broader conflict, and you will find none in this book. I take no comfort in knowing that few others seem to have any insight or wisdom as well.

This volume is divided into several sections that cumulatively attempt to capture the major themes and processes in emergent Israeli society that I outlined above. The first four chapters deal with the formation and background of Israeli society and include, in chapter 1, a review of the ways in which nation-building, population growth, and development emerged over the last decades. Against this historical review of trends, chapter 2 identifies the emergence of ethnic diversity among Jewish and Arab populations of Israel to help place into context the current ethnic divisions within the state of Israel as well as the Palestinian-Israeli conflict. Chapter 3 begins to disentangle the ethnic heterogeneity among Jewish Israelis, outlining the patterns, selectivity, and timing of immigration. Chapter 4 explores in detail the communities and minority status of Arab Israelis, focusing on structural factors of demography, growing economic dependence on Jewish Israelis, and the continuing distinctiveness of Arab-Israeli communities.

The second section focuses on structural and cultural features of Israel that form the basis of social change and inequality. Chapter 5 considers in detail the politics of community formation and the distribution of communities in urban areas. Urbanization is a key development nationally as are the diversity of community types and the shifting significance of residential concentration among Israel's ethnic groups. In chapter 6 we turn our attention to religion and religiosity among Jewish and Arab Israelis. From the results of a special survey carried out by the Central Bureau of Statistics, a comprehensive picture emerges of the intensity of religious identity, of religious ritual observances, and of attitudes toward the role of the state in religious activities. Judaism and Islam have often been described in theological and polemical language. In this chapter we take a more social-science and empirical look at religion and examine the growing secularization along with the growing religious fundamentalism that characterize Israeli society and its ethnic divisions. Having argued for the importance of gender differences in the development of societies we turn, in chapter 7, to analyze the changing roles of Israeli women and men in the process of transforming demography and development.

A third section focuses directly on social-class inequalities and stratification in addition to inequalities based on gender, ethnic, and religious characteristics. We turn in chapter 8 to a fundamental consideration of social class. Here we expand our view of inequalities in Israeli society by examining core variation over time in education and occupation. Our major concern is the generational transmission of social-class inequalities. In particular we examine the increasing educational achievements of all groups and address the question of ethnic-group convergences in educational attainment. The increasing social-class-and-income gap is of particular concern. The relationship between this gap and ethnic and religious heterogeneity is addressed. Chapter 9 pursues an analysis of another dimension of inequality by focusing on mortality trends among Jewish and Moslem Israelis. In particular we look at evidence on infant mortality and by inference the distribution of and access to health care that diverse populations have. The overall improvement in mortality control and the remaining mortality gap among groups in Israel are analyzed in this section.

Marriage and family formation are key elements analyzed in the final section. Chapter 10 explores in-depth family formation among Jewish and Arab Israelis to bring to a fuller discussion issues of ethnic-group assimilation and generational continuities. An analysis of increasing rates of ethnic intermarriage is often considered the prime indicator of acculturation and assimilation. Our reexamination of interethnic marriages points to important reservations and limitations in the use of intermarriage evidence as a basis for assessing ethnic assimilation. We conclude our exploration of emerging Israeli society by unpacking the influence of external factors. In particular we consider the role of the Jewish communities outside Israel and the influence of changes in Palestinian society on the West Bank in shaping issues within the state of Israel. We wrap up by returning to the critical question of which among the multiple forms of ethnicity are transitional.

There is no doubt that new data and new information will become available in the next several years. I am hopeful that the analysis presented will remain salient and interesting so that others can build on these foundations in their future research.

Calvin Goldscheider
Brown University
American University
Washington, DC
Spring 2014

Acknowledgments

Many persons have contributed to the ideas and research reported in this book. In addition to those cited in the chapter endnotes, I want to acknowledge the continuing input of colleagues at the Hebrew University in Israel, and of researchers at other Israeli universities, for their help in enhancing my understanding of Israeli society. I am especially grateful to Ilan Troen of Ben Gurion University in Be'er Sheva and Brandeis University who encouraged me to think about and prepare this volume so that it would fit into his series at Brandeis. Phyllis Deutsch, editor in chief of the University Press of New England, saw the manuscript through its editorial stages with grace and efficiency; Will Hively copyedited the manuscript with thoughtfulness and expertise and spared me several embarrassing errors.

Over the years important colleagues in Israel and in the United States have shaped my thinking about issues associated with immigration, ethnicity, religion, and family. They are too numerous to mention, but several should be singled out: in the United States, these include the late Alan Zuckerman, Charles Hirschman, Arland Thornton, Judy Lasker, Zvi Gitelman, and Richard Alba; in Israel in addition to Dov Friedlander and Barbara Okun, Judah Matras, Majid Al-Hal, Sammy Smooha, Jon Anson, Zvi Eisenbach, Nurith Yaffe, and Eliyahu Ben Moshe.

The Hebrew University (Departments of Demography and Sociology) was my intellectual home for fifteen years and had a major influence on the direction of my research. Brown University's Program in Judaic Studies and Department of Sociology have shaped and sharpened my social-science commitments and expanded my intellectual development. In the last several years, American University in Washington, DC, has offered me opportunities to be part of its expanding Israel Studies Program. I am particularly grateful to Laura Cutler, Russell Stone, Pamela Nadel, and their new director, Michael Brenner, for being supportive of me in every way.

Some of the conceptual thinking and organization of materials started in a series of my publications on Israel at Westview Press. These books provided challenging perspectives on Israel through the 1990s. I drew on some of that material but updated my thinking and the data on which it was based. I have altered the thrust of each theme and added new ones as both the Israeli context has changed and new themes of importance have emerged. I remain grateful to Westview and its editors for supporting over a dozen of my publications and my edited Population and Development series.

Fran Goldscheider has directly and indirectly shaped the content and direction of my research over the last three-plus decades. Words are insufficient to express my gratitude to her and to others for shaping my career. I dedicate this volume to my children and grandchildren, who have in recent years experienced Israel in new and old ways. May they continue to appreciate the Israeli experience.

Israeli Society in the
Twenty-First Century

1 | Nation-Building, Population, and Development

The state of Israel is one of the oldest new societies to have been established in the post–World War II era. Its roots are embedded in the very distant past of the Hebrew Bible and in centuries of anti-Semitism and the minority status of Jews in Christian and Moslem societies. Emerging politically out of the ashes of a European Jewry destroyed in the Holocaust, Israel was carved out of the nineteenth-century Ottoman Empire and its successor, British colonialism, and was based on European ideologies of nationalism and ethnic politics. Built on Western and Judaic foundations of justice, independence, and democracy, it has struggled continuously for political legitimacy among its neighbors, and its members have battled over its boundaries and territory, the distribution of its resources, and the treatment of its minorities. Committed to peace, it has been mired in warfare and ceaseless conflict. Though Israel is defined as a secular state and is dedicated to being an open, pluralistic, egalitarian society, religion has been an integral element of its politics, and it is a country divided by ethnicity and religion. Major sources of inequality continue to characterize Israeli communities and families in the twenty-first century. Gender discrimination and ethnic/racial prejudice are embedded in its institutions and its politics. Fiercely independent, Israel remains the major recipient of economic and military aid from the United States and from Jews around the world. Designed as a haven for the remnants of world Jewry, it contains less than half of the world's Jewish population after more than six and a half decades of statehood, immigration, and population growth.

Israeli society has integrated over three million Jewish immigrants from an enormous range of diverse countries, the majority from Europe, has invigorated an ancient language to form a common basis of modern communication, and has developed a rich culture of literature, theater, film, and scholarship. It has become a leader in agricultural innovation and rural communal experiments, even as it is one of the most urban and most technologically sophisticated of contemporary societies. The deserts have bloomed, and modern technologies have flourished in Israel; major revolutions in the family have occurred, and extensive health-care institutions have been organized. Israel has become a model state for many Third World nations and a major source of identity for Jewish communities around the world. Characterized by heterogeneity and by intense and continuous change, Israel is a small state occupying a disproportionate share of the headlines and stories in the Western press. Indeed, contradictions and paradoxes seem to be some of the defining features of Israeli society, as does its complexity.

This book considers these complex themes in an attempt to understand Israel's emergent society in the twenty-first century. I examine population and ethnic/religious processes, and social-economic-political-cultural developments, to describe the changes that Israel has experienced and to provide clues about the sources of these changes and their consequences. I focus on the linkages between nation-building and population growth and investigate the assimilation of immigrants from diverse societies and their mobilization into a coherent, pluralistic polity. I assess how religious conflict and cohesion blend to form one national diverse society. I document how resources are distributed and how external dependencies and internal conflicts are connected to clarify the basis of ethnic/religious and other inequalities. To grasp the complexity of the everyday life of its citizens, I review normal, recurrent life events—births, marriages and family formations, sicknesses, and deaths. I investigate the communities where people live, the jobs they have, the children they love, their schooling, and their resources, and the religion and institutions that give meaning to their lives. I outline developments in culture, politics, and religion; minority inequalities and the creation of new communities, their distinctiveness and differential access to opportunities; the significance of gender roles and the sources of family values; the relationship of Jews and Arab/Palestinians in their diasporas to Israelis and their society. Together, these themes provide a portrait of contemporary Israeli society, a canvas upon which to assess the historical roots of current patterns and the basis for conjecture about the future.

To carry out the daunting goals of understanding this complex society, I use some overall theoretical maps to orient readers with broad images in which to fit details into a coherent whole. I provide in this introductory chapter several points of entry into the complexities of understanding changes in Israeli society over the past several decades. Focusing on the first decades of the twenty-first century, I emphasize the links among nation-building, population processes, socioeconomic development, emergent ethnicity, and religious divisions. I end up with many questions challenging some of the ideas of the past and some guides for the analysis of future changes.

I make two core arguments about the patterns of nation-building in Israel: First, I argue that social-demographic transformations—changes in immigration, health and mortality, fertility and family structure, internal migration and residential concentration—have been critical in shaping nation-building and economic development in Israeli society and in that society's generational renewal. Second, I demonstrate how the sources of inequalities within Israel have changed over time and how new divisions among Jews and between Jews and Arabs are emerging. Population processes and social-structural factors are at the core of these changing inequalities, transforming communities in the process of nation-building. At the same time, religious institutions and ideological developments that often create a common set of values and core culture have been sources of conflict and polarization within the society.

In my examination of Israel's changing society, I note the tensions between its uniqueness and its commonalities shared with other countries. Social patterns are emerging in Israel that are similar to those of other small developing countries dependent on large and powerful nations for socioeconomic resources and political support. At the same time, other processes reflect the specifics of the Jewish condition in recent history and the relationships between Israeli and non-Israeli Jews and between Israeli Jews and Arabs. Still other patterns in Israel can be understood only in light of Israel's particular history, related to its development and its role in the Middle East region. Israel, as other countries, is unique in the forces that have shaped its history; it is also a microcosm of population, development, and ethnic/religious relationships. It is one country that comprises many communities—a political entity unified and organized, with official boundaries (however fuzzy at times) and administrative networks. Israeli society is an example of the processes of sociopolitical development, economic dependency, and ethnic/religious pluralism; it is at the crossroads of East and West, where Western democracy and capitalism, European socialism, and Jewish and Moslem religious fundamentalism blend with Middle East culture and society.[1]

Yet it is striking how the social and cultural processes that have come to characterize Israeli society parallel those that have emerged elsewhere, in old and new states, in more- and less-developed nations, in Western and non-Western countries. The analyses that I present provide a basis for understanding one fascinating case study; my conclusions should be informative for comparative studies. The unique features of the Israeli case, as well as more-general patterns of social change and social inequality, should emerge at the end.

Demographic Themes

Demography is not "destiny" but plays a powerful role in understanding the formation of Israeli society and the changes that it has experienced. Among the core demographic themes are (1) the centrality of immigration in Israel's population growth, (2) the links between increases in population size and economic development, (3) the tie between the geographic distribution of Israelis and the political legitimacy of the state, and (4) the ways that residential patterns have created ethnic and religious networks within a pluralistic society. There are other demographic themes of importance. The relative size of Jewish and Arab populations in Israel has been of central political importance. Population processes are associated with social inequalities based on ethnic origins, religion, and gender. Family values and gender roles are linked to the changing size of families; differentials in health and death are indicators of social inequalities. Population issues have been themes of Zionism, the national ideology of Israel, and cultural values and political conflict have revolved around population issues. I expand on these themes throughout my analysis. Here, I outline five basic principles of population analysis.

First, there are only two sources of change in population size—natural increase (the difference between births and deaths) and the net flow of migration. All social, economic, political, and cultural factors that affect the changing size of a population operate through these two sources. In turn, alterations in the social and economic composition of a population are influenced by the origins and selectivity of migrant flows and the differential reproduction of social groups. Entering and exiting processes indicated by fertility, migration, and mortality are the bases for understanding the changing social processes in Israeli society.

Second, communities and families, like the populations of states, are shaped by these demographic processes. The number of children people have, where they live, who their neighbors are, and their own health and welfare are important for the generational renewal of society, as are the family roles of men and women, the networks that families sustain, and the values that they convey from generation to generation. Communities shape the national society profile, and families are the building blocks of communities. Thus, our analysis focuses on changes in population size and distribution for the country as a whole, as well as for families, communities, and groups.

Third, demographic processes are interrelated: fertility, mortality, and migration (both internal and international) are linked to one another in dynamic ways. Changes in each process contribute to overall population-size changes and are likely to affect other processes. These population processes can be examined for their impact on demographic phenomena over time and in their different configurations. Each process influences the age and sex structure of populations and often cohort changes in socioeconomic and ethnic composition. Together, these interrelated demographic processes form a population system.

Fourth, marriage and family formation are significant in a demographic context, since these processes bind families together, linking the generations to each other in a web of relationships. Community is defined as a pattern of interrelated networks. The tighter the networks and the larger the number of linkages between families through marriage, residence, jobs, and cultures of origin, the greater the community cohesion and the stronger the identification with the community. Demography shapes the shared intensities of interactions within and between generations; in turn, population processes are at the core of societal cohesiveness.

Fifth, demographic processes do not operate in a vacuum. The key social dimensions of communal life—family-kinship networks and socioeconomic stratification—have systematic connections to population processes. As networks and resources change over time, demographic processes will be affected; as demographic processes unfold, social changes are likely to follow. Hence, when we examine basic demographic processes and focus on population changes, we are confronted with the fundamentals of sociological analysis. Issues of family continuity and social inequality are critical parts of the generational issues highlighted by demography.

These social-demographic themes focus attention on how population processes are at the core of nation-building, development, and national political integration in Israel's changing society. They point to the need to investigate the changing linkages among groups and convergences in social processes among communities. They suggest the importance of population processes in the formation of social-class variation among communities and the generational transmission of inequality among ethnic communities and continuities of religious traditions. Studying demography in the contexts of nation-building, inequalities, and community provides a powerful basis for understanding Israel's changing society.

Changing Demographic Snapshots

I begin empirically with a simple demographic profile of contemporary Israeli society in the first decade of the twenty-first century.[2] A snapshot, cross-sectional view reveals a total population size in Israel in 2013 of over 8 million people—approximately 6 million Jews (75%), 1.67 million Arabs (21%), and some 340,000 defined as "others" (4.2%). Twenty years earlier in 1993 Israel had a total population of 5.3 million—4.3 million Jews and fewer than 1 million Arabs and others.[3] The annual rate of total population growth was 1.9%, similar to that of the previous decades. In the 1990s, years with a high rate of immigration from the former Soviet Union, the average rate of growth was approximately 3% per year. In 2012, the rate of growth of the Jewish population was 1.7%; the rate for the Moslem population was 2.5%, for the Christian population 1.7%, and the Druze population 1.5%. The Israeli population is a relatively younger population than that of Western countries. In 2012, over one-fourth of the population was below age 15 and 10.4% was age 65 and over.

Israel is an overwhelmingly urban society: over 90% of the population live in areas so designated. During the decade between 1990 and 1999, almost 1 million immigrants arrived in Israel, over 90% from the former Soviet Union; an additional quarter of a million arrived between 2000 and 2009. Since 2005, an average of 17,000 immigrants have arrived annually, over half from the former Soviet Union. Birthrates in the state of Israel in the twenty-first century were higher than in most industrialized Western countries and lower than in Third World countries (an average of 21 births per 1,000 population and a total fertility rate of about 2.9 births per woman). Death rates were among the lowest in the world (5 deaths per 1,000 population, an infant mortality rate of fewer than 4 deaths among children under 1 year of age per 1,000 births, and a life expectancy of 80 years). The dominant ethnic-religious population in the state is Jewish, representing about 75% of the total in 2013, with a rather even split between those of European (Western) origins and those of Asian and African (Middle Eastern) origins. In 2013, about three-fourths of the Jewish population was born in Israel and over half of the Jewish population was third generation (Israelis born of Israeli-born parents). The Arab population in Israel is largely Moslem (about 8 out of 10) and is concentrated in particular regions of the country.

Changes in the demographic portrait of Israeli society can be sketched by examining these same elements in the year when the state of Israel was established. At the end of 1948, there were 872,700 persons living in approximately the same land area in Israel, mostly Jews (82%), and there was a low rate of natural growth. During the first several months subsequent to statehood, there were very high rates of immigration and a potential for continuous Jewish immigration from a wide range of countries. At the same time, there was an exodus of Arab residents as war raged between Israel and neighboring Arab countries. The state of Israel was established in part of the areas of Palestine, as territorial control was transferred from the British Mandate toward an emerging Jewish administration and political control. There was a low level of industrial activity in 1948 but a high level of urban concentration. Israel was a country without a secure future, as war and political-economic uncertainty marked its birth; it had an unknown capacity then to economically and socially integrate large numbers of immigrants. The Arab population became a demographic, political, and social minority as Jews became the dominant majority in the new state.

The demographic snapshots begin to be sharpened when one reviews the pattern of population growth. The path of demographic growth in Israel has been rather uneven since the 1950s, even as the rate has been high. Starting with a base of 650,000 in mid-1948, the population surpassed its first million within the first year and doubled to 2 million within a decade. By the end of 1970, Israeli society had over 3 million people; by 1982 it had added another million to its population. Over 5 million people lived in Israel by the end of 1992, representing a sixfold increase in the Jewish and Arab populations in 45 years. In the year 2000 there were 6.4 million Israelis and in 2012 there were 8 million Israelis, a tenfold increase in 65 years.

These core population shifts were major sources of social and economic transformations.

Questions of war and economic uncertainty remain; the cultural, economic, and social integration of Israel's immigrant/ethnic populations continue to be issues in the beginning of the twenty-first century. However, the dimensions have radically changed as the context of both immigration and the society have changed. Israel's status as an independent state is largely unquestioned internationally and is increasingly accepted by its Arab neighbors, even as the boundaries that mark its political borders remain tentative and controversial. So, while snapshots sketch formal beginnings and outline macro changes, they omit much that has happened in the society and miss the processes underlying these changes. Snapshots cannot adequately convey the detailed nature of social and demographic changes; the dynamics of change need to be examined directly in order to understand the society and fit the population processes of Israel into a broader historical and comparative framework.

Are Israeli Demographic Patterns Unique?

The demographic transformations in Israeli society appear to recapitulate in compressed form the demographic transitions in Western, industrialized nations, historically and comparatively. They also seem to parallel the demographic processes unfolding in Third World countries over the past several decades. When we place Israeli society in comparative context, we begin to disentangle that which Israel shares with other countries and that which is unique to its development. One key to understanding these processes is to explore how the high rates of population growth reflect different combinations of demographic sources for Jews and Arabs.

The Jewish population increased primarily as a result of immigration; natural increase accounted for most of the Arab population growth since 1948. These different sources of growth imply very different population trajectories and related social processes, even as the relative size of these populations has remained remarkably steady. The general patterns are well known and include several conspicuous features: Mortality levels have declined with improvements in public health services and have been extended to all sectors of the population. There has been a transition to nuclear family structure, an increasing use of efficient contraception, and the emergence of small family size. Reductions in mortality and the shift from high to low fertility resulted in a period of rapid population growth, followed by a slowing of the population growth rate. As the population has become increasingly urban in concentration, metropolitan areas have expanded as populations have moved to suburban communities. Immigration and ethnic residential concentrations have characterized the society over time, and significant socioeconomic integration of populations from diverse countries of origin has taken place. Welfare, health, and educational services have expanded to meet the changing needs of a population with a new ethnic configuration.

These demographic changes in Israel (as in other countries) have been linked to the expansion of economic opportunities, the changing roles of women, and the increasing political and economic dependencies of small periphery nations on a select number of large, powerful core countries. Israel's demographic uniqueness lies in the specifics of these processes, not in the transformations themselves. The importance of immigration in demographic growth rates, for example, is not unique to Israel, but the *rate* of immigration (relative to the size of the receiving population) has at times been unprecedented. Indeed, what is so fascinating about Israeli society is that its demographic patterns compress in microcosm all these transitions in a relatively short time span (see Berelson 1979; Friedlander and Goldscheider 1984). To take but one example: the transition to small family size that took over a century to unfold in Sweden's demographic history occurred within less than a generation among Israel's Asian-African Jewish population. This fertility reduction has taken place within the short span of a generation in a pro-natal normative context and without the use of modern contraceptives; mortality control has occurred within an even shorter period, indeed, noticeable for some populations before statehood and for immigrants in the period immediately subsequent to arriving in the state of Israel. The entire range of demographic transitions can be identified and the entire spectrum of transition stages can be documented for major subpopulations living in the same society at the same time. The rich demographic heterogeneity is neutralized when only the total society is examined, since the national "average" distorts the range of diverse patterns.

What about the geographic distribution of Israel's population? A look at a map of Israel's population points to major areas of residential density in Israel—the urban centers of Tel Aviv, Jerusalem, and Haifa. Since its founding as a state, Israel has been an urban society, similar to the European, developed-country model and unlike the more-rural Third World countries. Israel is small in population size and geographic spread and also in its sense of local community. In part, Israel's size makes it resemble a large extended community where each event has significance because of the connections among persons and families throughout the country. Israel, like other small states, has an intimate relationship with space. Thus, Israeli demographic patterns have both common and distinctive features that reflect its unique population history, ideology and values, politics, and the complex social mosaic that has emerged there in the last generation.

Development and Nation-Building

There is an economic cost to high levels of continuous population growth when the economy does not expand. Israel could not sustain its population growth rates, retain its population, and continue to attract new immigrants without extensive economic growth. Indeed, the growth of Israel's economy has widened the opportunities of and generated increases in the standard of living for a growing number of people. In part, economic changes were brought about through the increase of population size by way of immigration (the human capital and resources brought by the immigrants and their contributions to production and consumption) and the increased economic investments made in Israel from outside the country. Whether demographic changes generated the economic change or vice versa, both population size and economic production have increased over time.

The demographic transitions that I outlined occurred in the contexts of economic growth and an emerging national policy. Immigrants and their families were responsive to economic opportunities and affected economic change as they operated in a new national political system. Immigrant economic integration in the short run and reduced ethnic-economic inequalities in the longer run are strongly related to the opportunities that were emerging for the new Israeli-born generation. Changes in the economy and in the distribution of resources between the generations are critical factors in understanding the changing linkages among population, nation-building, and ethnicity. Economic conditions in the country as a whole have improved. I briefly review the sources of Israel's economic development, internal growth versus external investments; identify the industries and economic sectors that have expanded; and examine the distribution of economic activities among ethnic and social-class groups to study the connections between stratification and the emerging occupational hierarchies and their links to ethnic origin. Associated with economic growth are the transformations in the labor force and markets as the population becomes more educated, technology develops, and new sectors of the economy expand in a postindustrial world economy.

These complex issues are outlined below in broad strokes and are elaborated on as the analysis unfolds. Macro indicators of social and economic development in Israel show some dramatic changes that parallel the demographic revolutions that have occurred. At the same time, distortions may emerge when different patterns of socioeconomic change appear balanced at the national level but vary among major groups. National indicators of economic growth can be misleading if the distribution of growth is skewed in favor of some groups.

Overall Economic Measures. A range of economic indicators at the national level make it clear that Israel's economy has grown in terms of domestic production, technological developments, and labor-force improvements. From 1950 through the mid-1970s, economic growth was quite high, apart from recessions in 1953 and 1966–1967 and stagnation in the mid-1970s (Plessner 1994). During the quarter century from 1950, the national product rose ninefold, an average of 9% per year (Ginor 1979, 50). The sharp rise reflected an increase in capital stock (11% per year) and the number of employed (4% per year); hence, capital per employed increased 7% per year. The quality of the labor force increased dramatically after an initial decline (which reflected the ethnic and socioeconomic background of immigrants). Educational capital per employed declined by 7% in the first half of the 1950s, rose 22% in the period from 1961 to 1972, and continued to increase in the 1970s through the 1990s (Ginor 1979, 50–51). Gross domestic product (GDP) per capita at constant prices doubled between 1950 and 1965 and doubled again between 1965 and 1990. In the half century from the establishment of the state, the GDP increased four-and-a-half-fold. By the decade to 2012, the gross domestic product per capita had increased over 50%.

The share of agriculture in the domestic product rose in the first years of the state, then declined steadily with a modest rise in the share of industry.

The share of trade, finance, and personal services declined, and the share of public services rose, indicating the increased share in social services. The biggest rise in capital stock occurred in the shares of public services, transport, and communications, revealing the expansion of the infrastructure on a modernizing basis. These changes in economic growth have been directly correlated to changes in population (Ben-Porath 1986b).

Economic and Occupational Shifts. Economic shifts over time can be observed in the changing structure of economic branches and in occupations. The distribution of employed persons among economic branches reflects a combination of stability and change. The most striking overall feature of the years between 1955 and 1990 is the relative stability of the employment distribution among various sectors. The industrial branch remained relatively steady (at about 25% of the employed) until 1990–2000. Commerce, transportation, and personal services have also remained steady over time. The major shifts in employment have been the decline in agriculture, from 18% to less than 2%, and in construction, from 9% to 5%. At the same time, there have been increases in employment in the finance sector (doubling to 10% from 1970 to 1990 and increasing to 14% in 2000 and to almost 20% in 2012) and in public community services (from 22% to 31% and to about 40% in 2012).

A complementary picture emerges from an examination of shifting occupational distribution over time in Israel. There has been a clear and sharp decline in the proportion engaged in agriculture from the mid-1950s to 2012 (from 17% to less than 1%), modest declines in skilled laborers (from about 30% of the employed in the 1950s through the 1970s, to about 25% in the 1980s and 1990s, to 20% in 2000 and 14% in 2012). Service and sales workers have remained at about the same level over time, declining somewhat since 1990. The most conspicuous overall occupational shift has been the increase in the professional, scientific, and academic category (from 10% of the employed in 1955 to 28% by 2000 and to over 30% in the first decade of the twenty-first century).

Educational Changes. Along with these broad economic changes there have been improvements in the educational levels of the population. The median years of schooling for the total population in 1961 was 8 years; 9% of the population had 13 or more years of schooling. The median increased 2.5 years by 1980, and the proportion with higher education doubled to 19%. The average level of education in Israel in the beginning of the

1990s was 12 years. These increases are even more impressive when the educational levels of Arab Israelis are examined. Fully half of the Arab population age 15 and over in 1961 had no formal education, and only 1.5% had 13 or more years; four decades later, over 90% of the Arab population had some formal education, and 19% had more than a high school education; 21% of the Arab Israeli population had 13 or more years of education by 2012. Among Jews, the decline at the lower level of education, fewer than 8 years, was from 13% in 1961 to 3% in 2000, and the proportion at the higher educational level, 13 or more years, increased fourfold during the same period. By 2012, almost half the adult Jewish population had 13 or more years of schooling.

These educational shifts have transformed the employed population. In the early 1960s, 58% of the employed men in Israel had fewer than 8 years of education, and about one in ten had more than a high school education. By 2000, only one out of ten had fewer than 8 years, and four out of ten had 13 or more years of education. In 2000, only 4% of the women employed in Israel had low levels of education, and over half had 13 or more years of education. This distribution reverses the patterns in the 1960s, when 45% of the employed women had fewer than 8 years of schooling and 15% had 13 or more years (see also Amir 1986).

Standard of Living. Other economic indicators reveal the increased standard of living and the improved quality of life among Israelis. For example, indicators of housing and crowding reveal the increase in the amount of household space available from the 1960s through the first decade of the twenty-first century. Increasing possession of consumer goods also indicates improvements in the standard of living and the quality of life among Israelis. In 1950 only 2% of the Israeli households had an electric refrigerator, but one-half of the households had a refrigerator in 1960, and virtually all did by 1975. Seven percent of the households had washing machines in the mid-1950s, increasing to 43% in 1970 and to 80% in 1980. Only 4% of Israeli families owned a private car in 1960, 15% in 1970, 34% in 1980. These and more-recent data reveal the overall increase in the standard of living, access to modern consumer items, and the diffusion of these to major sectors of the population.

Economic Dependency. As Israel's economy improved, there was also a growing dependency on external funds. In part, this is a direct result of the military burdens that Israel has experienced and the economic costs of building a modern defense system. Israel has devoted a considerable part of its economic capacity to defense, much higher per capita than in Western countries. Since World War II, the average defense expenditures of Western countries has been below 10% of GDP; defense outlays in Israel averaged 25% per year from 1969 to 1981 (Berglas 1986). In 1970 total U.S. assistance to Israel was less than $100 million, and 85% was in the form of loans. A decade later the assistance had increased to over $2 billion, with half as loans. In 1985 Israel received $3.3 billion of military and economic assistance from the United States, all of it in the form of grants (Rabie 1988, table 14). This assistance increased significantly in the last 25 years.

Israel has also received increasing support from the American Jewish community (as well as other Jewish communities around the world) and annual restitution payments from Germany (Halevi 1986). Estimates of external private and public support add up to over $8 billion annually, according to some, and considerably less on average, according to others (compare Rabie 1988 and Halevi 1986). The important point is that Israel has increasingly become dependent on other states and on Jews living outside the state for its continued growth. Israel's financial obligations abroad increased over threefold to $3 billion during the 1970s, jumping to $21 billion in the 1980s. By the beginning of the 1990s these foreign obligations fluctuated at about $33 billion. Even though the net export of goods from Israel increased from $211 million in 1960 to $5.3 billion in 1980 and to over $11 billion in the 1990s, net imports have increased even more sharply. These international flows are part of the economic dependency of a periphery country on a core country and have become an integral part of the economic structure of Israeli planning.

Overall macro economic, occupational, and educational shifts raise a number of questions about the distribution of these economic improvements among Jews and Arabs, among Jews of different ethnic origins and generations, and between women and men. These related economic development themes are analyzed in subsequent chapters when these indicators are translated into measures of the quality of life in Israel's communities.

Zionism, Development, and Conflict

Zionism—a combination of national ideology, political movement, and established institutions—has had an important relationship with social-demographic issues and with development directions. Zionism has not been a monolithic ideology, nor has the Zionist movement established a singular set of institutions, goals, and policy commitments (see among others Avineri 1981; Halpern 1961; Hertzberg 1960; Vital 1975, 1982, 1987; Shapira 2012). Nevertheless, all the Zionist variants have emphasized the centrality of Jewish immigration and the importance of building an autonomous Jewish community into an independent political unit. Zionists also viewed the Jewish condition as a minority community outside the state and debated whether that minority status was problematic.

At various points in time, Zionism shaped the rate and sources of immigration, the development and support of institutions that encouraged maternal and child care, and the welfare system that provided benefits to children and families. Zionist institutions and underlying ideologies were instrumental in the development of agricultural enterprises and in subsidizing agricultural communities and new towns. Zionist institutions also mobilized financial support for Israel among the Jewish communities outside Israel, linking Jews together in supporting the state as a national Jewish homeland.

This is not to argue that the state of Israel is a direct outcome of Zionism as an ideology. The variety of Zionisms did not provide a clear directive to carry out any activity, nor was Zionist ideology a major determinant of the processes underlining immigration to the state. Similarly, it should not be assumed that ethnic inequalities among Jews and between Jews and Arabs are traceable directly to Zionist ideology or that economic, social, cultural, or religious developments are direct outcomes of Zionist ideological movements. As a combination of ideology, social movement, and a set of organizations, Zionism has been both a legitimating ideology and a source of financial support for the development of Israeli society. Phrased as a complex question, one can ask, How have ideological and organizational aspects of Zionism influenced different aspects of Israel's changing society? I consider this question throughout the analysis.

Israel has emerged as a national state, has developed and expanded its population and economy, and has articulated its commitment to national goals, institutions, symbols, and culture. Israelis have become integrated politically and economically into the emerging nation-state. At the same time that a national society has developed, there have been signs of internal divisions and conflict among Jews within Israel and between Jews and

Arabs. Some of these divisions are observable in Israel, as in many societies, and are not specific or unique to Israel's development. Their form varies among countries, and their particular nuance reflects the historical and cultural context of places. These divisions are reflected in differences by religious commitment, by type of residence in regions of the country, and by age and generational exposure to the country as well as in the social and cultural construction of family and gender roles. Social-class inequalities have sharpened and economic conflict has become more conspicuous in the twenty-first century.

There are particular divisions within Israel that are more clearly a manifestation of local-regional contexts and specific historical circumstances. Two are obvious: divisions between Jews and Arabs and divisions among Jews by ethnic origins and by generation status. Another increasing set of divisions relates to the internal religious differences among Jews, especially between the *haredi* religious groups ("ultraorthodox" and those "religiously" identified), on the one hand, and the secular on the other. In subsequent chapters we consider whether and how these divisions have changed over time and whether they challenge the national integrity of Israeli society.

NOTES

1. I shall use the convention Moslem, not Muslim, throughout this book.

2. See the appendix for the statistical sources of these patterns.

3. I define the state of Israel within its formally recognized boundaries: Before 1967 it includes the state recognized internationally in 1948; after 1967 it includes the eastern part of Jerusalem. The territories added after 1967, the West Bank and Gaza, are defined as "administered territories," or those occupied by the state of Israel. In 1994 Gaza and Jericho on the West Bank were placed under Palestinian control. These political changes undoubtedly altered the demography and politics of the state of Israel. With minor exceptions, I do not use the biblical names "Judea" and "Samaria" for these territories and do not include data for them unless explicitly noted. All designations of these areas carry with them political significance and are social constructions. I do not want to convey a political statement or imply any judgment by my use of these designations. My goal is to be clear about the areas I am examining so that I can describe and analyze the processes occurring within them. I deal more explicitly with these territories and their relationship to the state of Israel in the concluding chapter.

2 | Ethnic Diversity Jewish and Arab Populations of Israel

Population changes and political developments altered the emerging society in Israel by radically transforming its composition and redefining the basis of power. With the establishment of the state, the Jewish community became the demographic majority and the source of political control. The transition from Yishuv (the Jewish settlement in Palestine) to Israeli society occurred in the context of a massive Jewish immigration from dozens of countries around the world, primarily from Eastern European and Middle Eastern countries. The Arabs in Palestine, devastated by war and depleted by mass and selective out-migration, became a minority in the emerging Jewish state. This recomposition of Jewish and Arab populations changed everything in the new state and created the diversity that characterizes contemporary Israeli society.

There are many forms of ethnic diversity within the complex society emerging in the state of Israel. Some of these forms are derived from the distinctive national origins of the population (countries and regions of the world); some are based on religious differentiation; still others are based on political constructions that have emerged in the new Israeli polity. The complex layers of ethnic differentiation (within which I include the ethnic divisions among Jews and between Jews and Arabs) are complicated further as some specific groups have assimilated and disappeared over several generations, though new ethnic-based sources of differentiation have emerged. My review of the changing meanings of ethnicity in Israel points to three central themes. First, no analysis of change and no investigation of differences within Israeli society can ignore the ethnic dimension, since it is a major aspect of Israel's pluralism. Second, ethnic differentiation is a changing and contextual basis of distinctiveness. Ethnicity cannot be regarded solely as primordial or a constant of birth or of cultural heritage, since it may change over the life course of individuals and is more salient in various contexts. Third, a core aspect of Jewish ethnicity is the generational question: how has ethnic distinctiveness changed among the children and grandchildren of immigrants?

National policy and cultural ideology favor the integration and total assimilation into the Jewish state of Jews from diverse countries of origin. Yet ethnic differences have characterized social life in Israel. Paradoxically, the integration of groups has at times led to increased ethnic distinctiveness rather than to total assimilation. The tensions between ethnic change and continuity and between ethnic pluralism and an ethnic melting pot are powerful themes in our understanding of Israeli society. I examine how ethnicity emerged and how it is sustained over the generations, specifying the contexts that reinforce and sharpen ethnic distinctiveness and those that have reduced ethnic differences.

The primary objective of studying ethnic differentiation is to identify how ethnicity is conveyed generationally and not to examine ethnic differences per se. Throughout, I illustrate how ethnic differences have been translated into inequalities—the unequal access of groups to the rewards and opportunities within the society. I demonstrate how the timing and selectivity of immigration and the continuing patterns of residential concentration have been critical in shaping the changing ethnic mosaic in Israel over the last several decades and are directly linked to the perpetuation of ethnic inequalities. I show how those ethnic differences, which are embedded in the structure of social life in Israel, tend to be perpetuated. At the same time, ethnic differences that are primarily transfers from places of origin are rarely sustained and only selectively reinforced. Hence, sharp ethnic differences that characterized groups in the past have narrowed considerably as exposure to Israeli society has increased, and they mainly reflect socioeconomic factors. At the same time, ethnic distinctiveness in new arenas has emerged as an unintentional consequence of social processes within Israel.

Ethnic Categories Construction and Definitions

I set the stage by examining the social construction of ethnic categories and describing the ethnic mosaic in Israel. These provide a basis for identifying the contexts of ethnic intensity and the basis of interpreting ethnic differences. Ethnicity captures a mixture of religion and ethnic-national origins in Israel and goes to the heart of who is a member of the society. The two major axes for defining ethnic factors in Israel are the internal ethnic divisions within the Jewish sector based on national/cultural origin and the differences between Jewish and Arab populations based on reli-

gion and political criteria. Ethnic divisions among Jewish and Arab populations have been formed from very different sources and are differentially
linked to political, economic, and social factors. These differential sources
of ethnicity have implications for their continuity into the next generation.

Jewish Ethnicity

Jewish ethnic differentiation in Israel reflects a combination of social
and cultural origins of immigrant groups and the effects of social conditions in Israel. Ethnic divisions among Jews do not derive from Zionist
ideological sources or explicit Israeli policies. To the contrary: the national
ideology, Zionism, denies the salience of ethnicity as a continuing factor
for the Israeli Jewish population. National-origin differences among Jews
are viewed as a product of the long-term dispersal of the Jewish people
in the diaspora; returning to the homeland, it is argued, will result in the
emergence of a new Jew—untainted by the culture and psychology of the
diaspora and freed from the constraints and limitations of experiences in
places of previous (non-Israel) residence (see Hertzberg 1960 for a review
of different Zionist ideologies; see also Shapira 2012).

Zionism's construction of Jewish peoplehood, therefore, involves the
assignment of ethnic origin to the minority experiences of Jews outside
Israel and, hence, requires its devaluation. Zionism rejects both the assimilation of Jews in communities outside Israel and the retention of ethnic
minority status as viable solutions to the position of Jews in modernizing
societies. The long Jewish diaspora of 2,000 years is viewed simply as an
empty interlude between the origin of a Jewish nation in the biblical land
of Israel and the return of Jews to that land of their ancient origin. Hence,
Zionist ideology posits that Israel is the national origin of Jews. Their
countries of "interlude," that is, their ethnicities during the diaspora, are
not the source of their Jewish-national identity: Israel is. It follows that
the recognition of ethnic origin as being the country of diaspora ancestry would be, in part, a denial of the "return" home to Israel. To recognize
the continuing salience of diaspora ethnicity would be to treat coming to
Israel as immigration in the normal demographic sense, not as *aliya*, the
imperative "ascent" to the Israel of Zionist ideology. To deny "returning"
to Israel would be ideologically and politically untenable, as would the ac-
knowledgment of the value and salience of ethnic origins. The continuing
distinctiveness of ethnicity among Jews in Israel is perceived, therefore, as

temporary, reflecting the past, diminishing in the present, and expected to disappear in future generations. Zionist ideology as it is manifest in contemporary Israeli society constructs the obvious evidence of Jewish ethnic differences in Israel as transitional and largely irrelevant to the longer-term goals of national Jewish integration and nation-building.

The consensus within Israel about the value of bringing Jews to Israel from diverse diaspora countries and the resulting policies encouraging this "in-gathering" are consistent with Zionist ideology, as is the anticipated integration of immigrants with these diverse ethnic backgrounds into the national culture and polity. To hasten achieving this latter goal, explicit policies were designed and implemented to "absorb" Jewish immigrants into Israeli society.[1] Along with the deliberate policy of building the nation through immigration, the goal was to mitigate social splits along lines of national origin. These goals have been at the top of the national agenda from Israel's earliest days. A great deal of effort and extensive resources were aimed at closing the gaps among Jews of different socioeconomic backgrounds in the hope of achieving rapid integration and equalization. This social policy has been reflected in Israel's particular development as a welfare state and its related economic system (Ben-Porath 1986a; Doron and Kramer 1991).

Israeli policymakers fully expect the total assimilation of Jews from diverse diaspora countries as the third generation emerges, distant from external ethnic origins, socialized into the national polity and culture by exposure to educational institutions and the military, and raised by native-born Israeli parents. The ethnicity remaining among third-generation Israeli Jews is expected to be marginal, cultural remnants of no economic or social significance celebrated in museums as relics and curios of the past. Nation-building in the ideological and policy contexts of Israeli society is expected to remove the diversity of external ethnic origins as new forms of national Israeli loyalty emerge, focusing solely on Jewish peoplehood. Religious similarity, military service, and "collective consciousness" derived from Israel's security situation, it is argued, operate to dilute ethnic differences (Ben-Rafael 1986). Ethnic cleavage becomes a "problem to be solved," not a cultural trait or a source of generational socioeconomic inequality.

Nowhere is the ideology that denies the salience of Jewish ethnicity more poignant symbolically than in the way ethnic origin is treated in official government statistical publications. Ethnic origin among the Jews in Israel is almost always categorized in terms of the place of the person's birth (i.e., some "objective" fact that is ascriptive and unchanging). For the Israeli-born, the place of one's parents' birth (usually the father) is obtained, also an unchanging characteristic. In that context, ethnic origin is simply limited by time (until the third generation) and is descriptive of the immediate past. Using this definition, generational distance from foreignness or exposure to Israeli society marks the progress toward the end of ethnicity and ethnic self-identification (in the particularistic sense). The question of the ethnic origins, or in the Western sense the "ancestry," of the third generation (the native-born of native-born parents) has not so far been addressed by officials in Israel. Indeed, to judge solely by the way official government bureaus in Israel present their texts, members of this third generation have no differentiating ethnic origins of significance — they are simply Israeli-born of Israeli-born parents, with no need to pursue retrospectively the previous origins of those two most recent generations.[2]

Information collected on specific country of origin (i.e., birthplace of parents) is recategorized into broad divisions by continents—Europe, America, and Asia-Africa (with a third category, Israeli-born of Israeli-born parents). This ethnic categorization is unique historically among Jewish communities of the world and is constructed only for Jews living in the state of Israel. It clearly reflects a distinction between Jews of "Western" and "Middle Eastern" origin. It is a rejection of the more widely used, and historically more complex, division between "Sephardic" and "Ashkenazic" Jewries, although there is some overlap. The latter distinction has been retained only to identify the political designations of the two chief rabbis of Israel. The Rabbinate is the only legitimate, governmentally recognized, and reinforced arena for Jewish "ethnic" diversity (chapter 6). This designation is largely political and serves as a cultural division within the secular government of Israel.

Contemporary analysts portraying Jewish ethnic variations include a wide range of groups within the "ethnic" rubric. Some include Jewish ethnic subpopulations by specific countries of origin rather than by broad geocultural areas, and this has particularly characterized some anthropological analyses (see, among others, Goldberg 1977; Morag-Talmon 1989; Hertzog et al. 2010; Mizrachi 2013). As distance from immigrant origins increases and mixed ethnic parentage becomes more common, the boundaries defining and delimiting ethnic origins have become fuzzy. Who is in and who is out of the group has become variable over time, depending in part on how affiliation and group identification are defined, even among major ethnic categories. The fluidity of ethnic boundaries over time has also resulted in varying definitions among research studies and the resultant difficulties in comparing the same group, historically and among communities. Anthropologists argue on cultural grounds for the importance of distinguishing among immigrants from Middle Eastern countries by specific places of origin (Goldberg; Morag-Talmon). Whether ethnic origin is rooted in specific countries (e.g., Poland or Yemen) or broad regions of origin (e.g., Eastern Europe or Asia), or whether new forms of ethnic categories are becoming salient in Israel (e.g., Europe-America or Asia-Africa), remain empirical questions.

Most of my review of materials on ethnic variations and ethnicity focuses primarily on the dichotomy between broad Western (European-American) and Middle Eastern (Asian-African) origins. Of course there are variations within these groups, but my focus is on social processes, not on cultural variations in places of origin. My goal is to identify emergent and changing values that are reflected in two (or three) major ethnic blocks or aggregates.

Arab Ethnicity

The difference between Jews and Arabs is another basis of "ethnicity" in Israel. As constructed in government documents and in politics, these "ethnic" differences are based on religious affiliation, reflecting variations among Judaism, Islam, and Christianity. The core of Arab-Jewish differences is not viewed as based on national origins or ethnic characteristics, but religion. The distinction between "religion" and "ethnicity" as the basis of the Arab-Jewish differentiation in Israel lies centrally in the quagmire of a series of political and ideological debates: Are Jews a nation or a religion? What constitutes Arab nationalism? What is the relevance of commonalities among religiously diverse Arabs (Moslem, Christian, and Druze)? The treatment of Arabs in Israel in religious categories denies (symbolically) their ethnic national identity ("Palestinian") and their political relationships to Arabs (or Palestinians) elsewhere in the region.

The Arab-Jewish distinction is designated on the identity card carried by all adults in Israel and characterizes all transactions between Arabs and others in Israel. The Arab-Jewish distinction is therefore clearer publicly and socially than the more-ambiguous ethnic differences among Jews. Arabs are often identified by the majority as the "other" and the category "non-Jew" had been used explicitly in official government publications to reflect this otherness.[3] The formal designation of "minority" in Israel (along with government bureaus of minority affairs) is a category allocated to non-Jewish "religious" groups; their communities have their own "religious" organizational character, with appropriate religious leadership positions and institutions supported by government allocations.

Some might argue that the Arab-Jewish distinction is not another case of ethnic differentiation, because of the unique history and political status of Arabs in Israel, the particular forms of tensions that have long characterized Arab-Jewish relations, and the forms of residential segregation that have emerged. However, the Arab population within the state of Israel has citizenship rights without formal political constraints and with recognized rights enunciated in Israel's declaration of independence. The politics of the region, though, result in less than full rights of participation (e.g., in the military), limited political expression, geographic-regional concentration, and powerful informal rules about geographic mobility and residence, marriage, and social activities, and hence about access to economic opportunities, social integration, and quality education. Until 1966, Israeli Arabs lived under a military administration within Israel and were confined to specific geographic areas, resulting in their sharp differentiation from the Jewish population. In contrast to the political and institutional attempts to reduce ethnic-origin diversity within the Jewish population, Arab-Jewish differences have not been a direct target of policy in Israel. Many of the developments within the Arab sector that have improved the welfare of that population have been an indirect consequence of changes in the Jewish sector (Ben-Porath 1986a).

In the period subsequent to the large migration to Israel from the former Soviet Union, an additional religious category has emerged: "Other." These are non-Jewish, non-Arab Israelis of largely Russian origin who have not met the religious criterion of the Rabbinate for Jewish designation (having a Jewish mother) and are not of another religion. It is indeed a status of uncertainty and ambiguity. In 2013, "Others" in Israel numbered 333,000, having increased from 95,000 in 1995, the first time that designation was used.

Ethnic Identity Variation and Change

Some have argued that in general ethnic categories should be treated as ascriptive—primordial, fixed at birth, and constant throughout the life course (Glazer and Moynihan 1975, among others). In the Israeli case it has been argued that ethnic encounters "take place on the basis of shared primordial historical and religious attachments that preserved the individual communities in their diaspora histories" but that ethnic convergences have tipped the scale in favor of "bridging gaps through a constant effort to draw on what is shared by all" (Morag-Talmon 1989, 37).

However, such an emphasis may be misleading, since it treats ethnicity as a "constant," unchanging over the life course of individuals and between generations, an ascriptive category that is "objective." In contrast, I treat the classification of persons into ethnic categories as a social construction that varies with who is categorizing, whom is categorized, and in what contexts these categories are applied during the life course. Thus, for example, Moslem Israelis may define themselves as Palestinians when joining those on the West Bank in political protest but as Israeli Arabs when they vote; they may be viewed by Israeli Jews as "Arabs" or categorized as "non-Jews." Similarly, third-generation Israeli Jews of Yemenite origins may be classified in Israeli government records as Israelis, born of Israeli-born parents (i.e., without ethnic origins). In a local community they may be classified as of "Middle Eastern" origin (or of Asian-African origin) or classified by family members as Yemenites of a particular regional origin. American Jews living in Israel may be referred to by some as Westerners, European-Americans, Anglo-Saxons, or New Yorkers. When they are touring Europe or visiting family in the United States, they may be labeled "Israelis" (see C. Goldscheider 2001a).

These labels are neither correct nor incorrect but are constructions designed by different "others" in an attempt at social classification and definition. Ethnic categories designated formally or informally can, of course, change over time—in the historical sense of time and in its life-cycle meaning. Young adults living alone may be less likely to identify themselves ethnically, whereas families with young children may be linked to ethnic communities through networks, jobs, schools, friends, and neighborhoods. The salience of ethnic identification may increase as new families are formed or as transitions occur—marriage, childbearing, death—that link the generations. Ethnicity may be reinforced through family networking during particular seasons of the year, holidays, and celebrations. Since the boundaries dividing some ethnic groups tend to be flexible, people are able to shift between groups most commonly at particular points during the life course. Multiple social identities have emerged in modern pluralistic societies; the salience of any one identity varies with the particular context, of which life-course transitions are of special importance because of the link between the life course and family networks.

The life-course perspective emphasizes the treatment of ethnic classification as variable, focused on family networks and intergenerational connections, not as a fixed individual identity or a group ascriptive trait. As transitions occur in the life course — as persons marry and form new families, as they become ill or seek medical treatment, as they have children or when they die — issues of community and family support, of local institutions and networks based on ethnicity, become more salient. In contrast, at points in the life course where there is an emphasis on independence and autonomy, or on broader national identity, ethnic networks are likely to be less valued.

Life-course transitions occur in a generational or a cohort context. Consider, for example, ethnic variation in terms of who has relatives and family available to be supportive in times of health-care needs. The availability of these ethnic family members reflects the fertility and family history of the group, whether marriage has been interethnic or intraethnic, the family's history of migration (who lives where and near whom, revealing degrees of generational family access), and the pattern of family structure and work (the extent of divorce and remarriage, the changing proportion of women working). An examination of different ethnic generations should reveal exposure to integration, distance from origins, and connections to cultures. Combined with the effects of particular time periods, the generational or cohort perspective is of particular importance in the study of ethnic differentiation over the life course.

A final point about terminology: I refer to ethnic categories, communities, and groups as a basis for the classification and categorization of individuals. I am also concerned about the intensity of the connection between the individual and the group. At times, ethnic categories do not capture the range of effects, because categories are static constructions and do not take into account the intensity of ethnic commitments and the variety of attachments within ethnic communities. Generation status or foreign-language use are obvious bases for identifying greater ethnic intensity among some groups. The ethnic composition of neighborhoods and the participation in an ethnic economic enclave are other bases of ethnic intensity. I refer to these indicators of intensity as ethnicity, paralleling the examination of religiosity as the intensity of religious activities or religious commitments of members of different groups.

The Changing Ethnic Mosaic in Israel

Despite the ideological and political denial of Jewish ethnicity in Israel and the concomitant reification of religion as the only basis of cleavage, there is significant ethnic differentiation (at one point in time) and ethnic stratification (over time, between the generations) within Jewish groups. Despite the categorization of diverse groups as "Arab" or "non-Jews," there is also significant variation among Arab Israelis. As we shall document, there is also substantial evidence of convergences among Jewish ethnic groups in some areas of social life. A central theme in the details that I examine in subsequent chapters is how some forms of ethnic differentiation diminish over time and how new forms of distinctiveness emerge for both Jewish and Arab ethnic communities. Underlying and reflecting these emergent ethnic patterns are complex and changing social-demographic processes.

As a prelude to investigating the sources of ethnicity in Israel, I sketch the ethnic composition of the Israeli population and outline the major changes that have occurred. A snapshot, cross-sectional view of ethnicity in Israeli society reveals a complex mosaic of ethnic groups (table 2.1). Out of a total population size of over 8 million in 2012, Jews were the dominant subpopulation, representing 75% of the total, a decline from earlier years, when the Jewish portion of the total was over 80%. Reflecting their immigration history, the Jewish population of 6 million has become increasingly native-born: about one-fourth of the Jewish population was foreign-born in 2012 compared to 65% in 1948. Of the foreign-born in 2012, more than two-thirds were born in Europe or America, 20% were born in Africa, and 12% were born in Asia. More than half (56%) of the fathers of the native-born Israelis were also native-born, 20% were of European or America origin, 13% of African origin, and 11% of Asian origin.

The specific country-of-origin composition of the combined first- and second-generation Jewish Israeli population in 2012 reveals that those

TABLE 2.1

Ethnic and religious composition of Israel's population, 1948–2012

Year	Size of Israel's Jewish population (000s)	Portion of Israel's total population who are Jewish (%)	Portion of Israel's total Jewish population who are foreign-born (%)	Portion of Israel's Arab population who are Moslem (%)
1948	717	82	65	—
1961	1,892	89	62	69
1972	2,753	85	53	76
1983	3,413	83	42	77
1990	3,947	82	38	78
1995	4,522	81	38	81
2012	5,999	74	26	83

Ethnic composition of Israel's foreign- and native-born Jewish population, 2012

	Native-born father's origin (%)	Foreign-born place of birth (%)
Native-born	56	—
Europe/America	20	68
Africa	13	20
Asia	11	12
Total	100	100

Note: Before 1995 Arabs included "others" and were defined as "non-Jews."

Source: These data are drawn from the *Statistical Abstract of Israel*, 2013, especially tables 2-2 through 2-8 and previous yearbooks. Data on early years are in Goldscheider 2002 and Friedlander and Goldscheider 1969.

originating from Western countries (Europe and America) were overwhelmingly from the former Soviet Union, and the rest were from Romania, Poland, and North America; those originating from Africa were mostly from Morocco, Algeria/Tunisia, and Ethiopia; those originating from Asia were from Iraq, Iran, and Yemen. The rank order of these countries of origin has remained the same for well over a decade.

The relative population size of the third generation (Israeli-born of

Israeli-born fathers) is increasing, representing 56% of the Jewish population in 2012. Its ethnic origins can only be estimated, but given past immigration patterns, third-generation Israelis are currently dominated by Jews of Eastern European origin. When the state of Israel was established, there were 716,700 Jews at the end of 1948, representing about 82% of the total population within approximately the same land area as in the twenty-first century. Most of these first Jewish citizens of the state were foreign-born (65%) and of European origin (85%). Thus, while Israel remains ethnically a Western or European state, the Jewish population has increasingly become Israeli-born and distant from immigrant roots. At the same time somewhat less than half of the Jewish population finds its ethnic origins in Asia or Africa.

There were 1,387,500 Moslems in the state of Israel at the end of 2012, almost all of them members of the Sunni branch of Islam. Moslem Israelis were 17% of the total of about 8 million persons in Israel in 2013; 158,400 of the total population were Christian (2%), most Greek Orthodox or Greek Catholic; and 131,500 (1.6%) were Druze. The Arab population has become more Moslem over time, increasing from less than 70% in 1948 to 83% at the end of 2012.

These snapshots, whose beginning and end are 65 years apart, reveal an outline of the story about ethnic compositional changes but miss the processes underlying these changes. Thus, for example, there was a rather stable Jewish-Arab population ratio for over half a century from the founding of the state, despite the rapid population growth of both groups. This stable ratio reflects the growth of the Jewish population through immigration, combined with the indirect effects of the fertility of the immigrants; the growth of the Arab population has been largely by natural increase—the excess of births over deaths (Friedlander and Goldscheider 1984). How have these different demographic factors shaped the emergence of ethnic groups and the processes of ethnic-group integration in the context of nation-building in Israel? What are the important implications of these differential processes for the nature of political, social, and cultural change?

Contexts of Ethnic Differences
Methodological Considerations
Ethnic differences characterize social life in Israel, as in other pluralistic societies. The question is what are the contexts that sharpen or dimin-

ish these differences generationally? Answering this contextual question requires addressing several sources of complexity in the examination of ethnic groups. First, ethnic differences vary over time, as the distinctiveness of groups changes and as differences among them in some areas of social life narrow or widen. Second, the importance of ethnic differentiation relative to other characteristics—for example, education, region, or occupation—changes over time as well and may be more pronounced among some groups. Third, convergences in ethnic differences in some areas of social life do not necessarily imply convergences in all areas. These features suggest that ethnic differentiation may be discontinuous over time and from one social dimension to another. In turn, the similarity among ethnic groups in the past or in one sphere of activity does not necessarily imply continued similarity under all conditions. Thus, the changing contexts of ethnic differences need to be explicitly considered.

Although general theories of ethnicity have not been fully specified, social scientists have suggested some historical, economic, political, and social factors that are important in the study of ethnic continuity and change in general. The identification of these factors offers the first clues for understanding the changing contexts of Israeli ethnic patterns.

Of critical significance in studying the changing importance of ethnicity in society is to examine changes in socioeconomic opportunities and the differential access of ethnic groups to these opportunities. The concentrations of ethnic groups in particular jobs, neighborhoods, industries, and schools imply at times socioeconomic disadvantage and inequalities. The ethnic–social class overlap almost always indicates more-intensive interaction with members of the ethnic community than with those outside the ethnic boundaries. The overlap of ethnic factors and social class connects to the importance of family and economic linkages. Social class combines with broad family-economic networks to establish bonds of community and generational continuities. Hence, the generational transmission of inequality becomes the key to understanding ethnicity over time. The importance of formal and informal, explicit or subtle forms of discrimination in jobs, housing, schools, and government allocations are among the primary factors that reinforce ethnic communities.

Changes in the generational reproduction of groups and their general demographic characteristics are also important in understanding the dynamics of ethnic-group change. Population size, structure, and cohort succession are structural features that delimit ethnic marriage markets and family formation, childbearing, schooling, and the socialization of the next generation into the ethnic community. Migration (and for some groups, immigration) is of particular importance in the generational continuity of ethnic groups at the national and community levels.

Ethnic intensity is likely to be greater when the ethnic origins (and hence the intergenerational bonds) of a couple are the same. When ethnic family members live close to one another, when they attend the same schools, have similar jobs and leisure activities, marry within their ethnic group, and are involved in ethnic social and political institutions, then ethnic attachments within groups are more intensive. Examining the intensities of ethnic attachments reinforces the notion that ethnic classification should be treated with movable boundaries over time; the degree of involvement in the ethnic community will vary over the life course.

In addition to the socioeconomic and demographic factors connected to ethnic groups, there is the important role that the state may play, including the development and implementation of ethnic-specific policies. The state may indirectly shape ethnic communities through policies affecting education, real estate and housing, business practices, jobs, public welfare, and health systems. The entitlement systems common in modern welfare states and their links to ethnic factors, therefore, influence ethnic continuities and change. These systems can encourage and reinforce ethnic political mobilization and may often become the basis for the institutional expressions of ethnic interests (see Glazer and Moynihan 1975; C. Goldscheider 1995).

These "external" contexts are often complemented by the reinforcing role that ethnic institutions play in sustaining continuity. Some of these are family based and others are political, social, and cultural institutions that create a more-intense ethnic community. In the absence of economic discrimination or ethnic markers that distinguish groups in the eyes of others, ethnic institutions become the major constraint on the total assimilation of ethnic populations.

My investigation of the changing ethnic factor in Israel, therefore, disentangles cultural from social-class linkages; separates factors that reflect attitudes from those that are primarily issues of access and availability; distinguishes technological factors from those embedded in the social, demographic, and economic structure; and analyzes those factors that reflect intergenerational continuities and those that are cohort-specific. I separate as well individual-based factors of ethnic identity from those that relate to the family and household, the community, the state, and the broader society. Operating between the life course of individuals and the impact of the state on ethnicity are families and households, with their extensive patterns of exchanges that I refer to as community. Community and family factors are powerful and conspicuous bases of ethnic continuity, shaping the ways individuals identify themselves ethnically.

Ethnicity based on immigration has often been assumed to diminish with time and exposure to the new place of destination. As generations exposed to places of destination increase, the impact of origins recedes in memory and diminishes in effect on the life of the group. As the third and fourth generations are socialized and integrated into the economy, are dispersed residentially and geographically, are exposed to the influences of educational institutions and mass media, and interact with others on a basis other than ethnic origin, their ethnicity melts away—they are homogenized into the larger culture and become undifferentiated through intergroup marriages and broader national political identification. This view assumes the centrality of the past for the continuity of groups in the present and de-emphasizes the roles of family and community. When ethnicity is viewed primarily through the past, the driving questions are, How much of the past is retained in the face of pressures toward integration and cultural homogenization? How long does it take before ethnicity becomes only "nostalgia" or symbolic and hence difficult to transmit generationally?

This perspective appears to distort the questions that I address about the ethnic phenomenon. In contemporary Israeli society, ethnicity is constructed (or reconstructed) out of the present circumstances, shaped not simply by what was, but by what is, incorporating selectively from the past within the present. Ethnicity revolves around institutions, those that reduce and those that sustain ethnic communities. In the process, new ethnic forms appear as different institutions develop to reflect these emergent cultural forms. Even when cultural differences weaken, institutions can be retained and can continue to shape communities. These institutions include family and kin, and social, economic, cultural, and political organizations. Ethnic groups that have retained, developed, and extended institutions have more-cohesive communities compared to those whose search for individual identity or for cultural forms of the past take precedence over social institutions.

Interpreting Ethnic Differentiation
General Orientations

The identification of factors associated with ethnic groups and ethnicity is a starting point in my examination of Israeli society. To consider how these various themes fit together as a whole requires the presentation of some map or theoretical framework to organize how ethnic differences have been interpreted and to provide guidelines for the analysis of ethnic variation. The three types of interpretations that have been used to analyze ethnic variation are cultural, social-class, and community networks—each emphasizing a different dimension of social organization and together providing a helpful orientation to studying ethnicity.[4]

Culture as Ethnicity. The first framework emphasizes the cultural aspects of ethnic groups and posits that ethnic variation reflects the culture or the values of groups. An emphasis on cultural themes focuses attention on indicators of values and foreignness and on closeness to the sources of ethnic cultural origins. Ethnic differences are reduced over time as acculturation into the mainstream of society occurs. The process of becoming culturally similar to the dominant group advances through increased educational attainment and contacts with others in schools, neighborhoods, and on the job; through changes in the use of a foreign language; and through adopting local cultural values. The salience of ethnic distinctiveness recedes as groups of diverse cultural origins embrace similar values. Remaining ethnic differences reflect the legacy of the past that is temporary and transitional; differences may be maintained by the state through multicultural policies.

This source of ethnic distinctiveness is more likely to characterize the foreign-born and their immediate family members, those who speak a language other than the national language, and those who have received most of their socialization elsewhere. The second and third generations, socialized formally in places of destination, are more distant from their cultural roots. Ethnic groups that are culturally closer to the native population (i.e., those whose values are from areas that most closely resemble their place of current residence) are more likely to lose their cultural distinctiveness compared to others whose cultural roots are less similar.

Social Class and Ethnicity. A second explanation treats ethnic distinctiveness as a reflection of the social-class composition of ethnic groups. The association of ethnic differences with socioeconomic disadvantage and inequality has a long history in social-science research. The argument is that ethnic differences—whether generated by discrimination and racism or by unequal access to opportunities, or whether fed by immigration and the lower occupational and educational origins of ethnic immigrant groups—reflect the disadvantaged socioeconomic status of the group as a whole and the inequalities in the overlap of social class and ethnic origin. Observed differences among ethnic groups are therefore primarily social-class differences. Occupational mobility and education are the key processes that eliminate ethnic distinctiveness. Ethnic groups that are not concentrated generationally in particular social-class categories and that no longer have a disadvantaged socioeconomic status become integrated and assimilated into the society. Ethnic continuity, therefore, implies generational inequality and persistent socioeconomic gaps between ethnic groups.

In its more-extreme form, this social-class argument views a focus on ethnic differences as distorting the underlying socioeconomic disadvantages of disenfranchised groups. The analysis of ethnic differences, it follows, should examine correlates of poverty and inequality and social-class discrimination and competition. The reduction of economic discrimination—changes in the overlap of social class and ethnic origin through equalized education and job opportunities and through residential mobility and generational discontinuities in socioeconomic characteristics—should diminish and eventually eliminate the basis of ethnic distinctiveness.

Both the cultural and social-class perspectives tap important dimensions of the differences among ethnic groups in Israel. Ethnic differences become the combined consequence of cultural and social-class factors; when social-class factors are neutralized and discrimination is minimized, the remaining ethnic differences are "only" cultural. These unmeasured, residual cultural factors are minor and tend to weaken generationally. Cultural factors are reinforced by the disadvantaged socioeconomic position of ethnic groups, which reflects discrimination, blocked opportunities, and economic origin (including the occupational skills and lower educational levels of the first generation acquired elsewhere).

In more-complex interactions, cultural forms of ethnicity are considered more intense among the less-educated, poorer social classes, since social mobility and the attainment of middle-class and higher status minimizes the salience of ethnic distinctiveness.[5]

Both perspectives, in their own way, project the steady reduction of ethnic differences over time in Israel when cultural integration occurs, usually with the length of exposure to Israeli society. With linguistic homogeneity, educational equalization, and the reduction in ethnic job discrimination and residential segregation—and, in general, when social-class factors are more equalized among groups—ethnic distinctiveness should be reduced or eliminated.

The cultural and social-class perspectives assume that ethnic particularism and discrimination are likely to diminish over time because of the ideological and institutional commitments of the state toward the integration of groups into a political and economic system based on merit, achievement, and universalism. Hence, with political modernization, the social-class basis of ethnic differentiation declines, and cultural differences are homogenized. In short, the salience of group differences diminishes. Indeed, the Arab exception in Israel is often used to prove the rule. When discrimination blocks the integration of groups and their access to economic opportunities, continued inequality and distinctiveness are reinforced. When residential segregation and family patterns are reinforced by state policies, ethnic differentiation is likely to persist generationally. Hence, political and social factors reinforce Arab cultural distinctiveness.

Ethnicity as Community Networks. An alternative and complementary view to the cultural and social-class arguments, and the third framework, places emphasis on the structural networks and the power of a community and its institutions to reinforce ethnic distinctiveness and identity. The networks of ethnic communities may be extensive. They are often tied to places of residence, connected to families, linked to economic activities and enclaves, and expressed in political ties, cultural expressions, and lifestyles. These networks are reinforced by institutions and organizations that are ethnically based. The key element of this argument is that the cohesion of ethnic communities is based primarily on institutions and networks. Hence, the intensity of community is facilitated by the intensity of social networks: the greater the social networks and the denser the institutions, the greater the cohesion of the ethnic community. Cohesion is reflected both in interaction patterns and in cultural expressions. The larger the number of spheres where interaction occurs within the ethnic community, the more cohesive the group; the greater the arenas of cultural particularities and activities, the higher the rate of ethnic attachments.[6]

According to this perspective, the basis of ethnic community is the extent of ethnic ties to the labor market over the life course, not simply the overlap of ethnicity and social class. Changing economic networks forge the greater interactions within ethnic communities, developing bonds of family and economic activities at different points during the life course. The support of kin and family and the concentration of ethnic groups in geographically defined areas become important bases of ethnic continuity. Whatever the values, common background, specific history, and unique culture are that may bind ethnic members together in a "primordial" sense, the key factors involved within this framework are structural — residence, jobs, schooling, and family. The cultural bases of ethnic groups reinforce and justify the cohesion of the community and are themselves variable, but they do not determine its continuity. Cultural distinctiveness and values occur in social contexts, and their construction changes over time as contexts change.

When networks and the communication within ethnic groups are strong, ethnic-group attachments are more salient. Viewed in this way, ethnic distinctiveness is not limited to unacculturated immigrant groups or to ethnic groups that have experienced discrimination or are economically disadvantaged. Ethnic communities are sustained by informal institutions and networks, are often reinforced by local politics and policies, and are enhanced by extended family connections.

The network perspective emphasizes that national attachments do not necessarily imply the reduction of ethnic-group distinctiveness, even when discrimination diminishes and social mobility occurs. Under some conditions, nation-building reinforces distinctiveness, particularly when there is increased socioeconomic competition among ethnic groups, intensified forms of economic concentration, and residential segregation. Often ethnicity is reinforced rather than diminished when acculturation takes place, when the values among ethnic groups become more similar, and when socioeconomic competition among groups becomes sharper. Ethnic social mobility through improvements in education and jobs may increase economic concentration at the upper levels of socioeconomic status, just as ethnicity was associated in the past with concentration at lower socioeconomic levels.

Under some conditions, nation-building results in the total assimilation of ethnic groups through the erosion of community and family-based institutions, through residential integration and intergroup marriages, through open-market forces and universal schooling, and through state policies that provide access to opportunities and that enforce nondiscrimination. But not always, not for all groups, and not as an inevitable by-product of urbanization, economic development, nationalism, and social mobility. The specific contexts must be studied to examine these patterns so as not to infer them from broad patterns of societal change.

Treating ethnicity as networks implies that ethnic groups may not necessarily be transitional or unimportant features of modern societies. Ethnicity may be embedded in the institutions, politics, and economy in ways that are likely to have a significant impact on the lives of people. The reinforcement of ethnic connections through continuous patterns of immigration ensures that ethnic origins remain important factors that distinguish communities for an even longer period of time. Community, not individual, identity is the most fruitful unit for an examination of ethnic expression in Israel. Therefore, I argue explicitly against those who would examine ethnicity among Jewish Israelis mainly as a reflection of transitional immigrant categories and individual ethnic identity.

Using community and networks as the framework, I emphasize in upcoming chapters how policies within Israel have reinforced generational continuities among some ethnic groups, and I study the role of external factors in the evolution of ethnic communities (e.g., changing immigration patterns and the Israeli-Arab conflicts in the Middle East region). The documentation of continuing ethnic differences in a variety of social, economic, and political spheres and the estimation of ethnic convergences over time in other social and demographic arenas provide the basis for assessing ethnic communities in Israel.

NOTES

1. The word used in Israel to describe Jewish immigrant integration is "absorption" (*klitah* in Hebrew). This is a rather unusual description of assimilation. The concept of assimilation is almost always used in Israel to designate the integration of Jews as a minority in communities outside the state. From a Zionist ideological

perspective, it has a negative connotation of "total" assimilation—the loss of community, continuity, and identity as Jews.

2. In the Israeli censuses, there are no provisions to directly ask ethnic ancestry. For many younger persons of the third generation who are Israeli-born and living with their parents, ethnic identifiers are indirectly available only through place-of-origin data on their parents. For young adults of the third generation not living with their parents, no ethnic identifiers are collected.

3. The designation of Arab as "other" or "non-Jewish" precedes the establishment of the state. The Balfour Declaration of 1917 specifying the commitments of Britain to the establishment of a "national home for the Jewish People" in Palestine explicitly notes that the civil and religious rights of the "non-Jewish communities" should be safeguarded.

4. As in all generalizations, this is oversimplified, although it is useful for a broad orientation (see C. Goldscheider and Zuckerman 1984; Smooha 1989).

5. On the cultural basis of ethnicity see various essays in Hertzog et al. 2010.

6. For an application of this argument to the historical and comparative conditions of one ethnic-religious minority in Europe and America, see C. Goldscheider and Zuckerman 1984; C. Goldscheider 2004; see also Alba and Nee 2005.

3 | Immigration, Nation-Building, and Ethnic-Group Formation

Israeli society has been shaped by immigration patterns more than most other countries. Changes in the rates of immigration and in the characteristics of immigrants are critical for understanding each of the major themes that guide this analysis—nation-building, ethnic and religious continuities and change, and socioeconomic inequalities. The ethnic mosaic and ethnic integration processes in Israeli society have been affected directly by fluctuations in the volume of immigration over time from different places of origin, as have all the major social and demographic transformations involving the immigrants and their children. Social, economic, cultural, and political developments in Israel and the internal conflicts among Jews and between Arabs and Jews are linked to the changing intensities of immigration and to the socioeconomic and demographic characteristics of those migrating. Moreover, immigration ideologies and policies have been at the core of Zionist ideology, political movements, and institutions for over a century, predating the establishment of the state and changing with its development. In this chapter, I outline the main contours of immigration patterns over time, their fluctuations and selectivity, and sketch some of the issues that will emerge and are the detailed foci of subsequent chapters.

Ideology and the Uniqueness of Immigration to Israel

Immigration has been a major strategy of nation-building in the state of Israel: the Zionist movement since the nineteenth century and the state of Israel from the time of its establishment have sought to gather together in one country those around the world who consider themselves Jewish by religion or ancestry. The processes, patterns, and policies of immigration have been unique. The conditions in Europe preceding and following the Holocaust and World War II, the emerging nationalism among Jews around the world, the conditions of Jews in Arab-Moslem countries, and the radical changes in the 1990s in Eastern Europe with the breakup of the Soviet Union have been among the most obvious external circumstances influencing the immigration of Jews from a wide range of countries to Israel. The emergence of a large and integrated American Jewish community that has not immigrated in substantial numbers to Israel is an additional factor in understanding the selectivity of Jewish migrations to Israel.

There are, of course, internal developments in Israel that have influenced the pace and selectivity of immigration. The demographic expansion of the Jewish community in pre-state Palestine, the attractions of economic opportunity and Jewish political control, Israeli cultural developments, and religious activities have been important factors influencing decisions to immigrate. War and military victories have generated national commitments and euphoria that encouraged immigration (as in the post-1948 and post-1967 periods), but they have also caused fear and anxiety about living in uncertain and dangerous circumstances.

Immigration to Israel is also special because of the sociocultural diversity of the immigrants, their overwhelming importance in the formation and development of Israeli society, and the concentration of immigration in the first three years after the establishment of the state and in the 1990s. Immigration—in its ideological, policy, and behavioral forms—has symbolized the renewal of Jewish control over national developments and is a core value shared by Jews around the world. At the same time, it has been one of the core symbols of the conflicts between Jews and Arabs in the Middle East (Al Haj 1992; Friedlander and Goldscheider 1979; C. Goldscheider 1990, 2001b; Smooha 1991).

Not surprisingly, immigration has been perceived very differently by Jewish and Arab populations in Israel (Al Haj 1992; Smooha 1991; Smooha 2012). An overwhelming majority of Israeli Jews are committed to the continuation of further Jewish immigration as an implementation of the Zionist agenda and a justification of their own national commitments. The Israeli Arab population views further Jewish immigration as part of the asymmetry between Jews and Palestinians, as a further diminution of their political power, and as a dilution of limited national economic resources. Immigration is central for understanding Israeli society because it shaped the ethnic composition of Israel's Jewish population and redefined the position of its Arab minority. Thus the immigration of Jews to a country of their own has been more than the process of moving people from one place to another. It has meant the building of a Jewish state, reinforcing national goals, and the expansion of an entire set of institutions. It has also meant converting the Arab population from a majority population before the establishment of the state to a minority group when the new boundaries of its population were drawn in 1948 (Al Haj 1987).

Yet the strategy of nation-building through immigration has been used by many countries (Alonso 1987). Parallels with the role of immigration in other countries should not obscure the fact that immigration for Israel remains special because of the ideological centrality of immigration and its overwhelming importance in the formation and development of Israeli society, and the fact that Jews "returning" to the state of Israel descended from ancestors who had not lived there for almost 2,000 years.[1] As it was for the United States at an earlier period of its history, immigration is Israeli history.[2] Understanding the basic contours of who immigrated to Israel, when and from which areas of the world they arrived, what happened to them in their integration into Israeli society, and what the connections are between places of origin and destination will go far in clarifying the changes in Israeli society since the establishment of the state through the first decade of the twenty-first century. Pick any thread of social life in Israel—family, social mobility, residential patterns, politics, religion, stratification, culture—and the role of immigration will be important. Identify any social problem—Arab-Jewish relationships, inequality, economic dependencies, ethnic-religious conflict—and the continuing effects of immigration become clear. Here, I document core features of immigration and sketch their importance in nation-building—economic development, demographic growth, and ethnic compositional changes. I begin with a brief overview of the historical context.

The Historical Context
Jewish Immigration to Palestine
Jewish immigration to Palestine and Israel has been rooted in theological aspects of Judaism for centuries and in secular Jewish nationalism, Zionism, since the middle of the nineteenth century. The beginnings of modern international immigration to Palestine, and subsequently to Israel, may be traced to the end of the nineteenth century, when organized groups of Jewish immigrants entered Palestine to build a national Jewish homeland. This migration was part of a much larger-scale immigration out of Eastern Europe, mainly in the direction of the United States and

other Western, industrialized nations (C. Goldscheider and Zuckerman 1984). Ideological factors were central to the immigration of this small segment moving to Palestine, since social, economic, and political conditions in Palestine were not conducive to immigration. The migrants to Palestine were a small, select, relatively well-educated, secular, urban group entering a different cultural milieu, with the goal of working in agriculture to develop barren wastelands in order to create the basis of a new Jewish society (Horowitz and Lissak 1989).

The First Immigration Waves. Two major waves of immigration occurred during the late nineteenth and early twentieth centuries (Friedlander and Goldscheider 1979). First, from 1882 to 1903, an estimated 25,000 Jewish immigrants arrived in Palestine, doubling the 1880 Jewish population there. During these years, the revolutionary migrants lacked funds and had little or no agricultural skills. They were rescued by outside capital, particularly from Jewish foreign investors. Over time, they hired Arab laborers and became administrators. Paternalism and inefficiency, along with disillusionment and emigration, became the dominant characteristics of these first settlers. The initial Jewish settlers were colonialists in their economic dependency on Jewish capitalistic interests outside Palestine and in their relationship to local Arab labor.

A second wave of immigrants, estimated to number between 40,000 and 55,000, entered Palestine during the decade beginning in 1904 and built on the foundations of the first wave. Many had been part of the organized Zionist movement in Europe and had been active socialists in Russia. Their goal was to shape a new social order in Palestine based on socialist principles and secular Zionist ideology. The growing Zionist movement recruited, organized, and financed the immigrants, facilitating their migration and easing their economic accommodation and the purchase and development of land. The new immigrants in Palestine expanded existing agricultural settlements and founded new urban and industrial communities. They were educated, politically articulate, and skillful organizers. The activities and principles of those immigrants in this second wave were at the heart of the social, cultural, political, and economic settlement of Jews in Palestine and subsequently the state of Israel (C. Goldscheider and Zuckerman 1984). The entry of these migrants into Palestine was opposed by the formal policies of the Ottoman government of Palestine. The opposition was ineffective, since the administrative apparatus to control and regulate immigration and to implement the formal policies was largely defective (Mandel 1976; Friedlander and Goldscheider 1979).

Thus, these two early waves of immigration to Palestine did not follow the established out-migration pattern in European modernization. The heavy reliance on outside capital, dependence on external economic and political support, shifts of urban workers into agriculture and rural residence, and the lack of conspicuous economic opportunity as an incentive for immigration were exceptional features. Whereas most of those who emigrated from Eastern European countries were motivated by the relatively better economic opportunities available at their destinations and were moving into areas of urban industrial development, Jews immigrating to Palestine were guided by ideological commitments and political-nationalistic goals.

The British Mandate. Two major immigration policies dominated the British Mandate period in Palestine after World War I (Friedlander and Goldscheider 1979). Until 1936, the guiding British policy was the regulation of selective types of immigration based in large part on economic criteria. The number of migrants subsidized by Zionist organizations was adjusted to what became defined as the "economic absorptive capacity" of the country. This regulation of immigration varied over the period but cumulatively allowed the entry of 300,000 Jewish immigrants, half of whom were subsidized and over 90% of whom were from European countries. (See fig. 3.1 in C. Goldscheider 2002 for patterns of Jewish immigration to Palestine, 1919–1948.) Nothing in this British policy prevented wide annual fluctuations in the volume or composition of immigrants. Changes outside Palestine—in particular, the changing quota restrictions on immigrant entry into the United States, political changes in Poland and later in Central Europe that directly affected Jews economically and culturally, and the economic depression in Europe—were major factors shaping the ebb and flow of migration.

The second period of the British Mandate, from 1937 to Israel's declaration of statehood in 1948, was characterized by increasingly restrictive British immigration policies. These were directed toward greater British control over the total volume of Jewish immigration, using political and demographic criteria (the ratio of Jewish to Arab populations). During this period, 175,000 Jewish immigrants arrived in Palestine, the majority legally. British policy prevented an even larger number of immigrants from entering, particularly refugees from the Holocaust. Increasingly, toward the latter part of the period, British policy directly controlled the timing and volume of immigration. By the end of the British Mandate period, most Jewish immigrants were entering Palestine illegally, and they became important symbols in the struggle for Jewish national independence.

Throughout the pre-state period, there were ambiguous British political commitments to both Jewish and Arab nationalism. The emergence and strengthening of the Zionist movement—with an emphasis on immigration, settlement, and development—occurred alongside the growing momentum of Arab nationalism. Improved economic conditions in Palestine, changes in immigration policy, and Zionist political ideology were not the main determinants of changing immigration patterns. Although ideological factors were clearly operative and important in the immigration of the early Zionists, it is incomplete to argue, as some have (Horowitz and Lissak 1989), that the waves of Jewish immigration were ideologically motivated during the British period. Ideology played little direct role in the Polish and German migration of the 1920s and 1930s and was hardly the major factor through 1948. Instead, the deteriorating political situation of Jews in Europe after the rise of Hitler and Nazism in the 1930s was a major push factor. The absence of attractive (or available) alternative destinations, facilitated the flow of these Jewish migrants to Palestine.

During the entire Mandate period, British policy was oriented toward the regulation and control of Jewish immigration. There were no clear policy guidelines on Arab immigration to Palestine. Arab migrants from neighboring areas were part of the movement of labor, often seasonal and temporary, in response to better short-term economic opportunities in Palestine. Most of the demographic growth of the Arab population in Palestine was through natural increase; immigration was the primary source of Jewish population growth (for documentation see Friedlander and Goldscheider 1979 and the discussion in Kimmerling and Migdal 1993).

Jewish Immigration, 1948 to the
Twenty-First Century Four Major Streams

Between 1948 and 2013, over 3 million Jewish immigrants entered the state of Israel, an average of about 50,000 per year (see fig. 3.1 for annual numbers). Of this total, over two-thirds were from European or Western countries and less than one-third from Middle Eastern (or Asian-African)

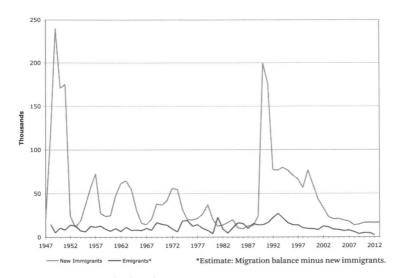

FIGURE 3.1   *Israel Migrations, 1947–2013*
Source: Israeli Central Bureau of Statistics, data compiled and processed
by Sergio Dellapergola (see Dellapergola 2013). Used with permission.

countries. The proportion of immigrants from Asian-African countries
shifted from over 70% in the period from 1952 to 1957 to less than 10% in
the early 1970s and 1990s. Immigration during the late 1980s and 1990s
was dominated by a large movement from Russia (and from the republics
of the former Soviet Union). Of the 956,000 immigrants to Israel during
the 1990s, about 90% were from Europe, most from Eastern Europe. From
2000 to 2012, 318,000 immigrants arrived, over three-fourths from Western countries (see C. Goldscheider 2002 for patterns of Jewish immigration to Israel, 1948–1999).

New policies of immigration were implemented after the establishment of the state of Israel, contrasting sharply with the immigration restrictions enforced by the British. There was a conjunction of social and
political pressures to open the gates of immigration widely to Jews coming from a variety of countries. As the highest priority, the state was to be
a refuge for the Jewish survivors of the Holocaust. The movement of these
European Jewish refugees to the new state was a critical part of the political rationale for its establishment, particularly since there were no alternative destinations for the thousands of stateless Jewish persons. Over
time, Jewish communities in several neighboring Middle East countries

and more-distant Arab states also began looking toward Israel for refuge as their minority populations became increasingly vulnerable following the Arab-Israeli War of 1948. Jewish nationalist ideology gained international political strength and increased legitimacy from the potential for large-scale immigration of persecuted and displaced Jews from Europe and the Middle East.

The formal context of Israel's immigration policy is contained in the Declaration of Independence (passed on May 14, 1948): "The State of Israel is open to Jewish immigration and the Ingathering of Exiles." This policy was combined with the first order enacted by the provisional Jewish government: to abolish the British restrictions on immigration and to define "illegal" Jewish immigrants retroactively as legal residents of the country. Together, these actions represented the foundation of Israel's immigration policy during the first two years subsequent to statehood. The Law of Return enacted July 5, 1950, granted to every Jew in the world the right to immigrate and settle in Israel, with minor exceptions related to health and security. These formal regulations do not convey the main thrust of Israel's policy, however, which was not only to allow such immigration but to actively encourage and subsidize the major phases associated with the immigration process (Friedlander and Goldscheider 1979).

From the establishment of the state of Israel in 1948 through the first decade of the twenty-first century, the rates of immigration and the countries of origin of the immigrants have fluctuated significantly and can be divided roughly into four main periods.

Mass Immigration, 1948–1951. The first and most dramatic immigrant stream occurred immediately after the establishment of the state and is referred to as the period of "mass" immigration. During the three years following the establishment of the state of Israel, in the context of war and the transition to national independence, a very large surge of Jewish immigrants from diverse countries of origin arrived (see fig. 3.1). The high rate of immigration doubled the size of the Jewish population—350,000 immigrants arrived in the first eighteen months after statehood and an additional 350,000 arrived during the following one and one-half years. It was a massive undertaking to provide the basics of settlement—housing, jobs, schooling, and health services—for immigrants who were not able to use the national language (Hebrew) and who often arrived from the depths of deprivation in postwar Europe. All the immigrants were arriving to a newly established polity, an expanding economy, and an emerging society. The immediate adjustment was complicated by the immigration of Jews from Middle Eastern countries, whose culture and language were significantly different from the European orientations of the emerging nation.

In the first period immediately subsequent to statehood, the immigrants were European in origin—Jewish refugees from the Holocaust coming to a predominantly European-origin society; in 1948, 85% of the 100,000 immigrants to Israel were of European origin. This pattern changed as Jewish immigrants from Middle Eastern countries joined this stream: in 1949 and 1950 only about half of the immigrants were from Europe; by 1951, over 70% of the immigrants were from Asian and North African countries, mainly Iraq, Iran, and Libya. The primary determinants of this migration were political and economic, with some elements of religious messianism among Jews from the traditional communities of the Middle East. The period of mass immigration established some of the basic contours of Israeli society—expanding major social, political, economic, and cultural institutions, including the development and extension of the welfare entitlement system.

North African Immigration. The second major stream of immigration to Israel occurred beginning in the mid-1950s, when over half the immigrants were from North African countries, particularly Morocco, Tunisia, and Egypt. Coming on the heels of mass immigration and the subsequent strains of nation-building and immigrant adjustment, 165,000 immigrants arrived between 1955 and 1957. The occupational skills and educational backgrounds of these immigrants differed significantly from those of the earlier European-origin streams. Immigrants were now arriving with fewer occupational skills and lower levels of education and were not easily integrated into the labor market. Selective immigration quotas and regulations to control the negative economic impact of large-scale migration were imposed by Israel during this period. Immigration continued slowly and picked up again in the early 1960s, when half of the 228,000 immigrants from 1961 to 1964 came from North African countries.

Soviet and Western Immigration, Post-1967. The third major immigration wave began after the 1967 war, mostly from Eastern Europe (the Soviet Union and Romania) and from Western countries, mainly the United States. These areas contained the largest Jewish populations outside Israel; therefore, they were the major potential sources of Jewish immigration. Between 1972 and 1979, 267,582 immigrants arrived in Israel, 51% from the Soviet Union and 8% from the United States; of the 153,833 immigrants to Israel between 1980 and 1989, 65% were from Europe and the United States, 11% from Ethiopia, and 6% from Iran. Restrictions on the emigration of Jews from the Soviet Union and the option of alternative destinations (particularly the United States) reduced the flow of Russian immigrants to Israel until 1989. This third wave of immigrants entered Israel in the post-1967 period of economic growth and geographic extension, which was also characterized by a new national political and military self-confidence.

Higher standards of immigrant integration within the society emerged during this period. Attention to adequate housing, jobs, and provisions for university-level education for the children of immigrants contrasted with the elementary health care and minimum living accommodations provided to previous immigrant waves. The contrast between the subsidies offered to the new immigrants, particularly among those entering voluntarily from Western countries, and those available to the immigrants of the second period from Middle Eastern countries was conspicuous. The political challenge remained to provide resources in order to encourage new immigration and to ensure the immigrants' "absorption"; nevertheless, some immigrants of previous waves and their Israeli-born children remained disadvantaged.

Russians: The New Masses. The latest immigration stream to Israel began in 1989 and has continued into the twenty-first century. Significant numbers of Russian Jews emigrated from the former Soviet Union. (Immigration restrictions reduced the number of Russian Jews entering the United States during this period.) Of the 1 million Jewish immigrants who arrived in Israel during this period, the overwhelming majority were from areas of the former Soviet Union. The number of immigrants was the largest since the period of mass immigration half a century earlier (although not the rate relative to the base population in Israel). This immigration stream is the largest ever to Israel from any one country during such a brief time period.

In addition to these four main waves of immigration, there have been other notable trends. During the 1980s, 17,000 Ethiopian Jews were airlifted to Israel, and an additional 40,000 entered Israel from Ethiopia in the 1990s. Although few in number, these immigrants symbolize Israel's continuing commitment to be the political haven for refugee Jews from around the world. Ethiopian Jews have a significantly different cultural, religious, and economic background compared to other immigrants and to the native Israeli-born population, with a lower level of exposure to the educational, health, and welfare systems of Western nations and a lower level of formal education. They have occupational skills that need to be translated into the competitive postindustrial, service economy of Israel. At the end of 2012, the Ethiopian community numbered 131,000, of whom 85,000 were born in Ethiopia; the rest were born in Israel of Ethiopian origins. They are highly concentrated in the central and southern districts of Israel and almost all (90%) marry within their own communities. Only in one community do Ethiopians constitute as much as 10% of the local population (Kiryat Malakhi, 16%). There is a declining trend in the number of immigrants from Ethiopia; fewer than 2,500 arrived in 2012.

Non-Jewish immigration is another trend. During the 1990s, over 80% of the immigrants from Russia were defined as Jewish. Rather suddenly, though, the proportion of non-Jews entering Israel from the former Soviet Union increased to almost 50% in 1999–2000. The volume of Jewish immigration from Russia to Israel has since declined, reflecting the reduced size of the Jewish population there and the increased Jewish activities reemerging in Russia. On the other hand, conditions in Israel have also changed, as economic and political problems make immigration less attractive. A significant number of Jews still remain in Russia, living under uncertain economic and political conditions. They are the potential for future immigration to Israel. Meanwhile, labor demands in particular industries in Israel have resulted in the importation of temporary workers (non-Jewish) recruited from Romania, Thailand, and the Philippines who arrive on special work permits. These skilled and unskilled laborers have replaced the large pool of Palestinians from the administered territories who, starting in 2000–2001, were no longer part of the commuting labor pool working within Israel.

The new immigration in the twenty-first century represents a continuing challenge to Israeli society. As in the past, serious short-term problems of housing and education have been generated by the volume of Russian immigration. It is likely that the descendants of previous waves of immigrants, particularly those who are disadvantaged economically, will have negative reactions to these newcomers and to the government subsidies they receive. Clearly the Arab Israeli population will continue to view the Russian immigration negatively and as competitors for government funds and benefits. Ethnic competition, if not ethnic conflict, is likely to result. Russian Jews who have arrived in Israel are well educated, with professional occupations and high socioeconomic aspirations for their children. They tend to be relatively uneducated in Jewish history, religion, and culture, having come from a secular society that had for decades denigrated the role of religion and limited the development of Jewish institutions. As we shall document (chapter 6), their levels of religiosity in Israel are significantly lower than those of other groups within the Jewish population. Also, the experience of Russian immigrants with non-Russian forms of political democracy has been weak, which could lead them, one might think, to greater vulnerability in the Israeli political system. However, for the first time in Israel's political history, one ethnic group has successfully organized to form powerful political parties as a basis for political mobilization and power sharing. Russian political parties have become the third-largest bloc in Israel's political system. There is every reason to assume that the adjustment problems among this latest immigrant wave will be short-term and transitional, as they have been for previous waves of immigrants.

Given a choice of destinations, many Jews leaving Russia have turned to the United States. For those emigrating from the Soviet Union in the 1980s, well over half (and in the late 1980s, close to 90%) rejected immigration to Israel in favor of the United States. A comprehensive study of Russian immigrants concluded that had they all had the choice of destination, about half would not have immigrated to Israel and most would have selected the United States (Al Haj and Leshem 2000; see also Gitelman 2012). Increasingly, significant numbers have moved to Western European countries. The degree of economic and social integration Russian immigrants achieve will influence whether they remain in Israel and whether their relatives will join them. A peaceful resolution of the Israeli-Arab conflict or continuation of the violence that began in 2000–2001 will affect the amount of further immigration and the possible return migration or forward migration of the Russians who have already arrived in Israel. Economic and family networks pull new immigrants from the former Soviet Union and retain those who had moved earlier.

The lack of rapidly expanding economic opportunities to match the high educational and occupational skill levels of the new immigrants and

their high socioeconomic aspirations for their children may result in selective remigration from Israel and a reduced flow of immigrants from
Russia. Unlike those who arrived between 1948 and 1951, more-recent immigrants from Russia were greeted by former residents of the Soviet Union
who had arrived before them in the 1970s. This fourth wave was also met
by a more-developed set of institutions that were introduced in the established political regime to deal with their integration. In the longer run, the
economic consequences of this immigration are likely to be positive, given
the human capital and resources of the immigrants.

The movements to Israel from the former Soviet Union and from Ethiopia cannot be understood without attention to the conjunction of international crises and economic opportunities in Israel in the context of
Zionist ideology encouraging immigration. In contrast, there has been a
steady but small stream of immigrants to Israel from Western countries—
particularly from the United States, which has the largest Jewish community in the world—that has not been tied to particular crises or to the
relatively greater economic opportunities in Israel. This immigration can
only be understood as reflecting the importance of ideology, secular and
religious Zionism, in the context of some economic opportunity. In some
cases, discrimination and anti-Jewish (anti-Israel) actions in countries of
origin have played a role in selective emigration to Israel from some European countries (e.g., France). Clearly, this migration is selective of the
Jewish population of origin: it involves, disproportionately, Jews who are
religiously and ethnically committed and of higher socioeconomic status
(education and occupation) relative to those who remain in places of origin and to the Jewish population of Israel. The voluntary nature of this
migration, along with the retention of family and friendship ties in places
of origin, results in high rates of return to the United States and to other
countries of origin.

Many immigrants to Israel from Western countries bring financial support from family members remaining in their places of origin. A paradigm of immigrant integration needs to be developed to understand the
integration of these high-socioeconomic-status immigrants in Israel who
have options of returning to their places of origin. That model should include the socioeconomic and cultural selectivity of immigrants and their
continuing ties to families and networks in their places of origin, for the
second generation as well as for the immigrant generation. These factors,

in somewhat modified form, also need to be taken into account to understand the integration of the more educated and occupationally skilled Russian immigrants of the 1990s.[3]

Although commitment to Jewish nationalism, Zionism, is among the determinants of immigration to Israel, ideological factors always operate in social, economic, and political contexts. Ideological changes do not account for the changes in the rates and sources of immigration over time. Similar to international migration elsewhere, economic factors have been critical in voluntary immigration to Israel; political factors have been central in refugee and nonvoluntary types of movement. Changes in the political condition of Jews in countries outside Israel and the options available for migration to alternative destinations have shaped the fluctuating rates of migration to Israel and the changes in the national origins of immigrants. Zionist ideology is a necessary but not sufficient determinant of immigration to Israel. Those political and social factors that have been critical in determining immigration to Israel are mostly beyond the control of the Jewish polity, either inside or outside Israel (Dellapergola 1986; see also Friedlander and Goldscheider 1979; Al Haj and Leshem 2000). As such, policies in Israel are not likely to have a major impact on the rates and sources of Jewish immigration.

The Conspicuous Consequences of Immigration

Changes over time in the rate and composition of immigration to Israel have reverberated throughout the society, in terms of the integration of the immigrants themselves and their impact on previous immigrant streams as well as on the social and demographic structure of the society as a whole. Much of the discussion in subsequent chapters is related to the variety of the structural consequences of immigration to Israel in the process of nation-building. Here, I review several long-term demographic implications of these patterns, including the roles of immigration in national population growth and in the formation of ethnic communities in Israel.

Immigration and Population Growth. The most conspicuous and direct effect of immigration has been on the increase in the population of the country. The size of Israel's population doubled between 1948 and 1951, and doubled again between 1951 and 1971, increasing to almost 5 million by the end of 1991 and to over 8 million by 2012. The Jewish population component increased almost sixfold from 1948 to 1990, from 717,000 to almost 4 million; the number of Jews in Israel at the end of 2000 was close to 5 million, representing about 80% of the total population of Israel. Had there been no immigration, the size of the Jewish population of Israel in the 1970s would have been less than 1 million instead of 2.7 million, and the proportion of the Jewish population would have been 65% instead of 85% (Friedlander and Goldscheider 1979, table 7.6). In contrast, the Arab minority in Israel has grown by natural increase, since immigration has remained in large part restricted to the Jewish population. Almost half of the total growth of the Jewish population between 1948 and 2000 was a direct result of immigration, but 98% of the growth of the Arab population was due to natural increase.

Therefore, population growth and immigration are intimately and directly connected in the development of Israeli society. To the extent that population growth is linked to economic development, immigration has been indirectly associated with developmental processes (through its impact on population increase). Other indirect consequences of immigration for demographic growth are tied in with who immigrates and what demographic "baggage" (i.e., fertility, health, and mortality patterns) and social characteristics (family structure, educational level, and occupational skills) immigrants bring. These more-subtle effects are important in assessing the longer-term population-growth implications of immigration. Some immigrants tend to come from high-fertility countries, and these immigrant streams were in large part composed of young adults and families. Those arriving from more-traditional Middle Eastern Jewish communities had higher fertility levels than those from European countries, which contributed disproportionately to Israel's population growth.

In addition to population growth, the changing volume of immigration, particularly mass immigration, had a ripple effect through the age structure of Israel at different periods of time—first, in the bunching up of births; several years later, in the schooling of children at younger and older ages; then in the enlarging of the number of men and women in their middle ages and in the workforce; and finally, in the increasing entrance of cohorts into the older ages (Ben-Porath 1986a; Friedlander and Goldscheider 1979). This burst of age effects and its subsequent contraction has placed particular strains on a political and welfare system that attempts to address population needs and provide age-related services. The changing compositional effects of these age cohorts, particularly their ethnic origins and related socioeconomic correlates, exacerbate these strains.

Ethnic Composition and Demographic Change. In addition to issues of population growth and age structure, immigration from a wide range of countries has resulted in the ethnic diversity of the Jewish population of Israel. The ethnic composition shifted from an overwhelming European-origin population to a more-balanced composition of Western and Middle Eastern origins (see chapter 2). Given the overlap of ethnic origin with social and economic resources, political orientations, and culture, the ethnic compositional shifts have had, and will continue to have, major implications for the social, economic, and demographic developments of Israeli society. Ethnicity in subsequent generations is associated with relative economic and educational status, differential access to economic opportunities and networks, and the generational transmission of ethnic stratification. I also explore whether new ethnic configurations have emerged among the third generation and have become less linked to specific countries of origin. I review in subsequent chapters evidence that identifies the economic, demographic, and cultural bases of ethnic differences in a wide range of social processes in the twenty-first century.

I expect that emergent Jewish ethnic communities in Israel are significantly different from those in places of origin, since the contexts of their lives and of their children's lives have been dramatically altered. For example, occupational patterns have become more diversified for all immigrant groups, educational levels have increased, mortality has declined, and family size has become smaller. Ethnic communities have experienced social mobility and occupational and educational transformations. Even as they are of diverse origins, Jews are united nationally by externals—their culture, history, and sense of peoplehood, as well as by their relationship to the Arab minorities in the state of Israel and in the territories administered by Israel (C. Goldscheider 1986a; Smooha 1978). Ethnic immigration groups over the generations have been transformed and should not be considered simply as transplanted populations from countries of origin.

Indeed, the major changes that all immigrant groups have experienced have resulted in the emergence of new Israeli patterns, neither fully "Western" nor "Middle Eastern" (see chapter 2). Although Jewish ethnic differences remain salient and generational distance from the immigrant generation continues to be an important factor in understanding social change in Israel, the critical question is whether there are structural features that continue to differentiate Israel's ethnic groups (C. Goldscheider and Zuckerman 1984). These features include the overlap of ethnic origin with educational attainment, residential concentration, and political orientation. Do higher levels of education and occupation continue to characterize European-origin populations of the third generation? Does ethnic residential concentration continue by region (e.g., living in a development town versus a major urban center) or by neighborhood that is linked, in turn, to job and educational opportunities? Are there continuing high rates of intraethnic marriages and ethnic self-identification? How do the children of mixed ethnic origins identify themselves? As in other pluralistic countries, we can assess whether an "Israeli" national identity has emerged, not only in myth but in fact, that negates or minimizes the longer-term legitimacy and significance of ethnic origin or ancestry.

Ethnic pluralism has emerged in Israeli society as a result of immigration and its consequences. This pluralism is in tension with increasing Jewish national unity and integration among the diverse immigrant streams. Exposure to educational and military institutions has been an almost universal experience for the Jewish population and has served as an important mechanism of national integration. The Hebrew language has become a major integrative force nationally, linking Jews of different national origins and of diverse linguistic backgrounds to each other and to the emergent national culture as well as to pre-state history. External hostilities and continuous conflict with Arab countries have also resulted in the relative unification of the Jewish population of Israel and have linked Jews to Jewish communities around the world. Thus, there are tensions between ethnic integration and assimilation, on one hand, and a new form of ethnic stratification and distinctiveness, on the other.

The occupational skills, educational background, and family and ethnic ties of the European immigrants facilitated their entry into Israeli society and their access to resources and opportunities. Europeans could build successfully on their connections to the European-dominated Israeli society and economy. Immigrants from Asian-African countries came from societies that were less modern economically and demographically, and they were less able to compete initially with the European immigrants in Israel. The different timing of these immigrations and the cultural differences between groups in places of origin reinforced these structural factors. Immigration patterns created two new ethnic communities among Jews in Israel—"European-Americans" and "Asian-Africans"—and they have been sustained over the generations. The divisions have been marked by social-class concentration and linkages to distinctive cultures. In part, these have been connected to places of origin and the ethnic networks that sustain them. However, most specific country-of-origin differences have declined in significance.

Immigration to Israel has resulted in the convergence of ethnic differences in some areas of social life, as well as ethnic continuities in others (see my discussions in subsequent chapters; see also Schmelz, Dellapergola, and Avner 1990). The question remains about the relative balance of these changes in current patterns, their implications for the next generation, and the factors that sustain ethnic distinctiveness. Commonalities and convergences in one dimension of social life do not necessarily imply commonality (and assimilation) in all areas. Thus, I explore whether convergences in some demographic characteristics result in the declining significance of ethnicity and ethnic communities in social behavior. Put analytically, I ask under what conditions ethnic communities retain their salience, and what are the contexts that facilitate ethnic assimilation, particularly under a regime of converging demographic differentials.

Some new ethnic forms may be Israeli-made products, not simply the legacy of origins, background, and immigrant selectivity. It is therefore important to disentangle the ethnic variation that is the result of "origins" (i.e., the characteristics that immigrants brought with them) from the factors that were shaped by their exposure to Israeli society. Although every ethnic group has been characterized by social mobility, the question remains whether the socioeconomic gap between ethnic groups has diminished. Inequalities may persist even with rapid development and economic growth and the opening of new opportunities within a relatively open stratification system. The questions raised by large-scale immigration in pluralistic societies are related to immigration's impact on overall societal growth and macroeconomic development as well as to the distribution of economic opportunities among groups and the access immigrants and subsequent generations have to economic mobility. The combination of country-of-origin differences plus those reinforced, institutionalized, or created by the state are the critical dimensions in the transition from immigrant to ethnic group.

One final note about the salience of ethnicity relates to the links between religion (in this case Judaism) and ethnicity. Immigrants brought to Israel a variety of forms of Judaism from their different cultures of origin. Developments in Israeli society militated against the retention of some forms of religious practices and customs. Some of these changes in religion may be considered under the rubric secularization but better described as transformation. New features of religious expression have emerged in Israel, building on the specific ethnic cultures of the past and redefining and transforming the nature of religious culture. Three aspects of these forms of Israeli Judaism will be discussed in subsequent chapters: (1) the role of the ultraorthodox or *haredi* groups in Israel and the singular power of the Orthodox rabbinate in issues of marriage, divorce, and Jewish identity in a secular society; (2) the organization of Sephardic, or Middle Eastern, Jews into a religious party (Shas) and its political, economic, and educational power; and (3) the role of religion among the Jewish settler population in the administered territories. These themes connect ethnicity and religion in Israel, reinforcing the ethnic cultural features of Judaism, the political and social context of religious expression, and the ways that the forms of Judaism result in ethnic and religious conflict. Just as the overlap of ethnicity and social class reinforces the salience of ethnic communities, so the overlap of ethnic origin and Judaic expression reinforces the diversity of Israeli Judaisms and their anchor in ethnic origins.

Emigration

For a long time, demographers have observed that all migrant streams have counterstreams (C. Goldscheider 1971). This is no less true for immigration to Israel, but it involves an ideological twist. In a society that has experienced massive and diverse immigration patterns and has fundamental ideological and policy commitments to immigration, it should not be surprising that emigration from the country is viewed negatively. Hence, whereas the Hebrew word used to describe Jewish immigration is *aliya*, or ascent, the word for emigration is *yerida*, or descent. To Israelis, the significance of immigration and emigration for loyalty to the state and to the values of the society is unambiguous, and the negative connotations of *yerida* are unmistakable. Nevertheless, one would expect that the major streams of immigration to Israel would produce counterstreams of emigration, if not to the country of origin, then to areas of better economic opportunity. The concern expressed in Israel over emigration far exceeds the actual volume of out-migration and can only be understood in its deep-rooted ideological contexts (Lamdany 1982; Sobel 1986; Lustig 2011; Dellapergola 2011).

Ideological concerns spill over into definitional problems. When is someone who leaves a country to be treated as an emigrant? Although many countries define an emigrant as one who intends to remain abroad for over one year, such a declared intention in Israel violates the fundamental ideology of the state and the shared norms of the Jewish population. Given the stigma associated with emigration from Israel, that declaration cannot be the major basis for identifying emigrants. Indeed, over time the rate of emigration defined by declaration has declined and represents a negligible component (Lamdany 1982). Yet also, over time, the negative implications of emigration from Israel have declined, as emigration has brought about new forms of transnational family and economic networks.

Estimates of emigration are based on the number of residents departing Israel minus the number of arrivals during the year. This figure maximizes the estimate of emigration. At most, there were 340,000 emigrants from Israel between 1948 and 1979, an average annual rate of emigration of 4.6 residents per 1,000 residents, or 225 emigrants per 1,000 immigrants. Of these, 318,000 were estimated to be Jewish. The factors affecting Jewish and Arab emigration are different, and the magnitude of emigration as well as the propensity to emigrate differ over time for the two populations. A lower-bounded estimate of emigrants is the number of residents abroad for more than 10 years; by the end of 1979 that number was 145,000 and had increased significantly by the twenty-first century (Lamdany 1982, Dellapergola 2013).[4] There are no official figures on emigration from Israel that are released annually. The data on emigration in figure 3.1 have been compiled by Dellapergola on the basis of annual publications of the Central Bureau of Statistics. The estimates are rough and are based on the total of new immigrants annually minus the net migration balance. In the longer view these data provide results similar to other indirect methods. There appears to be a rather flat rate over the long period since the establishment of the state (see fig. 3.1). Indirect observation suggests an increase in emigration following the mass immigration of Russians and the movement out of Israel among younger native-born Israelis. There are several studies of Israelis in the United States and Europe documenting the strong connections of emigrants to the state and the power of international networks (Rebhun and Lilach 2010; Gold and Phillips 1996). Perhaps the most significant change in emigration patterns over time is the movement of native-born Israelis out of the country (for substantial periods of time), sometimes with their families, rather than the turnaround of immigrants who have not adjusted to Israeli society.[5]

Emigration had been much more voluntary and individual compared to immigration. Employment opportunities outside Israel and the potential for greater professional advancement, along with higher personal income and a better standard of living, have been the critical factors shaping the migration from Israel (Lamdany 1982; Sobel 1986). The unusual military burden Israel has placed on its citizens on a continuous basis may have also influenced the decision of some to leave. Yet, it is likely that neither economic opportunity nor military concerns fully account for emigration, since relatively few Israelis leave and since there has been a small, continuous stream of immigrants to Israel from Western countries. It is likely that family, social, and economic networks in Israel and the linkages between Israelis living in Israel and in other countries are important factors in accounting for emigration rates. Political and religious changes in Israel may have been important push factors increasing emigration in the recent period.

Variations in emigration rates from Israel are related empirically to changes over time in economic conditions, the security situation, and integration of new immigrants. Changes in actual and expected standards of living affect the propensity to emigrate; emigration varies with changing levels of consumption per capita and follows the economic cycle, declining with prosperity and increasing during periods of economic stagnation. Economic factors are likely to affect the timing of emigration but not necessarily the decision whether to emigrate. Economic expectations, rather than economic conditions per se, have a strong effect on emigration. Aggregate data do not reveal much about who emigrates. Estimates are that young adults, single males, and immigrants from Western countries have higher rates of emigration (Lamdany 1982). Return migration to places of origin is more likely among immigrants to Israel from Western Europe and the United States. In general, it is likely that emigration rates are higher among those who moved voluntarily to Israel. Again, the changes that have occurred over the last decades have involved the emigration of young native-born Israelis in search of better economic opportunities.

In all, however, the return rates and emigration (remigration) rates from Israel are relatively unimportant at the societal level and do not threaten the longer-term social demographic consequences of immigration. They challenge the ideological basis of one form of Zionism that negates the viability of Jewish communities outside Israel. When native-born Israelis of the third generation emigrate, the ideological challenge intensifies. It is likely as the rates of emigration change, new communities of Israelis living in other countries have increased and in turn have begun attracting Israeli friends and relatives to those new communities, if not for permanent residence then for longer-term visits. Over time new networks have emerged between Israelis in Israel and those abroad as transnational flows have continued in both directions.

Nation-Building, Zionism, and Immigrants

Israel is a changing society of immigrants, shaped by ideology and altered by immigration from diverse sociopolitical and cultural areas of the world. As immigration helped form the nation and guided its development over time, it was and continues to be the basis of ethnic cleavages and conflicts. Immigration has drawn on communities outside Israel and has resulted in enriching the social and cultural diversity that is at the core of Israeli society. Immigration has provided the basis for the formation of new communities in Israel and has helped Jews to forge linkages with communities outside Israel that resulted in new economic and social dependencies and networks.

As the basis of Jewish population growth and the social construction of an Israeli Jewish identity, immigration has long been a potent symbol of the Jewish-Arab conflict. The Arab population in Israel views Jewish immigration as a continuing threat to the political and economic aspirations of its community and the Palestinian people. As in the past, this powerful symbol of Jewish nationalism is a source of tension and conflict with Palestinian and Arab nationalism.

There are different components to the Zionist imperative about immigration. First, there is the great success of the Zionist emphasis on immigration as the fundamental step in the nation-building process. Jews from dozens of countries around the world, many as refugees, immigrated to Israel to reestablish Jewish sovereignty and control there. But the Zionist movement has failed to bring all or even a majority of Jews to the new state, as millions of Jews voluntarily continue to resist this feature of Zionist ideology. The United States symbolizes the alternative community, where Jews live as a minority with full rights, open opportunities for social mobility, high levels of education, and diverse avenues of cultural and religious expression. Although American Jews have rejected *aliya* as an imperative, they have articulated their sense of peoplehood and their culture in the form of common institutions and in their support of the Jewish state.

Some have argued that a new Zionist ideology needs to take into account the realities of the twenty-first century and the continuities of an assimilating community in the United States and in other places. Jews in Israel and in communities outside Israel should, they assert, form new bonds and new ideologies that reinforce the symmetries between communities rather than the centrality of one over the other. This belief may be more characteristic of Jewish communities in Western, democratic societies, where most Jews lived in the first decade of the twenty-first century. Yet there continue to be, as well, groups of people with both religious and secular nationalistic ideologies that view Israel as central to their lives. New ideologies have already developed that legitimate both types of Jewish communities inside and outside the state of Israel and that posit a new basis for interrelationships that builds on the strengths of both.

My major questions about immigration do not revolve around the future estimates of immigration or speculations about the future of Jewish communities in areas outside Israel (see C. Goldscheider 2002). Instead, my focus on immigration and its aftermath in Israeli society concerns (1) its impact on population growth and ethnic differentials; (2) the residential concentration of immigrant communities and the geographical distribution of populations in the country; (3) patterns of marriage, family, gender roles, and interethnic interactions; and (4) the distribution of education, occupation, and income among ethnic groups over time. These themes of the transition from immigrant to ethnic groups are explored as I examine the lives of the foreign-born and later generations of Jews and disentangle the effects of ethnic origins and the changing Israeli context on the lives of those living under its political and cultural auspices.

NOTES

1. Some have argued that the long Judaic tradition emphasizing "return" to the land of Israel makes the culture and the underlining ideology unique. Explicitly,

they suggest that Israel is different from other new states that were established after World War II since Israel is not a new nation in an old society but rather a new state and a new society for an ancient people (Horowitz and Lissak 1989). That may be the case; however, my focus is not the source of the ideology but the uniqueness of the immigration process.

2. When Oscar Handlin wrote the saga of American immigration, *The Uprooted*, he reported that he had set out to write the history of American immigration but had discovered that immigration *was* American history. A similar argument could be made for the history of Israel.

3. For a review of American immigration to Israel, see Avruch 1981; Dashefsky et. al 1992; C. Goldscheider 1974; Sobel 1986; Waxman 1989.

4. The numbers of emigrants do not include their children. From the point of view of the sending country (Israel), these are "losses"; the next generation is counted from the point of view of the "gains" to receiving countries.

5. A review of the issues involved is in Dellapergola 2011. His argument about emigration data from Israel is convincing especially as it disputes the polemics of Lustig 2011.

4 | Arab Israelis Demography, Dependency, and Distinctiveness

Social-demographic issues were in the forefront of the conflict between Arabs and Jews in Palestine from the end of the nineteenth century through and after the establishment of the state. In the pre-state period, there were political conflicts over the relative size and growth rates of Arab and Jewish populations defined in terms of the number of Jews permitted to enter the country relative to economic opportunities and rates of Arab population growth. The issue of the Jewish-Arab population ratio has continued to be controversial in Israeli society as the Jews increased their numbers through immigration and the Arabs increased through natural increase (the number of births minus the number of deaths). Along with the geographic distribution of both populations within Israel, the ratio of Jews to Arabs has been the most conspicuous demographic concern under several political regimes and within different territorial configurations. Almost always, the analysis of Arab demographic patterns has been placed in the context of the Arab-Jewish conflict, rather as a basis for understanding Arab social structure.

In this chapter, I focus on several issues associated with the distinctiveness of the Arab community in Israel. I outline the changing levels of inequality between Arabs and Jews in Israel, the role of large family size in reinforcing the position of women in the Arab community, and the centrality of residential segregation in sustaining the social, political, and economic dependency of Arab Israelis. These issues are integral to the understanding of the Arab community in Israeli society taking into account the religious, social-class, and regional heterogeneity within the Arab Israeli population.

The dominant religious group among the Arab Israelis is Moslem, representing 83% of the Arab population of Israel at the beginning of 2013, up from less than 70% in 1948. When not identified specifically, "Arab Israeli" or "Israeli Arab" will be treated as approximately equivalent to "Moslem Israeli" or "Palestinian Israeli." Each of these references has a political significance, as does the categorization of Arabs as "religious" (not national or ethnic) groups and their grouping in the past as "non-Jewish" in official publications of the state. In general, Christian Arabs have smaller families, lower rates of mortality, are more urbanized and better educated than Moslems in Israel.

As Israeli society has evolved, as state policies have developed, as the economy has expanded, and as the sociopolitical conflict between Arabs and Jews has changed, Arab communities and their institutions have been transformed. In particular, research documents how the "integration" of the Arab minority into the Israeli economy has resulted in their increased dependency on the Israeli Jewish population and continuing inequality. A core theme in this process has been the residential segregation of Israeli Arabs and the links between this residential concentration and limited economic opportunities, reinforcing the limited independence of women and the economic role of men. Formal government policies and informal social constraints have thereby resulted in discrimination against Arab Israelis.

We shall employ the concept of "dependency" in the sociological sense, referring to the power exercised by the majority population and its control over the opportunities available to the minority Arab population. I examine the underpinnings of the changing allocation of socioeconomic resources in Israel and the access Arabs have to the resources available. Dependency does not necessarily reflect legal or political inequalities, but it implies the continued distinctiveness of the Arab minority within Israel and socioeconomic inequality. Discrimination associated with dependency is structural and institutional, reflecting the particular location of the minority in the broader community. The structural evidence of discrimination against Arab Israelis is reflected in the economic returns to education (i.e., the kind of jobs that Arabs can obtain with higher levels of education) and in the costs of residential concentration in limiting access to economic opportunity.

Arab Israeli Structural Issues

Each of the major issues outlined below is linked to the changing social, economic, and political contexts of Arab communities in Israeli society. Together these help define the changing economic dependency of Arab Israelis and identify the sources of structural discrimination and disadvantage.

Arab-Jewish Population Ratio. The issue that has been at the core of the history of Arabs in Mandate Palestine and Israel has been the changing Arab-Jewish population ratio. This often has been considered *the* issue of the Arab-Israel conflict, with powerful political, economic, and ideological implications for the emerging Jewish state. The relative size and the growth rates of Jewish and Arab populations had been considered a key problem, recognized by all three political actors before the establishment of the state (Jews, Arabs, and the British). It became a different, but no less critical, issue in the years following the mass Jewish immigration from 1948 to 1951 and in subsequent periods, when the volume and rate of Jewish immigration to Israel fluctuated. The problem of the Arab-Jewish population ratio emerged in more dramatic form after the 1967 war, with the inclusion of Arab areas and populations under Israeli administration and control (see extensive discussions and analyses in Friedlander and Goldscheider 1974, 1979, 1984).

The demographic sources of the differential growth rates of Jewish and Arab populations tend to be viewed in the traditional framework of demographic transition theory. Some have argued that the Arab demographic pattern has reached the stage of "transition," with low levels of mortality and higher rates of fertility that only began to decline during the 1970s. In contrast, the Jewish demographic pattern has already reached a later stage of low levels of fertility and mortality rates—hence, low population-growth rates due to natural increase. This pattern characterized the first generation of the European Jewish population in Israel and subsequently characterized second-generation Israeli Jews of Asian and African origin. Thus, it is argued that younger cohorts of Jewish Israelis are moving toward zero or low levels of population growth and the Arab Israeli population remains in the higher population-growth stage. It does not take much demographic orientation to imagine (and exaggerate) the sociopolitical consequences of a rapidly growing minority population and a relatively low-growth majority population.

The issue of the relative sizes and growth rates of Israeli Jewish and Arab populations and the implied challenge of Israeli Arab population-growth rates to the political control of the Jewish majority is a profound ideological construction but without a firm demographic basis (see table 4.1). Since the establishment of Israel, the Arab proportion of the total population of the state has fluctuated around a narrow range, from 18% in 1948 to 21%

TABLE 4.1

Arab population of Israel by religion, 1948–2012

Year	Total Arab population (000s)	Arab portion of Israel's total population (%)	Non-Jewish subpopulation size (000s)		
			Moslem	Christian	Druze
1948	156	17.9	112	34	15
1952	179	11.0	123	40	16
1962	263	11.3	183	53	27
1972	472	14.6	361	74	38
1982	690	17.0	531	94	66
1992	953	18.3	725	141	87
2002	1,264	19.0	1,038	140	109
2012	1,647	20.6	1,388	158	132

Source: These data are drawn from the *Statistical Abstract of Israel*, 2013, especially tables 2-1 and 2-2. Data on early years are in Goldscheider 2002 and Friedlander and Goldscheider 1969. The 1948 data by religion are 1949. Before 1995 Christians included those not classified by religion.

in 2012. The lower proportion in the aftermath of the establishment of the state reflects some of the out-migration of Arabs from Israel and the mass migration of Jews to Israel. It did not take very long for the Arab population to catch up. In the long view, Arab growth reflects a more than tenfold Arab population increase in 64 years (from an estimate of 156,000 to 1,647,000) but a major increase as well in the Jewish population (from 717,000 to 6 million). No reasonable assumption of future demographic dynamics would lead to an Arab Israeli demographic "threat" to the Jewish majority, without the political incorporation of Arab populations currently not Israeli citizens—for example, those living in Gaza and the West Bank—or the mass emigration of Jewish Israelis from the country. Focusing on Israeli Arabs, not on Palestinians living outside the state, and assuming that mass emigration of Jews from Israel or mass immigration of Arabs to Israel are very unlikely (and hence unpredictable) events reveals unambiguously that, at the national level, the Arab population is likely to remain a permanent demographic minority in both the short and longer run.[1]

The evidence points in the opposite direction at the regional community level. There are regions within Israel that have a majority Arab population and areas within regions that have high levels of Arab population concentration and segregation. Hence, it is at the local community level where changes in Arab population size shape the labor supply and demand in an economic market and set up the potential for local market expansion, as well as for the retention of some specialized skilled labor and professionals. The regional and community importance of Arab Israeli demography emerges from the differential growth rates of these populations, not the national Jewish-Arab population ratio or the Arab demographic challenge to Jewish majority status.

Arab Selective Out-Migration. The growth of the Jewish Israeli population has been the direct result of immigration, combined with the indirect effects of the fertility of the immigrants, particularly those from high-fertility Middle Eastern countries. The high growth rate of the Jewish population has been more or less balanced by the natural increase of the Arab population, reflecting the Arab population's larger family size and declining mortality rates (Friedlander and Goldscheider 1984). Simply put, higher Arab fertility was the counterweight to large and continuous Jewish immigration. Several additional considerations are necessary to understanding these different sources of growth. The first relates to the *selectivity* of post-state Arab populations relative to pre-state Palestine. The Arab population remaining in the newly established state in 1948 was different from the pre-state Arab population in both its smaller size and its lower socioeconomic characteristics (Smooha 1989). The residual Arab population in Israel had a significantly higher level of fertility and mortality than the pre-state Arab population of Palestine. Hence, it had a subsequent demographic trajectory different from that of Palestinians living outside of the state. Some of the Arab demographic changes in Israel are the result of processes of population development and the transformation from a majority population to a demographic minority. Other changes resulted from the selectivity of Arab migration to areas outside of the state and a shift from an autonomous and somewhat diverse economic sectoral structure to a more homogeneous, agricultural, dependent sector under military administration in the larger Jewish economy (Al Haj 1987). The economic dependency of the Israeli Arab population emerges from the selective migration issue, as does its demographic minority status.

The decline in Arab mortality began before the establishment of the state and preceded the decline in fertility. The Arab mortality decline was slower than that among Jewish Israelis, and infant mortality remains over twice as high. (Infant death rates among Israeli Jews in 2012 were 2.7 per 1,000; among Moslems it was 6.9.)[2] The relative inequality of Arabs and Jews in Israel and the disadvantaged status of Arab Israelis become apparent when we examine the mortality gap between populations in the same country. The mortality decline is significant because of the gap between Arab and Jewish Israelis, despite improvements in both populations. The contribution of mortality decline to the population growth issue is secondary to the broader implications of mortality differences for issues of inequality.

The fertility transition among Israeli Arabs was slower and later than mortality declines, resulting in rapid rates of population growth. Since the 1970s, lower levels of fertility among Moslem Israelis have been recorded. The decline in family size occurred earlier among Christian Israelis than among Moslem or Druze Israelis. Moslem women who married immediately before the establishment of the state (that is, between 1944 and 1948) had an average of over 9 children after 30 years of marriage. The total fertility rate in the 1960s (an estimate of average family size) among Arab Israelis was over 9 children; by the 1980s, it was less than 5 children. In 2012, the total fertility rate of Moslem Israelis was 3.5; for Jews it was 3.0; the total fertility rate was 2.2 for Christian Arab women and for Druze 2.3.

Costs of High Fertility. The importance of differential Arab and Jewish fertility for population growth is unmistakable. And the significant reduction of Arab fertility in the last decades is no less remarkable. Largely neglected is the examination of two issues: those associated with the impact of large family size on role of Arab women within their communities and families and the consequences of high fertility on the socioeconomic opportunities available to the next generation of Arab Israelis. In large part, the traditional role of Arab women has almost always been treated as one of the determinants of sustained high fertility, following the argument that unless the status of women changes to non-childbearing roles, there is little likelihood of significant changes in fertility. But the causal direction might be reversed: one consequence of large family size is the continuing traditional role of Israeli Arab women.

Large family size sustained the family-oriented roles of Moslem women and high Arab fertility reinforced women's childbearing roles (Friedlander, Eisenbach, and Goldscheider 1979, 1980). The disadvantages of high fertility are clearly present at the family and community levels. The most recent data in the second decade of the twenty-first century point to a significant reduction of Arab fertility in Israel and the potential for the decreasing control of Arab men over Arab women. Combined with educational changes among Arab Israelis and their impact on smaller family size, there is every indication that the long-standing argument over population growth differences between Israeli Jews and Arabs is disappearing. To the extent that the size and growth of the Jewish relative to the Arab population is invoked it refers in large part to the growth of the Arab population living in the territories administered by Israel (the West Bank) or at local Israeli community levels.

The determinants of mortality change involve the extension of health care and public health facilities in Arab communities. The significant remaining mortality differences between Arabs and Jews reflect, in part, their individual characteristics (for example, their educational levels and occupational concentrations) and, more important, the context of their communities. The distribution of health and related services to more-isolated Arab communities in Israel and the differential access of Arabs to the more-extensive health care facilities in Jewish areas are critical factors sustaining higher Arab mortality. The Arab-Jewish mortality gap is clearly associated with, and a sensitive indicator of, social inequality in Israel.

The overall declines in mortality and the low rates of infant deaths have also had an impact on the goal of reducing family size. Family size has also been affected by a continuing increase in the educational attainment of Moslem women. Less than 10% of the Arab women who were married between 1964 and 1968 had any formal education after the ninth grade, compared to about half of those who married in the early 1980s. The decline of Arab fertility in Israel has also reflected the increase in the participation of Arab women in the formal and informal labor force and the exceptional growth in the participation of educated Arab women.

These societal-level changes and individual-level factors combine with the economic activities of those working outside of Arab residential areas. This is most conspicuous in the pattern of male employment and is tied into the economic "integration" of Arabs in the Jewish economy where there has been a continuous process of leaving agriculture to commute to jobs in the Jewish sector. Increases in the standard of living and education, along with the benefits from the welfare state and the increase in the opportunity structure, suggest that the economic futures of younger couples are more independent of their extended families. Thus, from the point of view of the Arab community, fertility levels are important, not primarily because they are linked to population growth, but because fertility is part of family, which is part of community and the organization of society. Fertility trends reveal, even more directly than do mortality changes, critical aspects of the social organization of communities and families.

Fertility patterns have had an impact on gender roles in households and on the hierarchy implied by the largely segregated roles of Moslem women. The distribution of household labor connects to both the circular movement of male Arab laborers in the Jewish sector of Israel and the substitute roles that Arab women have as unpaid laborers in agriculture. Thus, high fertility had bound Arab women to the household to take care of their families and places them in the control of the extended family and of neighbors. Arab women and young adults have increased their dependency on Israeli Jews. As Arab women have increased their education and moved into teaching and health related jobs, the limits of opportunities become readily apparent.

The dependency role of young adults, particularly women, is further illustrated by the pattern of living arrangements. Moslem young adults generally live with their families until they marry and move from one family role (as child) to another (as spouse). Few unmarried Moslem Israelis live alone, compared to increasing proportions of Jewish Israeli adults (F. Goldscheider and Fisher 1989; Okun 2013). Therefore, Arab dependencies in Israeli society are manifested at the level of economic activities and the dependencies of Arabs on Israeli Jews. There are also gender dependencies of Arab women on Arab male control, and the younger generation's dependency on adults and extended families.

Arab Migration and Residential Concentration. Most of the demographic studies of Arab Israelis have focused on the interrelationships of mortality and fertility issues and have ignored the role of internal migration and the urbanization of the Israeli Arab population. In particular, the critical role of residential concentration has been neglected. The overall political control over internal migration limited the voluntary movements of Arab Israelis through the mid-1960s; informal constraints (including the lack of accessible housing, limited economic networks and discrimination) continue to limit their internal migration. The major form of mobility, however, rarely captured and almost always underestimated by standard official migration data sources, is commuting—the daily movements of Arabs who work in Jewish areas. This circular or daily commuting pattern of Arab Israelis substitutes for other, more-permanent migration forms. Hence, commuting slows down changes that would have occurred under a different, more-open internal migration policy. The absence of large-scale internal migration directly reinforces the dependency status of Arab women on Arab men, of Arab men on Israeli Jews, and of the younger generation on the extended family and the community. The regional concentration of the Arab Israeli population and the development of commuting as a substitute for internal migration exacerbate the economic dependency of Arabs on the Israeli Jewish population. The absence of Arab relocation has reinforced Arabs' local ties and the powerful influences of kinship and family networks. Arab population growth without migration or territorial expansion as outlets has had major economic and social consequences, particularly since there are pressures on the opportunities available in local areas because of the increasing numbers. The regional concentration of the Arab Israeli population exacerbates Arabs' economic dependency on Jewish employers and on jobs in economic sectors controlled by Jews.

The residential concentration and segregation of Arab Israelis from Jewish Israelis is thorough. There are over 100 communities listed in the Israeli census; the proportion of Arabs in the 7 mixed localities ranges from 6% to 30%, and the others are either totally Arab (35 places) or totally Jewish (61 places). The high rates of residential segregation have been well documented in the past (Semyonov and Tyree 1981) and continues into the twenty-first century. Segregation is only part of the story, since the nature of the places where Arabs are concentrated also implies a controlled and limited opportunity structure and the constrained access of Arabs to economic markets. In most of the Arab communities, job opportunities are scarce and economic and infrastructural developments are limited (see also chapter 5).

There are some obvious consequences of the residential concentration of Israeli Arabs. The extent of health facilities, the nature of educational opportunities, and other social and economic infrastructural developments

—combined with the patterns of geographic isolation in these places and their small size—conspire to affect the role of Arab women, their dependency on men, and the relative economic dependency of Arab men on the Jewish economic sector. Because Arab residential segregation has an impact on educational opportunities and the translation of educational levels into appropriate jobs, the potential for the next generation of young adults to improve their standard of living is constrained. This is particularly the case when options for out-migration are limited and there is an expanding population base.

The economic and labor force consequences of residential concentration for Arab men and women are critical, as are the effects of segregation on such infrastructural issues as education, job opportunities, and organizational and institutional developments. The dependency of Arab communities on the Jewish economic sector is a direct outcome of the state's segregation policies and the subsequent increased discrimination in the labor market. The lack of adequate schooling and, most important, the lack of independence and autonomy are linked to the residential constraints on Arab Israelis (for one illustration see Al Haj 1987).

The increased dependency has been referred to as a form of internal colonialism (Zureik 1979). This shift toward dependency among Arab Israelis permeates the system of stratification among Arabs, influencing their status in the community, primarily their powerlessness. Patterns of dependency are an integral part of the educational system and the curricular orientation of Arab schools, of the Israeli values that inform Arab lives, of the national character of their communities, and of the general feeling that their communities are linked to an Israeli society that dismisses their culture as political and their independence as the basis for potential terrorism. Research systematically demonstrates how the dependence of the Arab population increased in direct relation to the rise in the standard of living in one Arab community (Al Haj, 1987). Arab segregation has an impact on the Jewish population, since contacts between Arabs and Jews are limited in large part to asymmetrical work relations, with separate local networks and kinship relationships.

From the point of view of the broader Israeli society, particularly the Jewish community and its political structure, the economic position of the Arab minority has been improving over time. At the same time, and less well-appreciated, Arab economic dependency on the Jewish economic

sector has become institutionalized. The changing economic relationships between Jewish and Arab Israelis have been the result of structural
realignments of economic and population distribution patterns. Some aspects of kinship structure and control have increased among Israeli Arabs,
at the same time that the specific economic roles of these kin groups have
been substituted by the power exercised by Jewish control. These changes
have resulted from pragmatic requirements and structural constraints
rather than from ideological or cultural commitments.

Arabs and Jews compete for jobs in the "integrated" Israeli economic
sector, and Arabs are less likely to succeed at obtaining employment. They
are likely to pay a heavy price for occupational integration, since they will
have to seek appropriate jobs outside their segregated sector in competition with better-educated and well-connected Jewish persons. It is reasonable to assume that, in the near term, Arabs will not be the advantaged
group or equal in this competition. Unlike in the past, when educated
Arabs were in demand in the Arab sector (replacing those who left the community in the 1948 war), more of the better-educated Arabs are now being
pushed into the Jewish sector and into blue-collar work. Thus, through
the early 1980s, there had been a nice fit between higher education and
high-level white-collar work among Arabs. But a continuation of increased
educational attainment without the expansion of high-level white-collar
job opportunities in the Arab sector has resulted in a decline in the economic opportunities appropriate for the educational level attained by the
younger generation. The lack of translation of education into jobs is one
form of structural discrimination.

There may be economic benefits to residential concentration, since
there is less direct discrimination in labor market terms when Arabs work
in Arab communities instead of in Jewish economic sectors. But this is not
likely to be case when economic opportunities in Arab communities are
not developing to accommodate the next generation. The increasing educational attainment of Arabs over time produces new cohorts of educated
young men and women whose opportunities are constrained both by residential segregation and by their economic dependence on the Jewish sector. Even if segregation was beneficial for some in the past, it is likely to
have more-negative consequences when the increase in population size
outstrips the available local economic opportunities. To the extent that a
gradual reduction in economic dependency on the Jewish economic sec-

tor is desirable, an expansion of diverse economic opportunities in Arab communities will be required. Although such an investment may improve the occupational returns to education and increase the autonomy and independence of the population as a whole, it will likely reinforce the extended family's control over the lives of younger persons and limit the shift to more-egalitarian gender roles. The trade-offs between increasing the economic independence and autonomy of the Arab population on the one hand, and the entrenchment of gender inequalities on the other, pose the dilemma confronting the shapers of local and national policy.

There are costs of residential segregation for Israeli Arabs in the context of the changing economic structure, a segregated labor market, and increasing levels of education. Together they operate to the disadvantage of Arab Israelis. Arab Israelis cannot escape the broad-ranging, high costs of residential segregation and regional concentration. These costs are economic, social, and educational, and they include the poorer income returns to education and unmeasured social and psychological disadvantage. The new jobs that are opening in Israel demand more education, which further places Arabs in a disadvantaged position. So, increased educational levels actually *increase* disadvantage instead of reducing the capital returns gap. Vulnerability among Arab Israelis stems from the fact that segregation intensifies and magnifies any economic setback and builds deprivation structurally into the socioeconomic environment. The costs of segregation are exacerbated by the economic dependency of Arab Israelis.

The Arabs' residential concentration in Israel in this structural context, therefore, has resulted in their continuous economic powerlessness, leading to an Arab underclass. The expanded work opportunities that occurred in Israel in the post-1967 period did not change the status of Arab Israelis. Their increased segregation—resulting from their increased population growth and the limited expansion of the area where they could live—yielded increased levels of economic deprivation, hopelessness, and deterioration, precisely at the time when objective conditions were becoming better relative to what they had been. Residential segregation makes the Arab minority vulnerable and conspicuous—vulnerable in the sense that they are subject to economic changes, not to political harassment, and conspicuous because their distinctive lifestyle characterizes their communities and clearly identifies them as Arabs.

Policies that increased their level of educational attainment and the availability of some jobs in the market, as well as the Arabs' traditional supportive family structure, may have spared Arab Israelis some of the dire economic consequences of their residential segregation. The presence of West Bank Palestinians in the labor market may have also reduced Israeli Arabs' level of disadvantage. Again, the consequences of segregation for the quality of life have been profound for Arab Israelis. Residential segregation is a structural condition, making deprived communities more likely; combined with social class disadvantage, ethnic segregation concentrates income deprivation in small areas and generates structural discrimination.

Data show that Arabs working in the Jewish economic sector suffer detrimental consequences in terms of both occupational and income inequalities (see the discussion in Semyonov 1988; chapter 8). Arabs working in Arab communities are occupationally advantaged, reflecting group competition in local labor markets. Although segregation into ethnic enclaves excludes minorities from equal access to broader opportunities and rewards, it provides temporary protection from discrimination generated by competition. Segregated Arabs who live and work in Arab communities are disadvantaged relative to Jews, but are advantaged relative to Arabs who live in Arab communities but work in the Jewish economic sector or Arabs who live and work in the several mixed residential areas of Israel. Working and living with Jews—that is, fuller residential and occupational integration—appears to be the worst case for Israeli Arabs. Working in their own communities and controlling their own occupational opportunities has the highest economic rewards.

There may be a need to develop greater pluralism within Israeli society in the short run, in the sense that Jews and Arabs develop opportunities in separate sectors. This reinforced segregation in Israel may be necessary, given the argument that there is a great deal of mistrust between the communities (Smooha 1991; Smooha and Hanf 1992; Smooha 2012). Greater segregation may work to the benefit of both Jewish and Arab communities. This may be viewed as a transition stage until greater trust between the communities develops. Such segregation must include greater symmetry between Jewish and Arab communities, with freedom of economic and political control internally and with important links to the central entitlement programs of the state.

The dependency of Arab Israelis does not operate only at the macro-societal level, nor does it simply reflect an abstract economic position in a hierarchy. It is not solely a condition caused by socioeconomic stratification and the inequalities of politics and demography. Of course, it is all of these, but there is more. Dependency can and is often translated into the psyche of the individuals in the group.

Arab Israelis in Israeli Society and in Their Communities

The examination of Arabs in Israel focuses our attention on the salience of ethnicity at the level of community. The ethnic cohesiveness of communities becomes the basis of analysis, incorporating the complex role of the state and its policies, including issues of entitlements, ideology, and discriminatory policies that shape demographic continuity and change in Arab communities. Arab "identity" emerges from the structural contexts of Israel's Arab communities, as it does from external factors. Ethnic identity is not constant but is variable over time. Its salience varies during the life course as it relates to economic and family transitions as well as to a variety of political contexts. The importance of Arab Israeli distinctiveness differs between cohorts and between stages of the life course within cohorts. It is clear that "culture," primordial identity, and an internally imposed or externally influenced political status and identity do not provide adequate orientations to the changing meaning of "Arab Israeliness." Since ethnicity is an intensity as well as a categorical variable, those who are more involved with the community are likely to be different from those who are less involved. Thus, an analysis needs to reflect this intensity dimension, at a minimum to test its salience in the Arab Israeli context.

A new generation of Arab Israelis is growing up, with higher levels of education, lower levels of occupational opportunities, and increasing Palestinian national identity. They are being socialized in smaller families, with higher levels of consumption and aspirations. But they have nowhere to go and little to do, with fewer outlets of social, cultural, and political expression. These generational changes and experiences clearly document that demographic changes are linked to quality-of-life issues and that demography is a major basis for understanding changes in the social, economic, and political structures of communities.

What is the picture of ethnic relations that emerges from a review of Arab Israelis? Clearly, it is different from that of Jewish ethnic groups, because of the source of their population increase (natural growth versus immigration) and their internal history of seclusion and control in the state. Arabs and Jews in Israel have a different relationship to the society and its national symbols. Arab Israelis also have a different relationship than do Jewish Israelis to the neighboring Arab countries and to Palestinians in the West Bank, the Gaza Strip, and elsewhere in their diaspora (see chapter 11).

An interesting example of the internal dynamics of an Arab community can be gained from the examination of one Arab town in Israel.[3] Shfar'am was a central district serving twenty-two villages in the area. During the British period, the Christians were numerically dominant; Moslems were second in population size, with a small Druze minority. In 1948, drastic changes occurred, partly because of the massive evacuation of local families, who became refugees in other countries, and partly because of the reshuffling of Arab populations within Israel's borders, creating internal refugees (Al Haj 1987). From a community point of view, the Arabs entering Shfar'am were outsiders, not connected to sources of power and control that were internal to the community and certainly not linked to the former source of prestige and power—land ownership.

The shifting movement of the local population for the first several years after Israeli statehood and the disruptions of families that were organized by the Israeli government affected mainly the Moslem population. The influx of mostly Moslem internal refugees was significant numerically, constituting over one-fifth of the total population. These population shifts meant a major change in the demographic and religious composition of Shfar'am. During the 1950s, one-third of its population was Moslem, and Christians constituted about half of the population. By the 1970s, the distribution was equal, with Moslems and Christians constituting about 40% each. Because of the differential fertility patterns—in particular, the significantly larger family size of Moslems compared to Christians—the Moslem population increased to 45% by the 1980s, with a Christian minority of 37% and 18% Druze. This close interrelationship of demographics, minority-group factors, and sociopolitical control is seen in microcosm among the Arab communities in Israel.

The issues, of course, are not merely demographic, although demography has played a critical role in shaping the contexts within which the political, social, and cultural elements are expressed. There were class divisions within each of the communities, even during the British period

(Al Haj 1985). The Christians were the dominant community in the economic as well as the demographic sense, possessing most of the land. They were the dominant group in trading and commerce in Shfar'am and between Shfar'am and the surrounding villages. Prior to the establishment of the state of Israel, all the merchants and owners of businesses were Christians. Large landowners were both Christians and Druze, but hired workers and poor agricultural laborers were almost all Moslems. The Moslem community was therefore dependent economically on the Christian and Druze communities. Moslems were the suppliers of unskilled labor. Regionally, the surrounding Arab villages were also dependent on Shfar'am, with the dominant Christian community supplying services and trade.

This economic structure remained largely intact through the 1950s, but Shfar'am was losing its dominance over the surrounding villages. In large part, the changes reflected shifts in the Jewish economy of Israel during the first years of statehood. As a result, the nature of the economic dependency of Shfar'am changed: it was losing its former local economic base and developing no alternative base. From the point of view of the Jewish community of Israel, the economic position of the Arab minority was improving precisely at the same time that economic dependency on the Jewish economic sector was increasing. The first change within Shfar'am that occurred after the establishment of the state was the slow integration of the Arab refugee population that had been displaced from neighboring villages. Their integration was neither rapid nor complete, since the local population resisted full integration and since many Arabs expected to return to their former places of residence and their communities of origin. It took almost a decade for the refugee Arabs to plan for a more-permanent settlement.

After 1948, the occupational structure of Arab communities in Shfar'am changed to wage labor. The process of proletarianization was rapid and developed fully within a decade after the establishment of Israel, with a total economic and political dependency on the Jewish sector. The occupational structure fluctuated according to the economic conditions in the Jewish sector. In part, there were land confiscations that decreased the land available to the local Arab population; the internal migrants arriving landless contributed to the increasing search for wage labor outside the town. In 1981, only about 10% of the labor force over age 15 was working in agriculture, and six out of ten worked outside the town (Al Haj 1987, 43, table 2.4). None of the in-migrants to Shfar'am and few of the Christians were working in agriculture.

The social-class transformation under these conditions had significant implications for kinship and family structure, particularly for changing family relationships, the role of women, and the power of the Arab *hamula*, or kinship system.[4] These changes were the result of structural realignments of economic and demographic patterns and the changing nature of dependency between the Arab community and the Jewish sector. The Arab kinship structure has not declined with modernization but, in some ways, has been reinforced since 1948. Some aspects of *hamula* structure and control have increased at the same time that its specific economic roles and control have declined. The condition of the *hamula* is a direct outcome of statehood and the position of the Arab community in Israeli society.

The *hamula* system has become a key both to the local political system and to the marriage market. Social and demographic changes resulted in the restructuring of kinship groups such that the rapid increase in kinship size reflected the growth due to natural increase and in-migration in the confined residential area. This combination of growth in limited geographical space resulted in the increased solidarity of kinship groups for social and political activities; group size and consolidation became powerful factors in local politics. Marriage markets, economic opportunities, and the residential-housing market became severely constrained over time and were linked to the limitations imposed by the status of Arabs in Israeli society and their communities.

It is clear that under these conditions ethnic convergence between Jewish and Arab Israelis is not a likely outcome, given the residential concentration of Arab Israelis and their distinctive characteristics. Issues of convergence to the Jewish majority are also constrained in terms of standard-of-living and economic factors and the control exercised by the Jewish sector over the economy and over the opportunity structure. In contrast, issues of family, and perhaps women's status, are likely to have a local Arab (Moslem, Christian, or Druze) reference group.

Israeli Arabs in Democratic and Demographic Perspective

Israel has been described as an "ethnic democracy" in which the dominance of one ethnic group is institutionalized; this, in turn, has its own tensions and contradictions. Such a system extends political and civil-liberties rights to the entire population but, at the same time, attaches a superior status to a particular segment of the population (Smooha and Hanf 1992). Israel is a state of and for Jews and is recognized as such internationally; Hebrew is the national language, and the use of Arabic is marginal in the public domain. All the state symbols and national institutions are Jewish, from the national anthem to national holidays, from the symbols around which national unity is organized to political symbols, flags, monuments, art, and literature (Smooha and Hanf 1992).

The Arab Israeli population was abandoned in Israel in 1948 as part of the Palestinian people and the vanquished Arab world; it was regarded by the Jews as a fifth column, as non-Jews in a Jewish state. Israeli Arabs were part of a residual community; they had lost their leaders, middle class, urban sector, and most of their institutions. Primarily, they had lost autonomy and control; that is, they became a minority. Hence, Arab Israelis were vulnerable to Jewish manipulation and discrimination, since assimilation into the Jewish majority culture and its institutions was not possible. The Arab population in Israel has been granted civil rights and the status of a linguistic, religious, and cultural minority. Welfare services were extended, as were development funds. At the same time, it was also under military administration, largely exempt from military service. Large portions of Arab lands were confiscated (even though Arabs had also previously lost control of their urban sector). Israeli Arabs voted for Jewish political parties and protested minimally.

After 1967, their situation changed, as the overall military administration had been lifted. Palestinians in nearby territories were under Israeli occupation and increasingly worked in the state as day laborers. Israeli Arabs were more readily admitted to Jewish institutions and were encouraged to integrate into the working class of the Jewish economy. Their educational and occupational levels increased dramatically, as did their standard of living. At the same time that they developed a bilingual and bicultural Arab and Israeli orientation, they recaptured and enhanced their Palestinian identity when their contacts with Palestinians in the West Bank and Gaza increased. They developed a network of organizations, institutions, and leaders in their struggle for greater equality. But their leadership tended to be local—Israel has never had an Arab cabinet minister or even a director-general of a government office.

Palestinians and Israelis see Israeli Arabs as part of the state of Israel; hence, formal separation of Israeli Arabs as a regional or territorial independent unit is not an option. (In contrast, they argue that partition is the only likely way to handle the Israeli-Palestinian conflict because any permanent settlement must include Palestinians outside Palestine). The only legitimate political status for Israeli Arabs is as an integrated minority with some local autonomy but within the Jewish state. This political position must remain tenuous and conflicted, given the dependencies associated with this type of minority status.

Another perspective for understanding the role of Arab Israelis emphasizes their demographic context. One well-developed demographic argument has been that populations respond in a variety of ways to the pressures on resources generated by high population-growth rates. Population growth itself is a major force in the reduction of fertility when the welfare of the family is threatened and there are no adequate outlets to relieve that pressure through out-migration, the expansion of territory, or the more-intensive use of land for production. In extreme form, when population size increases (e.g., through mortality reduction), members of the community may increase production on the land, may increase the intensity of land use, or may migrate to new areas, often in nonagricultural communities, that provide new economic opportunities. When population growth is the result of in-migration, there is a more-immediate strain on the population-resource balance. The theory argues for the multiple responses of a population to the pressures of population growth (see Friedlander 1969; C. Goldscheider 1971).

The Arab Israeli population has experienced these population-growth pressures from a combination of high fertility and declining mortality, with a limited outlet through out-migration. The family-oriented system of the Arab community of Israel militated against high rates of nonmarriage or childlessness. State welfare programs in Israel prevented a reduced standard of living, which would have resulted from these demographic processes. Welfare programs, combined with the ability to commute to jobs outside their communities, minimized the costs of high Arab population growth. But clearly, the crunch was delayed more than alleviated, particularly with the rising younger generation of more-educated Arab Israelis who could find jobs in the Jewish economic sector, but not jobs that were commensurate with their educational levels. They could more readily and successfully compete with Palestinians from the administered territories working in Israel; they were and continue to be less successful when competing with Jewish Israelis in their labor market.

The combination of demographic and democratic tendencies requires a solution to the disadvantaged position of the Arab minority in Israel. If we take as our guide the value expressed by Israel's first president, Chaim Weizmann, that the quality of Israeli society will be judged by how it treats its minority communities, then Israel has a distance to go to improve the quality of life of its Arab minority and needs to set policies that diminish ethnic inequalities. At the same time, policies must recognize the powerful trade-offs between residential segregation and economic development, between cultural pluralism and national identity, and between the retention of a Jewish Israeli state and a tolerance (and supportive policies) for minority populations and pluralism. It is unlikely that the next generation of Arabs and Jews in Israel will experience minority integration. Whether Arab Israelis continue to experience economic disadvantage and whether inequalities are reduced and sociocultural distinctiveness remains are open questions at the beginning of the twenty-first century.

NOTES

1. Israel's inclusion of over 1 million immigrant Jews since 1989 (see chapter 3) and the relative stability of the Arab-Jewish demographic ratio reinforce this point about the permanent demographic minority status of Israeli Arabs.

2. See the discussion in chapter 9.

3. I draw fully on the details presented in Al Haj 1985 and 1987; see also Bar-Gal 1986.

4. The *hamula* is a patrilineal and patriarchal system of social and biological relatedness that is more formal and extensive than the extended-family system (see Al Haj 1987).

5 | Urbanization, Residential Integration, and Communities

A dominant theme in Zionist literature has been the need for increasing the Jewish population in the national home to establish the basis of a total Jewish society and to solve the Jewish problems of disadvantage, anti-Semitism, and assimilation experienced in countries where Jews lived as a minority. Jewish population growth was expected to increase the base for economic production and establish a greater political presence. And there was an emphasis on the need to increase the size of the Jewish population relative to the Arabs to assure Jewish political legitimacy and control. These were fundamental political concerns in the articulation of a national ideology and in the development of population policies (Friedlander and Goldscheider 1979; see the discussion in chapter 1).

No less important were political, economic, social, and cultural considerations about the spatial distribution of the Jewish population living in Palestine and in the state of Israel. There were obvious needs to legitimate the Jewish presence in the areas defined as part of the emerging Israeli state and a need to disperse the population to facilitate its economic development and national integration. Large-scale immigration, leading to rapid population increases, brought pressures to develop adequate housing, health care, education, jobs, and cultural activities in areas where immigrants settled. Population growth, economic development, and nation-building raised complex issues of immigrant integration, frontier settlement, and urban-rural concentration. Immigrants from diverse places of origin tended to settle where others of the same origin settled, leading to residential concentration of Jewish ethnic groups. Concomitantly, the territorial goals of the Jewish community brought questions of Arab population distribution to the forefront of policy and planning. Conflicts over land and territory were key elements in the ideological and political battles in Palestine and in Israel.

Ideological factors associated with elements of Zionism were in the background of the pressures for the territorial distribution of the population in Israel. Jews had been disproportionately concentrated in the urban places of their countries of origin (in Western and Eastern Europe and in the Middle East), often residentially segregated as a minority (C. Goldscheider and Zuckerman 1984). Their occupational patterns reflected these residential concentrations and the restrictions imposed on Jews in the societies where they lived. Some Zionist arguments emphasized that Jews should have a "normal" occupational distribution in their own state, a blend of rural and urban jobs spread throughout the areas of Jewish settlement in Palestine and Israel (Halpern 1961; Hertzberg 1960; Shapira 2012). In their national home, unlike in their places of origin, Jews should have an unlimited range of choices of residential locations. Many of the early Zionists in Palestine asserted the strategic and ideological value of a literal "return to the land" and argued for the de-urbanization of the Jewish population. Immigrants to Palestine in the early years founded agricultural settlements and stressed the political and economic need to develop the land areas of Palestine.

The emphasis on nonurban residential settlement and on a more-balanced residential distribution throughout all regions of the country was reinforced after the establishment of the state by two pressing considerations: the defense needs of the emerging Jewish state and the goal of economically integrating large numbers of immigrants. Population dispersal was viewed as necessary to reduce Israel's vulnerability to military attacks and as a basis to defend national borders. Settling the frontier areas was a statement about Jewish control over the whole country and became a strategic national goal. The emphases within Zionism on territorial control and on the settlement of frontier areas were used selectively to justify and rationalize this prioritizing of military defense.

The influx of a large number of immigrants provided an opportunity to implement these Zionist goals and political objectives. Most of the immigrants in the first years of the state were dependent on government intervention and support for housing, health, education, welfare services, and jobs, at least in the early stages of their adjustment. Immigrants had to be integrated economically and residentially; their geographic location dictated the distribution of economic activities. They were more likely to be manipulated and "planned" for than were longer-term residents or those with more capital who were already settled in urban areas or had contacts there. Therefore, the dispersal of the population to nonurban areas and new towns on the periphery of the country developed as a political strategy to ease the economic and housing pressures in central urban places and to settle persons on the borders as a defense strategy.

The planned distribution policy was more feasible for Jewish immigrants from Middle Eastern countries, who arrived with fewer resources and less economic and social capital to be able to manage on their own. Their greater dependency on the state facilitated their shift to areas of settlement away from the urban centers. Jews from European countries had immigrated to Israel in the earlier period of national development, when urban housing was more available. More important, they arrived with urban occupational skills and had contacts with persons of European origin in longer-settled urban areas. They were less often directed to the peripheral areas of settlement; when they were settled in distant locations, their resources and their ethnic networks allowed them to migrate to urban central areas much faster than immigrants from the Middle East. In general, the political and economic advantages of immigrant population dispersal moved from the ideological arena to practical economic and political policies; it is among the clearest expressions of the links between nation-building and urban-demographic processes.

In this chapter I examine the actual changing population distribution of Jews and Arabs in Israel from the establishment of the state to the first decade of the twenty-first century, evaluate how ethnic residential concentration enhances generational continuity among Jews, and assess how distribution policies affect the segregation of Israeli Arabs.[1]

Large Urban Places

I begin the larger picture by reviewing the extent of urban concentration of the population in Israel and its changing regional distribution. Using the Israeli definition of urban localities, about 85% of the population resided in urban places in 1948, a level that was maintained through the twentieth century. Over 90% of the population was urban in 2013, a very high level of urban concentration by international standards. The changes for the Arab Israeli population were particularly dramatic, starting at a lower proportion of urban concentration in 1948 and increasing to the same level as the Jewish population in the 1990s. By 2013 almost 95% of the Arab Israeli population resided in localities defined as urban. The Arab urban changes were mainly the result of population growth in rural places (which led to redefining their rural areas as urban) rather than internal migration to Israeli cities, a kind of urban growth "in place." And the urban places where Arab Israelis resided did not share all the important economic and political characteristics of urban places.

Overall, between 1948 and 2013 population size increased in all areas but more rapidly in urban than in rural areas. The rural population in Israel more than tripled in size, but the percentage of the total population living in rural areas declined. In comparative urban context, Israel was a fully urbanized society when it was established, and it has remained so. It is clear that the early ideological emphasis on the return to agriculture and the antiurban bias of the founders of the Jewish settlements in Palestine and Israel have had little effect on the forces that generate urban concentration (E. Cohen 1977). The causes of increasing urbanization in Israel are likely to be similar to those in other countries, including economic concentration and specialization, industrial production, availability of amenities, technology, and state investments.

The four largest cities (Tel Aviv, Jerusalem, Haifa, and, more recently, Be'er Sheva) have dominated the social, economic, and urban landscapes of the country. Data show the significant population increase in all these cities for the half century since 1961 (table 5.1)—Be'er Sheva increased the most, from 97,000 in 1961 to 637,000 in 2011, and was 61% Jewish; Jerusalem and Haifa had even higher proportions Jewish (Haifa 69% and Jerusalem 67%). Tel Aviv was an overwhelmingly Jewish city (93%).

Most of the Jewish population lives in the metropolitan areas surrounding the largest cities: Tel Aviv, Jerusalem, and Haifa. All three are ethnically dominated by Western-origin populations and contrast with Be'er Sheva's predominately Asian/African-origin population. Three-fourths of the Jewish population living in Haifa is of Western origin, as are two-thirds of the Jewish population of Tel Aviv and 60% of the Jewish residents of Jerusalem. In contrast, 57% of the Jewish population of Be'er Sheva is of Middle Eastern origins.

A general comparison of the two largest cities in Israel, Tel Aviv and Jerusalem, illustrates the potential impact of place on the next generation. Separated by about forty miles and connected by expressways, these cities dominate the country. Their metropolitan areas have spread geographically to accommodate their growing populations, but their urban cores have declined. Jerusalem is characterized by government activities, public bureaucracies, and by cultural, educational, and religious

TABLE 5.1

Population of the four major districts, Israel, 1961 and 2011

District	Population size (000s)	
	1961	2011
Jerusalem	192	968
Haifa	370	926
Tel Aviv	699	1,303
Be'er Sheva	97	637
Total	2,180	7,837

Source: Statistical Abstract of Israel 2013, table 2.17.

Regional distribution of Israel's total and Israel's Jewish populations

Region	Israel's population, 000s (%)			Israel's 2012 Jewish population, 000s (%)
	1948	1972	2012	
Tel Aviv	306 (36)	907 (29)	1,318 (17)	1,232 (22)
Central	122 (14)	580 (18)	1,931 (25)	1,695 (30)
Northern	144 (17)	474 (15)	1,321 (17)	574 (10)
Haifa	175 (21)	484 (15)	939 (12)	648 (11)
Southern	21 (3)	354 (11)	1,146 (15)	855 (15)
Jerusalem	87 (10)	347 (11)	987 (13)	660 (12)
Totals	855 (100)	3,146 (100)	7,642 (100)	5,664 (100)

institutions. Jerusalem, with its ancient and historical roots, has been the spiritual center of Jews for centuries and is spiritually important for Christians and Moslems as well. From 1948 to 1967, Jerusalem was on the Israeli-Jordanian border, geographically marginalized and divided into areas under Jewish and Jordanian control. Since 1967, the city has expanded and incorporated new and newly rebuilt Jewish areas and has included large Moslem and Christian populations. As the historical core of Israel, Jerusalem exhibits an ethnic and religious pluralism and has become a symbolic center for many religious groups. Jewish religious groups scramble for power in Jerusalem and represent heterogeneous and institutionally divided communities that are often ethnically segregated as well. Both Chief Rabbinates (representing Sephardic, mostly Middle

Eastern, and Ashkenazic, mostly European, religious traditions) are located there, as well as local *haredi* rabbinical courts and institutions that deny the legitimacy of the chief rabbis. Conservative Judaism, known in Israel as Masorti, and Reform Judaism have institutions and constituencies in Jerusalem, and other Judaisms are located there as well. The non-Orthodox groups are not recognized as legitimate Judaisms by the Orthodox rabbinate.

Tel Aviv is the commercial, industrial, and financial center of Israel. It is a more-diffuse city, structurally and geographically. It was established in 1909 by secular Zionists shifting away from its Yafo (Jaffa) neighbor, and is the political and secular center of the country (even though Israel's political institutions and formal parliament, the Knesset, are located in Jerusalem). In contrast to Jerusalem, secular struggles characterize Tel Aviv—the struggles for status, property, and material success (Kellerman 1993). Tel Aviv has its roots in secular Zionism as well as its institutions; Jerusalem draws its inspiration from traditional Judaic texts and is identified with history and spirituality. The images of Tel Aviv one typically sees are of beaches, cafes, and nightlife—the excitement of city life. Located in the hills, Jerusalem generates images of the quarters of the old city, archaeological discoveries, and people praying at the Western Wall. Jerusalem, with its religious pluralism and contested history, is a core arena of conflict between Israelis and Palestinians and among Judaic religious traditions. Tel Aviv is the leading center of Israel's postindustrial economy, facilitating the shift to high-technology industries, financial centers, and producer services. In many ways, Tel Aviv is the center of contemporary Jewish Israel, the focus of urban technological, economic, and cultural innovations. Jerusalem is the spiritual and bureaucratic center of the country, its administrative core, and historical-institutional center.

Jerusalem, Israel's capital, is special because of the inclusion of its eastern part into the state of Israel after 1967, along with its Arab population. In the Israeli-controlled part of Jerusalem there were only about 2,400 non-Jews in 1961; the 1967 reunification led to a dramatic increase in its non-Jewish population size and its continued growth. In 2012, Jerusalem had a Jewish population of 660,000 within a total population of 987,000 (67%). Jerusalem is also undergoing rapid suburbanization, extending into new areas away from the urban core. The population expansion in Jerusalem is a result of a combination of administrative expansion of government activities, new immigrant settlement (some from Western countries) and internal migration, along with higher-than-average fertility, particularly among ultraorthodox and religious Jews who are concentrated in Jerusalem. There are increasing demands for new housing, expansion of the transportation infrastructure, and more-intensive use of larger land areas surrounding the city. At the same time, the growth of the Jewish population has generated conflict and tension with the Arab communities, which have also increased since 1967 in the expanded areas of Jerusalem. The conflict is basically political, but there are complex economic, infrastructural, and social dimensions associated with the emerging political realities of the residentially divided city, which is economically integrated and politically controlled by Israel.

Regional Changes

Another way to appreciate the distribution changes over time is to examine regional changes (table 5.1, lower half). There have been increases in the population size in all six regions of the country,[2] reflecting both overall population growth and the powerful impact of immigration, particularly in the aftermath of statehood through 1951 and in the post-1967 period. The Tel Aviv District dominated the country in population size in 1948 and, together with the Haifa District, contained 57% of the total state population. There were only 108,000 people living in the combined Southern and Jerusalem Districts when the state was established, about one-third the number of people living in the Tel Aviv District.

Since 1948, the distribution of the population among the six districts has become more equal. The population in the Tel Aviv District declined relative to the total population from 36% to 17% in 2012; the population in the Haifa District declined from 21% to 12%. These relative declines occurred despite sharp population increases in these two districts—each more than quadrupling in size between 1948 and 2012—from 306,000 to 1,318,000 in Tel Aviv and from 175,000 to 939,000 in Haifa. The Central District increased from 14% to 25%; the population in the Southern District increased from 21,000 to over 1 million, and from 3% to 15% of the total population. The combined results of these regional growth patterns have converged toward an increasing balance among districts: the Tel Aviv District dominated the other districts demographically in 1948, with a relative population 15 times larger than that of the smallest district and more than twice as large as that of the next-size district; in 2012 the population of the largest district was less than double that of the smallest.

The shift over time toward greater residential dispersal has resulted in the evolution of a national, urbanized Israeli society. Urbanization and population distributional changes have linked Israelis into one national community politically, socially, demographically, and geographically. Population dispersal reduces the sense of local, relative to national, identity, even as the character of the older urban places, along with their economic and sociopolitical functions, has remained distinctive. The emergence of a national community implies that even those on the periphery and in rural areas are part of the urbanized society and are likely to be influenced and dominated by urban values and structures.

Ethnic Urban Concentration

As cities expanded in population size and as new areas were developed in Israel, what happened to the residential concentration of the immigrants? Did the shifting regional balances involve the redistribution of Israelis of Middle Eastern origin among those of Western origin and the new immigrants from the former Soviet Union? Did Jews and Arabs become more integrated residentially? What are the residential patterns of the Israeli-born children of immigrants, who attended local schools, developed local ethnic friendships and family ties, served in the military, and started new families? The question of ethnic residential concentration in Israel is a critical part of the analysis of nation-building. The evidence from studies in the early 1960s through the first decade of the twenty-first century points to an initial ethnic segregation by place of origin and time of immigration among the foreign-born and a continuing but lower level of residential concentration by broad ethnic categories among their children. The evidence from the first decade of the twenty-first century shows that immigration from the former Soviet Union changed not only the population size and ethnic composition but also the urban landscape of Israel.

Paradoxically, both residential segregation and integration characterize Israeli cities in the beginning of the twenty-first century. There has been a general decline in the level of residential segregation of the European and American-origin population as upwardly mobile Asian- and African-origin families have moved into the higher-status core areas of cities. At the same time, small clusters of what had been exclusively European- and

American-origin populations in new garden-suburban neighborhoods have been joined by Jews of Middle Eastern origins. Nevertheless, disproportionate levels of European/American concentration remain in the wealthier suburbs of cities and in veteran areas of settlement. Some Israelis of Middle Eastern origins have integrated residentially with those of Western origins, yet many Asian- and African-origin Israelis have become increasingly concentrated residentially, often in neighborhoods that are pockets of poverty. Those who have been left behind in the social mobility process have become a hard-core disadvantaged group with a high level of separation from the Western-origin population as well as from the upwardly mobile second-generation Asian/African population (Gonen 1985; Kirschenbaum 1992; Klaff 1977; Yaish 2001).

Continuing ethnic residential segregation is not only associated with poverty in large urban areas but has also become a major source of ethnic continuity for all groups. This is reflected in the regional variation in ethnic Jewish composition, with high levels of continuous Asian/African concentration in some neighborhoods within cities. Thus, both ethnic residential segregation and ethnic integration are occurring in Israel's cities, with cultural and communal costs associated with ethnic integration and socioeconomic and political costs associated with ethnic concentration. The volume and concentration of immigration from the former Soviet Union in the 1990s have resulted in the development of strong ethnic-based Russian-speaking neighborhoods and communities. Government-subsidized housing and work-related projects in and around the major cities have resulted in new forms of ethnic residential concentration (Leshem and Sicron 1999; Gitelman 1995; Remennick 2011.

An examination of immigrants from various countries by first district of residence in Israel in 2012 is revealing. Of the immigrants from the United States, 42% resided in the Jerusalem District, as did 38% of the immigrants from the United Kingdom, 34% from Argentina, and 28% from France. In contrast, only 1% of the immigrants from Ethiopia and about 5% of Russian immigrants resided first in Jerusalem. Russian immigrants were concentrated in the Central District and in Haifa, Tel Aviv, and the Southern District. Ethiopian immigrants were concentrated residentially in Zefat in the Northern District and in Ashkelon and Be'er Sheva in the Southern District.

The retention of residential clustering among some ethnic communities is a positive statement about the value of family, economic, and neighborhood networks. The overlap of neighborhood and ethnic origin is not a feature limited to the immigrant generations or their children and is not confined to areas of initial settlement. Ethnic residential concentration appears to be pervasive nationally, even as some types of integration are also extensive and neighborhood boundaries are increasingly blurred.

Whatever their sources, patterns of ethnic segregation have consequences for the socialization of the next generation. Growing up in ethnic families and neighborhoods, attending local schools with disproportionate numbers of students from similar ethnic backgrounds, marrying persons and joining families of similar ethnic origins, and working with and spending leisure time with family and friends who share similar ethnic cultures reinforce the cohesion of ethnic communities. In regard to the question of ethnic continuity, my assessment is that residential concentration reinforces ethnic generational continuity—when it occurs, ethnic cohesion is stronger; when it is less pervasive, ethnic cohesiveness is weaker.

The initial settlement of immigrant groups involved settlers coming from specific places of origin, and pockets remain of second and later generations from particular countries who have maintained ethnic residential enclaves. These enclaves tend to be composed of the larger ethnic groups (e.g., from Morocco) and located in select areas in Israel. Over time, particular locations in Israel have become less concentrated in terms of people's specific country of origin but characterized more by concentrations of persons in broader ethnic categories. Where ethnic residential concentration is maintained, new ethnic combinations have developed. Residents of neighborhoods or towns in Israel were less likely to be referred to as being from particular countries and more likely to be characterized as being of "Western," "Asian/African," or "Middle Eastern" origin. These are constructed ethnic categories that have been shaped by both economic and residential changes in Israel. They are Israel-made ethnic products that are unlikely to disappear generationally, since the third-generation Israelis have already been socialized in their ethnic families and in neighborhoods that are ethnically concentrated. In this sense, the reduction of the overlap of social class and ethnicity is but one of the several types of generational connections that foster ethnic continuity in its newer forms in Israel. The residents of the new ethnic enclaves that were formed as a result of the immigration of the 1990s are more likely than not to reinforce these ethnic divisions. Despite internal ethnic variation among immigrants from the former Soviet Union, they too are more likely to form a new ethnic community as "Russian-Israelis" than to retain specific place-of-origin identification. This consolidation of ethnicity is likely to be most conspicuous among the second generation.

The streams of people moving to central urban places and to various districts of Israel are the primary sources of urbanization. Their movement results in changes in the regional distribution of the population. Internal migration tends to be selective of those who are more likely to respond to educational and job opportunities and housing availability, and who are less tied to local communities and places of origin. Young adults and those who are searching for ways to translate educational attainment into jobs and those who are in transitional stages of the life course (getting married or dissolving a marriage, having children, joining or leaving the labor force) are the most likely to change places of residence. The educational background of Western-origin Jews makes them more receptive to opportunities in new locations, and hence they are more geographically mobile. Ethnic and family networks may play an important role in providing information and support to potential migrants. Relocation is tied in with other social changes, which are linked to changes in fertility, health, and family structure. In Israel, the links between immigration and internal migration are strong, and both are intimately connected to the process of nation-building and ethnic change.

Internal migration of Jews in Israel is influenced indirectly by government policies that provide subsidies in particular areas for housing and jobs. The state has provided these incentives to those who live in some areas (e.g., development towns) and to those who live in new territories developed by Israel after the 1967 war (e.g., the West Bank). The primary determinants of internal migration for Israeli Jews have been market-economic forces and the educational and occupational opportunities that vary among areas; housing availability and cost figure prominently among the factors shaping residential mobility. Along with family life-course changes, these are the key variables separating migrants from nonmigrants. Ethnic- and religious-community factors, net of these economic, demographic, and social factors, influence migration to a much lesser extent, although some ethnic and religious differentials in migration patterns operate through these other factors. The availability of jobs, housing, education, and transportation combine with individual resources (money, education, and networks) to shape migration patterns in Israel (see the systematic analysis of internal migration in Israel by Ben-Moshe 1989a).

Arab Residential Concentration

The regional distribution of Arab Israelis remains significantly different from that of the Jewish pattern. This is the result of Arab-population concentration and the incorporation of some Palestinians after 1967, not Arab immigration to Israel or internal migration. In contrast to the Jewish population's concentration in the Southern District, the Northern District remains the regional area of concentration of Moslem and Christian Arab populations. There is less dispersal of the Druze population, and their relative concentration in the Northern District has increased over time. In part, this reflects the incorporation of the Golan Heights and the inclusion of its Druze population in Israel after 1967. The impact of the 1967 boundary changes on Jewish and Arab populations of the northern and the southern regions emerges clearly.

While the internal migration of Jews relates to the basic "voluntary" nature of that movement, it does not apply to Arab Israelis. In the past and continuing in the present, formal restrictions in housing and economic choices for Arab Israelis have had an enormous impact on their population distribution. In the process, the Arab Israeli population has become a fully urbanized sector of Israeli society. Arabs have taken urban jobs as they have shifted from their heavy concentration in agriculture and in rural areas. Much of this shift was the result of changes in the land accessible to Arab Israelis after 1948 and the heavy state investments in, and control over, agricultural production and markets. These controls flowed from both the political and the economic interests of Israel and the commitment of Israeli governments to support rural Jewish agricultural enterprises. The increase in the proportion that is urban among Israeli Arabs, however, has resulted from the reclassification of rural communities as urban when these have increased in population size through natural increase. The administrative designation of areas as urban without migration or changes of residence, therefore, has resulted in urban concentration in a statistical, but not necessarily a sociological, sense. Clearly, the economic, political, and social meanings of urbanization for Israeli Arabs and Jews are significantly different.

Overall, in 2012 about 95% of the Arab population in Israel lived in areas defined as urban, but 41% lived in urban places of less than 20,000 population (compared to 10% of the Jewish population); 17% of the Arab population lives in urban places with fewer than 10,000 people (compared to 6% of the Jews). Of the 21% of the Arab population in the three largest cities, most (85%) live in Jerusalem. Almost 40% of the Jews live in urban localities of medium population size (50,000 to 200,000 people), compared to only 11% of the Arab population. Viewing concentration among regions in Israel demonstrates that in 2012, 37% of the Moslems, 60% of the Christians, and 80% of the Druze lived in the northern region of Israel, compared to 10% of the Jewish population. The high levels of residential concentration mean that almost 85% of Arab Israelis reside in village communities, towns, and urban neighborhoods where Arabs are the only residents, a pattern that has been the case for several decades (see also Al Haj 1995; Lewin-Epstein and Semyonov 1993; Semyonov and Tyree 1981).

Most Arab communities are small, semiurban places where economic opportunities are scarce and economic development and infrastructure are limited. Health facilities, educational opportunities, and other key elements of social and economic infrastructure are significantly weaker in Arab communities, and the state has disproportionately invested in other areas with heavier concentrations of Jewish populations. Their relative geographic isolation, small community size, and residential separation, combined with lower state investments, conspire to impoverish the everyday lives of Arab Israelis as well as to increase their powerlessness (see Al Haj and Rosenfeld 1990; Lewin-Epstein and Semyonov 1993; Semyonov and Lewin-Epstein 2004).

The economic and labor-force consequences of residential concentration for Arab men and women have been critical in maintaining their disadvantaged economic status through location-specific distribution of educational institutions, employment opportunities, and organizational and institutional developments. The dependency of the Arab communities on the Jewish economic sector is a direct outcome of state policies and the increased discrimination in the labor market. The lack of adequate schooling can be linked directly to the residential stability and geographic segregation of Arab Israelis, since residential changes were so restrictive. These patterns are clearly part of the Arab-Israeli conflict in the region and are related to the internal ethnic tensions in the state of Israel. They reflect the differential sources of Arab and Jewish population increase in Israeli society (immigration primarily of the Jewish population and out-migration of the Arabs from Palestine before, or immediately subsequent to, the establishment of the state) and the nation-building patterns of the Jewish state.

The increasing educational attainment of the Arabs over time has created a younger cohort of men and women whose opportunities are constrained both by residential segregation and by economic dependence on the Jewish sector. Residential segregation is more likely than not to have negative consequences when the increase in population size outstrips available local economic opportunities. In short, these forms of residential concentration entail high social, demographic, and economic costs to the state and to the Arab community.

Residential location for Arab Israelis, as for Jews, reveals important dimensions of community life. Where people live in relation to jobs and amenities, educational opportunities and services, ethnic and economic networks informs us about the lifestyle, life chances, and quality of life experienced by different communities. The history of immigration patterns for Jews and the integration of Arab Israelis as a minority in the state have in the past shaped the distribution of the population and have influenced the expansion and composition of neighborhoods. Several generations of Jews and Arabs have experienced these living patterns. Their children have been socialized under these circumstances. Their identities as ethnic and religious communities have been shaped by their areas of settlement and the institutions that characterize different locations. Because of the power of place, it is unlikely that local communities will lose their influence in the nationally integrated Israeli society of the twenty-first century.

Communities
Kibbutzim, Moshavim, and Development Towns

As in other societies, social life in Israel occurs in communities. These are often based on families and kinship groups and incorporate ethnic networks, religious groups, and political, economic, and social organizations. Some of these communities are characterized by ideological and cultural particularities associated with Israeli society, Zionism, and Judaism. All of them exist in settings and social contexts that shape how communities develop, who shares them, what amenities and institutions are available to improve the quality of daily life, and the values and norms that set them apart from others. By comparing the socioeconomic and demographic profiles of these communities, we explore the contexts that shape the lives of Israeli residents and provide a basis for an assessment of the impact of place on the Israeli population.

Kibbutzim. Kibbutzim—the plural form of the Hebrew word *kibbutz*— are settlements, located primarily in rural areas, with a collective system of production, marketing, and consumption. These communal settlements have been of major interest in the study of the evolution of Israeli society, and the image of the kibbutz community—small, simple, and egalitarian—has been among the most engaging conjured up by Israeli society. According to this image, people who live in kibbutzim are committed to the basics of agriculture, hard work, and communal sharing—selfless and dedicated to the highest ideals. This representation borders on the idyllic, of course, but among Jews living both inside and outside Israel, the kibbutz image has sometimes been taken as synonymous with the historical reality of the Israeli state as a whole or at least synonymous with its ideals. The ideological construction of Israel as a new society finds its clearest expression in the ideals of kibbutz life.

The kibbutz movement in Palestine and in Israel has been a continuing experiment in collective economic, political, cultural, and social life for over three-quarters of a century. Each settlement is small; when taken together, they comprise only a small proportion of the Israeli population. Nevertheless, the movement has had a disproportionate influence on the formation of the Jewish community of Palestine. Its origin may be traced to the first two decades of the twentieth century, when the movement's economic and ideological bases were developing, when kibbutzim were expanding and consolidating, and when members of Zionist youth movements were being recruited to populate rural collective settlements. The organizational structure of the kibbutz evolved in the context of a broader set of political controversies, economic fluctuations, demographic growth, and geographic expansion in the changing political and economic milieu of Palestine (see Near 1992; Rayman 1981; Talmon-Garber 1972). In its origin and development, the kibbutz was an integral part of the larger Yishuv (the Jewish community in pre-state Palestine) and the broader society.

There were powerful European intellectual sources of kibbutz ideology, which were central to developments in the Yishuv and later in the state. Socialism and nationalism were core themes in kibbutz ideology. The proper balance between religion (Judaism) and ethnicity (Jewish national secular culture) in defining Jewishness and Zionism were continuing sources of controversy in nearly every kibbutz; and the importance of agricultural activity, socioeconomic and gender equality, Jewish cultural renaissance, and the collective basis of responsibility were debated endlessly. Kibbutz activities were often viewed suspiciously and competitively, often with curiosity, and sometimes with hostility by other residents of Palestine — Arabs, Orthodox Jews of the old Yishuv, urban residents, and the colonial British. Kibbutzim were financially dependent on the Palestinian Jewish community and on external Zionist funds, and at times they relied on Arab labor and markets. These dependencies had implications for economic activities within the kibbutz, for ideological variations among them, and for institutions that were developing within the kibbutz movement. Kibbutz responses to the problem of generational renewal (the demographic challenge of replacing older members and expanding production to accommodate increasing numbers) were addressed initially by recruiting young members of Zionist youth movements and Jewish immigrants to Palestine. These sources of demographic growth meant weaker family and kinship-based networks in the kibbutz. The persistence of traditional gender roles and family life and the connections between these and work allocations directly challenged an ideology emphasizing gender equality and minimizing family autonomy.

The kibbutz movement is an expression of the values of labor Zionism rather than those derived from "Jewish" social traditions, as some have argued (e.g., Near 1992). The spirit of the small Jewish town (shtetl) of Eastern Europe and the values of biblical Judaism had little to do with the formation of the kibbutz, even though both were used selectively and imaginatively as sources for its legitimacy. The kibbutz movement constructed its ideological views most directly from the currents of European, not Jewish, thought. Developments in the kibbutz, its economic, political, and demographic successes and failures, were the result of the financial and institutional support provided by Jewish communities in Palestine and elsewhere. They were not the direct result of the power of kibbutz ideology or the salience of its lifestyle (see C. Goldscheider and Zuckerman 1984).

The kibbutz in Israel symbolizes the ideals of secular (and some religious) Zionist dreams: a return to the land, equality of gender roles in the family, and social-class equality in the distribution of goods and consumption patterns, energized by pioneering and communal-collective commitments, and by creative Jewish culture. It is remarkable that the kibbutz has been among the most successful of the communal utopian movements, as the second and third generations have carried on some of the major ideological imperatives of the movement and have generated new ones (Krausz 1983; Spiro 1979; Talmon-Garber 1972; Gavron 2000).

There has been a dynamic interaction between the kibbutz movement and Israeli society. As part of the society, kibbutzim were shaped by what was happening in Palestine and, for the past decades, in Israel. They were not isolated communities with minimal national roles. Indeed, the kibbutz influenced Israeli society far beyond its small size, as it was influenced by the state. A disproportionate number of kibbutz members have been active in party and national politics, becoming political and ideological leaders of Israel, prominent in the Knesset, and overrepresented as officers in the Israeli armed services. Kibbutz ideals include the quintessential symbols of national Zionist values. How have the demographic and ethnic transformations in Israeli society influenced changes in the kibbutz? Clearly, kibbutzim have changed over time, and some have shifted their emphasis away from collective family activities and from communal ownership toward the nuclear family, greater privacy, and individualism. There have been difficulties incorporating the next generations. At the same time, new members have been continuously attracted to them. There have been difficulties demographically with the processes of entering and exiting kibbutzim as well as with changes in their population size, age structure, and ethnic composition. The economic and political support kibbutzim have received from the national government has also varied considerably, faring better when the Labor party was in power (from 1948 until 1977) and more poorly under the Likud party regime. The economic structure of the kibbutz has changed in response to economic and demographic developments in Israeli society and shifts in political administrations and their priorities (Gavron 2000).

Kibbutz ideology has stressed equality among groups and the irrelevance of ethnic origins as a legitimate basis of differentiation or generational stratification. Kibbutzim were often seen as supporting the equal status of the Arab minority and the need to develop symmetrical relations with local Arab communities. Yet the ethnic composition of the kibbutz has been overwhelmingly "Western" or European in origin. Kibbutzim competed with Arab agriculture, used former Arab lands for their own agricultural development, and have occasionally employed Arab laborers. Some of them expressed and supported a left-liberal social, political, and economic ideology that was welcoming and accepting of Middle Eastern Jews and Arab Palestinians. At the same time, kibbutzim benefited from government controls and regulations that have affected the distribution of land and the production and distribution of goods and resources. Central government policies were supportive of kibbutz institutions while being detrimental to Arab populations and to Jewish immigrants from Middle Eastern countries. In all, the ideals of equality sustain the kibbutzim, and although people often view them as special, the reality falls somewhat short of that.

To be sure, not all kibbutzim are the same, since they are linked economically and organizationally to different federations and supraorganizational structures, which are tied to political organizations and parties and guided by different political and economic ideologies. There are secular, antireligious kibbutzim and religious kibbutzim that are hostile to secular lifestyles; there are kibbutzim that are primarily agricultural and others that specialize in the manufacturing of industrial products; some are involved in the production of goods for local Israeli consumption, while others are organized for the export market; there are kibbutzim of different-size populations, some newly established and others that are veteran areas of settlement. Some kibbutzim maintain maximum community control over children, collectively raising and educating them; others are much more individual and nuclear-family based. Many of the kibbutzim are egalitarian in ideology, although some have become more capitalistic. As a result of this diversity and of the changes over time in kibbutz life, it is difficult to generalize.

When the state of Israel was established in 1948, there were 177 kibbutzim with a total population of 54,200, representing 7.6% of the Jewish population. The rapid Jewish population growth through immigration and the settlement of most of the newcomers in urban places resulted in a decline in the proportion of Jews living in kibbutzim to less than 3% in 2012. This decline occurred in the context of the increase of the kibbutz population to over 147,000 within 65 years after the establishment of the state and the addition of 90 new kibbutzim in six decades. From the perspective of

Israeli society as a whole, their relative demographic importance has always been small and has declined over time.

The population structure of kibbutzim in the past tended toward the younger ages, younger than the Jewish population as a whole. However, the kibbutzim population has aged considerably—the percentage that is 65 years old and over had more than doubled from 1970 to 1991. By the beginning of the twenty-first century, the proportion of older persons in the kibbutzim in Israel was slightly higher than the proportions among the urban Jewish population. This aging has increased the economic strains of having sufficient workers, paying health costs, and finding jobs for older members of the labor force. Aging within this type of communal setting has social consequences as well, including the increased collective responsibility necessary to care for the elderly and the problem of incorporating multigenerational units within collective decision making. It also involves shaping new socioeconomic and cultural priorities for an increasingly top-heavy age pyramid. As a result, many kibbutzim have turned to foreign workers as health-care givers.

Another factor shaping kibbutz life is internal migration. Each decade, several tens of thousands of people move into and out of kibbutzim, pointing to important labor-force turnover and social integration problems in terms of commitments to the collective.[3] As a small ideologically oriented community, a kibbutz relies on a core of continuous residents to sustain its uniqueness, even as new members are socialized and returnees are resocialized. Work and social relationships disrupted by out-migration need to be repaired and readjusted. Indeed, in- and out-migratory flows require adjustments by those leaving as well as those remaining in a kibbutz. The proportion of the Israeli population who have had some kibbutz experience is thus much larger than the proportion currently residing in them. Migration to and from a kibbutz is therefore one of the sources of the integration of kibbutzim in the broader urban society of Israel, where economic and human resources flow in both directions. Kibbutzim and Israeli society affect one another directly through these migratory exchanges.

Unlike the ethnic composition of the society as a whole, which has changed as a result of immigration from Asian and African countries, the ethnic makeup of kibbutzim has remained highly skewed. Through the end of the twentieth century about 80–85% of kibbutz residents were of

Western origin, similar to the percentage of Western-origin population living in the country as a whole in 1948. These proportions are unlikely to have altered significantly by 2012. Thus, 65 years after the establishment of the state, after mass immigration and the children of immigrants had reached adulthood, when immigrants and their children from Middle Eastern countries were altering the composition of the Israeli population, the ethnic composition of kibbutzim remained close to that of their original streams from European sources. For Israeli immigrants of non-Western origins, with different economic experiences and ideological commitments, kibbutz life was less attractive than life in urban places, with their greater economic diversity and opportunities to establish different types of communities (Bachi 1977; Keysar 1990).

Moshavim: Cooperative Agriculture. Immigrants to Israel from Middle Eastern countries were not, in large part, channeled to kibbutzim but were directed to small, newly established cooperative farming villages called moshavim. Moshavim—plural of moshav—are rural agricultural settlements where marketing and purchasing are collective and consumption and production are private. (When only consumption is private, the settlement is officially referred to as a "collective moshav.") Unlike kibbutzim, moshavim have been economically, not ideologically, committed to collective organization.

These villages were designed for the settlement of some of the massive numbers of immigrants arriving immediately after the establishment of the state; they were modeled after the *moshav ovdim* (rural-worker collectives) that had been in Palestine. As a result of the government's settlement policies, by the mid-1960s the moshav became the dominant form of rural agricultural settlement in Israel populated by immigrants of diverse social and cultural backgrounds, the overwhelming majority of whom did not have farm background or experience (Weintraub et al. 1971).

Unlike the kibbutz, where the collective was the unit of production, consumption, and socialization, the moshav was a cooperative community of individual households of working family farms. Typically, the moshav was made up of a small community of about 100 family units, sharing responsibility for communal welfare and networks of economic resources (agricultural, credit, supply, and marketing). Moshavim were developed to solve a series of immediate problems in the new state: (1) integrating diverse immigrant populations; (2) settling rural lands and augmenting agricultural production by Jews, to replace displaced Arab farm laborers; (3) population dispersal, decentralization, and extending political legitimacy over sparsely inhabited border areas; and (4) the provision of immediate employment—all within the context of national ideals exemplified by the kibbutz movement. Between 1949 and 1958, 251 new moshavim were established, settling 11,350 households (Weintraub et al. 1971, table 1; Klayman 1970). In 2012 there were 442 moshavim, with a population of almost 300,000. The population on the moshavim has been significantly larger than the kibbutz population since the 1960s, and in 2012 was almost twice as large. Moshavim (as kibbutzim in an earlier period) never attracted the majority of new immigrants. Agricultural development was ideologically and politically salient but was not viable economically for most in an urbanized society.

The moshav met the government's commitment to greater population dispersal, particularly away from city centers with their high levels of population density, crowding, and housing shortages. Israel's establishment of moshavim was also consistent with the rural emphasis of Zionism and moved the new immigrant population from areas that were then characterized by a slow rate of industrial production. Over time, immigrants were directed instead to new towns, as the rural areas and kibbutzim and moshavim were unable to attract immigrants or to receive the necessary financial investments to make the economy of these rural places viable. The small-community structure of the moshavim may have had the potential to ease the immigrant absorption process for some in the short run, but it also became a basis of intense generational conflict, dependency on government supports, and reduced social and economic mobility. Those who wanted increased educational and employment opportunities had to seek them in the cities. Unlike the domination of the Western-origin population in kibbutzim, the moshav population was largely of Asian and African origin.

The contrasting ethnic composition of moshavim and kibbutzim underlines the fact that ethnic residential concentration has become entrenched even for rural agricultural areas. Indeed these ethnic divisions were reinforced by the settlement strategies of the national government, even though these policies reaffirmed the ideal of Israel as an ethnic melting pot. Although ethnic differences were rooted originally in places of origin, Israeli policies embedded new forms of ethnicity in the commu-

nities they created and supported. The policies designed for the socioeconomic absorption of immigrants from diverse places of origin resulted in
the formation of ethnic enclaves. Community and residential segregation
of ethnic immigrant populations shaped the overlap of ethnic origins and
socioeconomic status and perpetuated this conjunction for the next several generations. The emergent ethnic pattern is ubiquitous, since it en-
compasses veteran and newly established areas, ideologically egalitarian
and ethnically neutral communities, and third and later generations growing up in Israeli society in the twenty-first century.

Development Towns. Development towns are a heterogeneous categorization of relatively small urban places mostly established after 1948
and located on the geographic periphery of Israeli society or in distinctive
neighborhoods in metropolitan areas. These mostly began as residential communities, heavily subsidized by the government to attract newly
arrived immigrants, and they expanded rapidly in the 1950s. By the mid-
1950s, the rural areas of settlement were inadequate to absorb the flow of
new immigrants, and the larger metropolitan areas were already densely
populated. It became clear that a different solution for locating the great
waves of arrivals from Asian and African countries was needed. New urban
areas, referred to as "development towns," were planned—partly to complement the rural strategy of immigrant settlement, and with similar
goals of economic development and the dispersal of population to border areas in order to meet political and military needs. These new towns
were located in sparsely settled regions, particularly near the borders of
the state, to reduce original territorial imbalances. They were designed as
middle-size cities to absorb immigrants and would serve as a solution to
excessive regional population concentration (see Berler 1970; Kellerman
1993; an earlier analysis of the importance of these new urban frontiers is
reviewed by Matras 1973; Troen 2010).

The number of areas designated as development towns in Israel increased fourfold, from 4 in 1948 to 16 in 1950, doubling again in the next
decade. Most of these development towns are located in either the northern or southern regions of the country. Several development towns located
in the more-developed central region of the country (e.g., Rosh Ha'Ayin,
Ramla, Lod, Or Yehuda, Or Akiva, Yehud, Yavne) lost their designation as
development towns during the 1960s (Kellerman 1993, fig. 3.1). In 2012
there were 20 places designated as development towns: 9 in the Negev,

8 in the Galilee, and 3 in the Center. The number of development towns has remained relatively constant since the 1970s. The population living in these towns increased dramatically between 1948 and 1965, and then growth rates slowed. Starting with only 11,300 persons in 1948 and representing 1.5% of the Jewish population, the development towns grew almost eightfold, to 85,400 in 1950 (7.1% of the Jewish population), and then to 180,600 in 1955 (11.4% of the Jewish population). In 1961, the percentage of the Jewish population living in development towns surpassed that of rural communities. Their relative population growth peaked by the mid-1960s, reaching almost 20% of the total Jewish population, and fluctuated thereafter to about 18.5% in the last decades of the twentieth century. The proportion living in development towns is more than twice the combined proportion in kibbutzim and moshavim. The steady growth in the number of Jews living in development towns reflects a considerably higher fertility rate, balanced by continuous net out-migration from many of these towns. A significantly higher proportion of those in development towns than in other areas of the country define themselves as religious.

The population in development towns has been and continues to be disadvantaged socioeconomically. The third generation growing up in them are largely the children and grandchildren of Asian and African immigrants, less educated, in lower-ranked occupations, and with lower incomes and fewer resources than the Jewish population as a whole or than their ethnic cousins in more-central urban places. At the peak of the expansion of development towns, in the 1960s, research documented the extensive ethnic residential concentration in these areas of people from specific countries of origin and the tendency of their labor forces to be concentrated in specialized industries (Spilerman and Habib 1976). There was little industrial diversity among development towns, partly reflecting the small size of their labor force and the pattern of central government investments in particular industries. Patterns of ethnic-based enterprises connected to development towns continued through the 1980s. Selective out-migration of the more ambitious and successful young adults searching for better educational and occupational opportunities in the larger metropolitan areas left the residual ethnic population in development towns in an even more disadvantaged socioeconomic position, with even higher levels of ethnic occupational concentration. Out-migrants from development towns do not leave when they are poor but when they are doing better and the opportunities for further advancement are blocked. Hence, development towns that have increased economic growth are paradoxically more likely to be characterized by extensive out-migration. At the same time that moving away from the development towns enhances the social and economic mobility of the migrants, the socioeconomic disadvantage of the towns increases. Indeed, development towns that are more prosperous and attractive to investments and sufficiently attractive to stabilize the population and prevent further out-migration need to sustain a major expansion of economic opportunities so as not to generate aspirations among young adults that cannot be met (Berler 1970).

Administered Territories Judea, Samaria, and Gaza

Administered territories are new settlements on the periphery of Israeli society located in Judea and Samaria and settled by Jews since the 1967 Six Day War. They are located in what I have referred to as territories "administered" by the state of Israel. The Jewish populations living in these settlements are Israeli citizens, surrounded by a large majority of Palestinian Arab residents. The territories and populations living in the eastern parts of Jerusalem that were under Jordanian control between 1948 and 1967 were incorporated into Israel after the Six Day War; the area of the Golan Heights was formally annexed in 1981. Israel also took political and administrative control of large territorial expanses and populations in the West Bank, Gaza, and Sinai. The Sinai Peninsula was returned to Egypt as part of the peace treaty initiated by the leaders of Israel, Egypt, and the United States. Gaza and the city of Jericho were transferred to Palestinian administration in the mid-1990s. The controversial issues of population and territory center on the West Bank and the large Arab Palestinian population living there. Here, I review briefly the Jewish population growth and settlement in the West Bank and in the Gaza area, which occurred under the auspices of, and with financial subsidies from, the Israeli government.[4]

There are a variety of views about the legitimacy of Jewish Israelis settling in these areas. Some Israelis, associated in large part with Gush Emunim—Bloc of the Faithful—have advocated the full annexation of the West Bank to Israel; a smaller Jewish minority have argued for the annexation of these areas but not the Palestinian population living there.[5] A small number of Jews with Israeli citizenship, many of whom commute to jobs in the state of Israel, have settled in the administered territories. They are of considerable symbolic importance and a powerful demographic and political presence. Most Israeli Arabs, and probably all the Arab Palestinians living in these territories, view the Israeli Jewish presence in the West Bank as a foreign settlement in their territory. Jewish settlers there receive financial support from the Israeli government, as do their institutions. Their areas of settlement have developed ecologically and economically with Israeli government planning and support. They receive the full protection of the Israeli military.

Settlement of these areas has been viewed by some as the next phase in the Zionist territorial reconstruction of the land of Israel. These new Jewish settlements evolved as part of the continuous policies of the Zionist movement and Israeli governments to populate land areas in order to establish political legitimacy and control. Starting with the kibbutz settlements in the first decades of the twentieth century, the first new form of Jewish resettlement in the modern era, Israeli governments continued to subsidize the settlement of Jewish immigrants in rural moshavim and then in development towns located in peripheral border areas. In the post-1967 period, new Jewish settlements were supported politically and economically in parts of reconstructed West Bank and Gaza areas, the previously defined area of Palestine.

Counted formally in the 1972 census were 1,500 Jewish residents of the administered territories—Judea, Samaria, and Gaza—located in 15 settlements. At the next census in 1983, there were 22,800 Jews living in 76 settlements in Judea-Samaria and 900 living in 5 settlements in the Gaza area. By 1991, these areas and the Jewish population living there increased—to 90,300 in Judea-Samaria in 120 settlements, and to 3,800 in 13 settlements in the Gaza area. There were 334,000 Jews in these territories at the end of 2012, in 127 settlements. Together, the Jewish communities in these territories have the most rapidly growing population and one of the highest positive rates of in-migration per 1,000 population. More than half of the Jews in the administered territories live in urban localities. Many of the others are in urban occupations and commute to their privately owned suburban residences. Economic and ecological linkages have been forged between the largest of the Jewish settlements and the metropolitan areas of Israel, since a significant proportion of the population in these settlements lives in close proximity to Tel Aviv and Jerusalem. The urban-suburban character of most of these settlements contrasts with the relative regional and urban isolation of development towns and the rural character of the moshavim and kibbutzim.

Three-fourths of the Jewish population in these territories were born in Israel. Half of the foreign-born arrived in Israel during the 1990s, and half of those born in Israel were at least second generation. The ethnic origin of the settlers was predominately European and American (60%); the overwhelming majority (80%) of the Asian and African settlers are at least second generation; the majority (51%) of the European- and American-origin settlers were born abroad, and most of those (60%) arrived in Israel in the 1990s.[6]

Unlike earlier Zionist settlers, who were socialists and secular and espoused a Zionist ideology of a return to agriculture, the settlers in the twenty-first century have urban lifestyles and emphasize the private ownership of property. Their settlements were not always planned by the central government and sometimes were in conflict with formal policies, although they rarely, if ever, were built without government infrastructural and economic supports. The Jewish settlers' conflicts were often with the local Palestinian populations, and their activities inflamed the Arab-Israeli conflict and exacerbated the tensions between Israel and neighboring Arab communities. There has been a serious division within Israeli society about the future of these settlements. A significant proportion of the settlers are *datiim* (self-identified as religious), and the religious character of these areas infuses the Zionist ideology with a strong religious orientation (see chapter 6).

The Role of Place in Israeli Society

Each of the territories or ecological settings I have reviewed played its particular role in the evolution of Israeli society and was consistent with some form of Zionism. Each of these place types was an attempt to deal with a changing conception of territory and population that was informed by external and internal events. Each settlement was planned to create political facts and to establish a Jewish presence on the outer reaches of the borders that were defined as part of the resettlement of the historic land of Israel. Surely these areas were variously defined at different times in the history of Palestine and Israel, and each in its turn, and for different reasons, generated conflict and debates among friends and foes inside and outside the state. These territories also required enormous government investments and financial and political supports to sustain their developments and to ensure their survival. And, at least to some extent, each was viewed as a critical part of the Zionist pioneering effort to rebuild and settle the land, fulfilling some utopian or messianic imperative. These areas generated a reaction on the part of the Arab residents, since each settlement was threatening to them symbolically and culturally, as well as demographically, politically, and economically. In turn, each was only partially successful in solving the problems of territorial and demographic politics.

I have described Israel as a small, nationally integrated state that is subdivided ecologically and socially by a complex grouping of areas. Some of the divisions are common in most societies—rural, town, city, and metropolitan area; others are uniquely Israeli, fitting in with the history and culture of the society—kibbutzim, moshavim, development towns, and the Jewish settlements in Judea and Samaria. These geographic and ecological settings are important for understanding Israeli society because they are associated with lifestyles and values and with the social, political, and economic characteristics that differentiate Israel's population and affect its future generations, who are socialized there and have access to its institutions. These ecological settings often reinforce economic and social inequality. Areal differences are overlaid with ethnic and religious patterns and institutions that relate to current residents and that shape the commitments and distinctiveness of their children. Community-based differences in resources, economy, and ethnicity, along with ideologically motivated settlements, are likely to continue for the next decades. Beyond the esoteric, experimental, and ideological interests of the uniquely Israeli settlements, there is the conjunction of social class, economic opportunities, ethnic origins, and religion that matters in these places.

In a society that continues to value the freedom of internal movement—where people have choices about where to live and where to raise their families—differences among areas in economic opportunities, educational possibilities, and housing availability are of enormous importance. The characteristics of individuals and their families shape how these areal differences are translated into settlement responses. The choice of where to live is not abstract but embedded in social class, in kinship, in ethnic resources and networks. It is the state and its policies that have selectively and differentially supported these settlements and areas. Those who do least well are those with fewer resources and weaker economic networks. Areas that provide few educational or occupational opportunities—those local and central governments that do not follow through economically on their ideological and political commitments—reinforce differentiation and convert the unequal distribution of resources into the generational perpetuation of inequality.

Where people live influences their social and economic lives in profound ways, most importantly, in the generational transmission of the role of place to their children. It is the dynamic, long-term, and continuous impact of ecological space on future opportunities and institutions that makes the examination of social and geographic settings necessary and complex. These communities reflect the evolution of Israel as a society; they are likely to shape its future politics, economy, and culture.

NOTES

1. In chapter 4 we reviewed the residential concentration of Arab Israelis.

2. These six broad geographic divisions are defined in terms of districts based on official administrative divisions of the country.

3. Many of those who are moving in and out of kibbutzim may actually be return or repeat migrants. Some are volunteers who spend only short periods of time in a kibbutz for the "experience" or as national service. The net figures mask these various types of migrations. There are no systematic studies of the different types of movements or the selectivity factors of remaining in or leaving a kibbutz; that is, there are no socioeconomic or demographic data concerning characteristics of those who enter or leave a kibbutz.

4. The focus on the minority Jewish population in the West Bank follows from the fact that Israel subsidizes these settlements and the Jewish population living there have rights and obligations of citizenship (including military obligations) and the educational benefits and welfare entitlements of Israeli society. Unlike the Palestinian population in these areas, they are fully part of Israeli society, except that they are living in areas administered by the state of Israel and not formally or legally part of Israel.

5. For an analysis of the ideological and religious roots of Gush Emunim, see Aran 1990 and Waxman 1991. On the political governmental and nongovernmental organizations involved in Jewish settlements in the West Bank, see Peretz 1986.

6. I do not know of systematic studies of the ethnic origins of the Jewish popu-

lation of the administered territories. My guess is that, in the large areas around Jerusalem and Tel Aviv, there is a rather even split between those of European and those of Asian and African origin, reflecting the ethnic composition of third-generation Israelis. In smaller places, particularly in areas of more-nationalistic, ideological, and religious settlement, the proportion of Jews of Western origin is likely to be higher.

6 | Religiosity, Religious Institutions, and Israeli Culture

There are powerful historic connections between the religion of Jews (Judaism) and the concept of Jewish peoplehood (Zionism). Judaism had always incorporated a vision of a return to Zion in its construction of history and in its traditional religious liturgy. Politically, the state of Israel was established as a secular, democratic society, populated initially in large part by those who substituted their own national ideology, Zionism, for the Judaism and religious traditions of their parents and grandparents. At the same time, the Zionist founders recognized that they could not entirely escape the religious culture of their origins. Over time, Zionists developed new forms of religious expression, new national religious holidays evolved, and traditional religious holidays were given new meaning. Familiar religious rituals were reimagined and became sources of cohesion among secular Zionists. Among some of those in the Old Yishuv (the settlement before the influx of the secular Zionists) and among many of the immigrants were Zionists who viewed the establishment of the state as the fulfillment of the divine promise of a Jewish return to the land of Israel. There were religious Zionists who sought to combine the return to a national homeland with reinvigorated religious observances, and there were secular Zionists who selectively included religious symbols in national rituals. Religious political parties were organized, state-supported religious kibbutzim were established, and state-sponsored religious schools were founded by the secular state.

Religious institutions were established in Israel, synagogues and religious academies were built, rabbis were empowered (and subsidized by the state) to make decisions about secular matters; political parties and religious public schools were expanded by religious movements, and government coalitions were organized to incorporate religious political parties. At the same time, new forms of Israeli culture emerged that extended the meanings of religious ritual and developed particular cultural Israeli expressions. Among many examples were secular-socialist kibbutzim that redefined traditional Jewish religious holidays (like Passover, Hanukkah,

Shavuot) in new agricultural and national contexts. Even minor religious holidays such as Purim became associated with secular culture within the Jewish settlement in pre-state Palestine. A fascinating account of the beauty competitions for Queen Esther in conjunction with the Purim carnivals in Tel Aviv from 1926 to 1929 is but one of many examples of such a process of developing Israeli secular culture associated with traditional religious practice.[1] Some traditional ethnic/religious holidays have been reconstructed and widely celebrated nationally among Israelis (e.g., the Mimouna originally among Moroccans and then nationally).[2]

Even as the state was not "controlled" by the religious establishment or by Judaism, religion was everywhere. From the imposition of rules about kosher food in the Knesset and in the army and to limitations (in some Israeli cities) on public transportation on the Sabbath and on religious holidays, to traditional religious symbols in public buildings, some forms of Judaism emerged as dominant cultural themes. At the same time tensions between the secular and the religious in Israel have had a long history (a history written in large part by secular historians and social scientists, hence not always unbiased). Here we take a broader view and examine the role of Judaism in Israeli life and the relationship between the religious and the secular to better understand the evolutionary changes in Israeli society. As a starting point we note that there are a variety of forms of Judaism practiced by Jews and all Judaisms reflect the contexts in which they develop. Given Israel's changing social contexts, we need to keep in mind that Israeli Judaism is different from the Judaism practiced in diaspora countries of origin and twenty-first-century Israeli Judaism is different from Judaism at earlier points in time. Simple time and cross-national comparisons of changes and variation in Judaism are therefore fraught with difficulties of interpretation. Hence, we need to be skeptical when changes in Judaism are defined as secularization and the decline of religion and when variation in religious practice among Jews in Israel is treated as the diminishing of religious tradition. Social scientists have raised questions about the appropriate use of the concept secularization in the study of Jews as well as other populations (see especially Deshen 1990; Gitelman 2009; Gitelman 2012; Leichtman 2013).

There are several axes along which we can begin to explore questions about Judaism in Israel. The first axis focuses on the religious identity and religious ritual behavior of Israelis. Here we ask, How do Israelis identify religiously, What do they do religiously, and How do they connect to the institutions of religion and to secular daily activities? A second axis deals with the institutional context at the macro-societal level. Here the questions are, What are the religious institutions in the society, Who controls them, and How do religious institutions connect to families and politics, to economy and culture? We connect these two dimensions by asking whether Judaism in its diverse public forms has an impact on the private family and daily lives of Israeli Jews. What are the consequences of religious beliefs and identities for communities and families in Israel? This chapter will address the main features of these issues and assess the ways in which religion, in its institutional/macro dimensions and its identity/behavioral and individual/micro dimensions, is a source of cohesion, tension, and conflict within Israeli society. A review of the role of the intensity of religious identity among Moslems in Israel will conclude the chapter.

Institutions and Religion

The relationship of Israeli Jews to synagogues is voluntary and public, and formal membership in a synagogue is not required for any religious activity. Nevertheless, Israeli Jews must connect to rabbinic or religious institutions at various points in the life course. The Chief Rabbinate, through its council and administrative apparatus, has jurisdiction over many aspects of life for Jews in Israel, including personal status issues, such as Jewish marriages and divorce, Jewish burials, conversions to Judaism, regulation and supervision over Jewish holy sites, working with various public ritual baths, and religious academies (*yeshivot*). In addition, the Rabbinate has control over the religious rituals in public institutions such as the army, the certification of kashrut for public institutions (e.g., restaurants, the government, hospitals, museums) and food establishments in general, the location of synagogues, the appointment of local rabbis, local and national religious courts, and public transportation on the Sabbath. At the extreme, some neighborhoods/communities have become defined as "religious," with formal and informal restrictions placed on activities permitted and not permitted on the Sabbath and holidays (e.g., travel by car) and even the proper (modest) way for men and women to dress. The Rabbinate and its administrators are in large part *haredim* (ultraorthodox or at least the more-religious end of the religiosity continuum) and are a relatively small proportion of the religiously defined population. Hence, it is not surprising that there are tensions when the secular, the majority of Israeli Jews, interact with these institutions.

The Chief Rabbinate (the two chief rabbis) was organized in Palestine before the establishment of the state, following the practice in European communities. In Israel, the chief rabbis are the supreme halachic (religious/legal) and spiritual authority for Jews, and they do not always agree on particular questions of ritual or political practices. We note that the ethnic divide in the Rabbinate (between Sephardic and Ashkenazic) is the only formally recognized ethnic divide that is institutionalized at the state level in Israel. The Rabbinate and its Chief Rabbinate Council have legal and administrative authority to control religious arrangements for Israel's Jews. They also respond to religious legal questions submitted by Jewish public bodies inside and outside Israel. The council sets guidelines and supervises agencies within its authority. The chief rabbis are elected for ten-year terms. As of 2013, the Sephardi chief rabbi is Yitzhak Yosef and the Ashkenazi chief rabbi is David Lau; both are the children of previous chief rabbis.

The Rabbinate also oversees Israeli Rabbinical courts, which are part of Israel's judicial system and are managed by the Ministry of Religion. The courts have exclusive jurisdiction over marriage and divorce of Jews and have parallel supervision in district courts in matters of personal status, alimony, child support, custody, and inheritance. Religious-court verdicts are implemented and enforced the same way as verdicts in the civil court system—by the police, bailiff's office, and other civil agencies. Jews of all religious persuasions therefore must deal with the Rabbinate and its affiliated agencies in critical transitions throughout the life course. Clearly this is a source of power and control among the religiously identified population and its leadership; it is also a source of conflict among the secular majority of Israeli Jews.

Religious schools, public and private, are among the options available for students from early education through advanced schooling in colleges and religious academies. Some of the religious elementary and high schools are not available in local communities, but there are religious boarding schools and regional religious institutions. In large part students and their parents have the choice of a religious-oriented public-school education or a secular public-school education as well as a private religious or secular schooling.

Hence, at the institutional level, Judaism and Jewish religious authorities have considerable power over the lives of the Israeli Jewish population who are marginally religious or not at all religious in behavior and identity. This is particularly acute in life-course transitions and in the formal definition of who is Jewish in Israeli society. Considering oneself to be Jewish is not sufficient; one must fit the formal definition in order to have access to rituals associated with these transitions. Because the institutions of religion have such pervasive presence in the society, and employ large numbers of persons in various ministries, the costs to the society are high (and for some the benefits are also considerable). The institutions and their academies tend to perpetuate themselves generationally. Because of their place in the political sphere, they have played a disproportionate role in various governments as part of political-coalition formation in Israel.

The Judaism(s) of Israeli Jews

One way to explore the religion and the religiosity of Israeli Jews is to examine how Israelis define and identify themselves religiously. A helpful source of information on the religious identity of Israelis comes from a special survey carried out by the Central Bureau of Statistics of Israel in 2009 obtained from adults age 20 years and older.[3] The survey measured religiosity on the basis of subjective self-identification and the regular performance of traditional religious rituals. The survey documented the range of religious self-identities of Israeli Jews and non-Jews. The results provide a strong basis for an assessment of religion and religiosity in Israel. The survey was constructed to allow for some inferences about changes over time (by age and by generation in comparison with parents) and about variation among social subgroups (by social class and ethnic origin). The survey was used as part of an interesting and important set of population projections on the future composition of Israel's population among religiously defined Jewish and Arab groups (Ben-Moshe 2014). These projections showed substantial growth for the religious sector and a declining secular proportion in Israel's future population.

To gain an appreciation of the range of ways Israeli Jews perceive their own religiosity, we start by noting the categories that are used to self-describe religiosity. Starting at the most religious end of observance among Israeli Jews are *haredim*, loosely translated as "ultraorthodox," who are most likely to have distinctive dress and to attend special private schools (separate for boys and girls) with minimum exposure to secular subjects and Israeli culture. *Haredim* have formed their own political parties, some are anti-Zionists, and they tend to live in segregated neighborhoods and communities (especially in Jerusalem and B'nei Brak). Despite the considerable internal heterogeneity of *haredi* communities, all *haredim* tend to have patriarchal and large families, marry at an early age, and lead gender-segregated lives. At the other end of the religiosity spectrum are those who define themselves as *heloniim*, secular and nonreligious. *Heloniim* are likely to celebrate Israeli national holidays but not Judaic culture and rarely participate in public or private religious rituals (except for those life-cycle transitions that rabbis control). In between are those who define themselves as *masortiim* or traditional Jews, at times combining this with the generic other category *datiim* or just religious. *Masortiim* and *datiim* relate positively to religious political institutions, attend public schools that are defined as "religious and Zionist," and are committed to reinforcing the overall Judaic character of the state. In large part we shall use these categories to describe the ways that Jews in Israel define their own religious identity. As will become clear, these forms of self-identification are highly correlated with religious ritual observances and institutional connections.

The lines dividing the two extremes on the religiosity scale are very clear (*haredim* versus *heloniim*); the lines dividing *masortiim* and *datiim* are more blurred, as some *masortiim* define themselves also as "religious" and some as "not so religious." The blurring is often because many of those from Middle Eastern Jewish communities define themselves as traditional Jews, some of whom are not as (or have become less) religiously observant compared to their parental generation. Some use the labeling of *masorti* to imply ethnic/family rather than specifically religious traditions. Moreover, religious self-identity has at times become part of peoples' identification with the political party system in Israel, separating "religious Zionists" (and their political parties) from secular Zionists (and their political parties) and both types of political parties from those that are explicitly religious non-Zionists. Some political parties are "religious" parties tied to broadly defined ethnic communities (e.g., Shas, the Sephardic religious party). Contributing even further complexity are the sources of this political diversity. Religious political parties were founded originally in European and Middle Eastern countries of origin a century ago and reconstructed in Israel, reflecting a broad Sephardic Middle Eastern origin population and an Ashkenazic origin, or *haredi* agenda.

Below we present the basic outline of religiosity as adult Israeli Jews reported it at the end of the first decade of the twenty-first century, reducing the detailed complexities of variations within these categories and their political connections. The main findings point to the following religiosity profile for Israeli Jews. Overall, the major self-identification of Israeli Jews fluctuates between those who define themselves as "secular" and those who simply define themselves as "traditional." Specifically, using the categories that Israelis themselves use in identifying their religiosity, about four out of ten Israeli Jews define themselves as secular/nonreligious (*heloni/lo dati*, 43%), and a significant proportion define themselves as "traditional" (*masorti*, 38%). The latter category combines two equal subcategories, "traditional–not very *dati*" and "traditional-*dati*." There are two more-marginal categories of religious self-identification: those who simply categorize themselves as religious (*dati*, 10%) and those who define themselves as *haredi* or "ultrareligious" (9%). With some variation, this division of the Israeli adult population has been consistent in studies carried out over the last several decades (table 6.1).

The survey was based on responses to questions about the religious identity of individuals, not of families. Included as well were questions about ritual observances that were also addressed to individuals, although many of the items related to household characteristics. Judaism has many rituals that have been gender-specific, but detailed data by sex showed no systematic differences in the self-identification distribution of religiosity between Jewish Israeli men and women. While there is a general impression and some overall evidence of trends toward reduced levels of religiosity, which might signal the growth of secularization in Israel at the institutional and societal level, there is also evidence that new forms of religiosity have emerged. It is therefore somewhat surprising that the variation in religiosity by age shows a mixed picture of religiosity among the younger age groups (from ages 20 to 45) and no sharp increase among those who define themselves as secular. How this will work itself out over the life course is an open question.

One of the confounding factors in the examination of religiosity among Israeli Jews is the triangular link among secular education, ethnic origins, and religiosity. Variation by ethnic origin shows that Israeli Jews of Asian/

TABLE 6.1

Religious self-identity, the adult Jewish population of Israel, age 20 and over, 2009

	Ultraorthodox (*haredi*) (%)	Religious (*dati*) (%)	Traditional (*mesorti*) (%)	Secular/ not religious (*heloni*) (%)	Total (%)
Current religious identity of respondent's household					
	9	10	38	43	100
Religious identity of parents' household when respondent was age 15					
	6	17	39	38	100
Respondent's religious identity by current age					
20–24	14	17	32	37	100
25–45	8	13	37	41	100
45–64	3	19	41	37	100
65+	3	24	39	33	100
Respondent's religious identity by parents' ethnic origins					
Born in Israel	14	13	31	42	100
Asia/Africa	3	26	55	15	100
Europe/America	7	15	30	48	100
Former Soviet U.	—	5	21	74	100
Respondent's current religious identity by parents' religious identity					
Haredi	66	13	13	8	100
Dati	4	69	21	6	100
Mesorti	1	18	68	11	100
Heloni	—	3	20	76	100

Source: These data are drawn from a special social survey of the Central Bureau of Statistics, Israel, 2009, publication number 1433, 4/12/2011, especially tables 13, 15–30. Also the *Statistical Abstract of Israel* 2012, table 7.6.

African origins are most likely to identify themselves as "traditional" (over half), with only 15% who define themselves as secular. In sharp contrast, three-fourths of the recent immigrants from the former Soviet Union define their religious identity as secular. Part of this pattern documents the way in which ethnicity interacts with religiosity in places of origin and in families from particular ethnic communities. Over four out of ten Israelis of Israeli origin (third or higher generation) identify their parental household (when they were age 15) as secular, and almost half of Israelis of European background identify their parental household as secular. In contrast, the two ends of the religiosity spectrum are the Russians (*heloniim*/secular) and those from Middle Eastern origins (*masortiim*/traditional): only 15% of those of Asian/African origins define their parental home as secular; fully 74% of those from the former Soviet Union, who immigrated to Israel after 1990, identify their parental household when they were age 15 as secular.

In many countries, there tends to be a presumptive relationship between secular education and religiosity. Under the assumption that religion is the traditional culture of the less secularly educated, the expectation has often been that the more educated are less religiously identified in their behavior than those with lower levels of education. Consistent with this expectation, the relationship between education and religiosity shows that the most educated in Israel are likely to identify as secular (58%) and a disproportionate number of the least educated identify as ultraorthodox (18%). This may partly reflect the emphasis of the ultraorthodox on religious and not formal secular education. Data by income show a similar pattern: religiosity varies inversely with income, as those with the highest income are more likely to define themselves as secular and those with the lowest income are least likely to define themselves as secular; those with the lowest income are the most likely to identify themselves as ultraorthodox. Half of the high-income earners are from secular households and 22% of those from the lowest income group identify their parental household as ultraorthodox.

It is likely that the relationship between educational level and religious self-identification obscures a number of other factors, including the role of peers and community, the effects of different types of education (religious or secular), the tendency for adult *haredi* men to be formally unemployed (many are registered as students in religious academies), and the observation that significant proportions of "religious" Jews are well educated. Certainly additional research into the meaning of the relationship between socioeconomic class and religiosity needs to be carried out, or at a minimum we should be cautious in reaching the oversimplified conclusion that students' educational experience in Israel exposes them to secular values and results in and enhances secularization processes or secular self-identity. The causal connection may be reversed: religiosity may lead to lower levels of secular education rather than the reverse. Perhaps the negative association of secular education and religiosity is a pattern that characterized earlier generations when the generational transition occurred from parents who were more identified religiously to children who were becoming less attached to religion and becoming more secular.

A more-detailed comparison of the religious origins and current identity of the Israeli Jewish population (bottom section of table 6.1) is revealing and shows considerable continuity between the religious character of the parental home and current religiosity: Three-fourths of those who identify themselves as secular identify the households where they were raised as secular; almost 70% of those who are currently traditional come from households they identify as traditional; and almost 70% of the *dati/* religious and ultraorthodox came from similarly identified households. On this basis and on the basis of the data by age noted earlier, the evidence does not seem to suggest a significant shift generationally away from the religious character of the parental household. This may reflect how the current generation perceives the religiosity of the households where they were raised. It may also imply that the generational shift toward lower levels of religiosity occurred for an earlier generation, as religious behavior was associated with foreign origins and more-traditional communities. The stability or continuity of religious/secular culture is likely to be most characteristic of the orientation of the younger generation, raised in Israel by Israeli-born parents. (Note the similarity of the religiosity at age 15 between Israelis of European birth and those born in Israel.) As the ethnic composition of the third-generation Israeli-born population slowly changes from European origins to Asian/African origins, we should expect the generational trend to shift further away from parental religious origins. Most likely the impression of increased secularization in Israeli society reflects in part ethnic compositional changes, notably the significant increase in the Russian immigrant population and their children.

Based on detailed data showing the relationship between subjective religious self-identification and the observance of religious traditions, it seems that the simple subjective measure of religious self-identification captures the essential character of religiosity. Almost all those who define themselves as ultraorthodox or *dati* report that they observe the traditions of Judaism; over one-fourth of those who define themselves as traditional/ not very religious report that they only marginally observe the traditions of Judaism; over 70% of the secular report that they do not observe the traditions of Judaism. Over half of those who report that they keep the traditions define themselves as either *haredi* or *dati*.

If Israeli Jews have remained in large part consistently as religious and as secular as their parental household, do they change their religious orientation over their own life course? In response to a direct subjective question, about two out of ten report that over their life course they have become more religious, while 14% report that they have become less religious. Those reporting themselves as more religious over their life course define themselves as *haredim* or *datiim*; a significant proportion of those who are traditional have become less religious over their life course. Only a small proportion of Israelis (5%) report that they consider themselves "returnees" to Judaism. An examination of the returnees by current religiosity points to the higher than average percentage of returnees who currently define themselves as ultraorthodox (22%) or religious (17%) compared to those who identify as traditional (9%). Returnees do not simply go from secular to traditional to religious but when becoming more religious define themselves either ultraorthodox or *dati*.

Religious Knowledge and Observance

How knowledgeable are Israeli Jews about Jewish traditions? Over 70% of Israeli Jews characterize their knowledge of religion and tradition as good or very good. Jews who are not religious do not perceive the cause as being ignorant of the Judaic traditions. The only major exception is among the recent immigrants from the former Soviet Union; only about one-third assess their knowledge of religion and tradition as either good or very good. Indeed the recent Russian immigrants to Israel are outliers on almost all dimensions of religiosity, reflecting the limited religious education they experienced under the regime of the former Soviet Union, their more-recent immigration to Israel, and lower levels of exposure to Israeli society relative to other Jewish ethnic groups. Most importantly, when taken together, these data do not point toward either secularization or increased religiosity over time or major shifts generationally among Israeli Jews.

In addition to how Israeli Jews perceive their own religiosity, selected data allow us to explore levels and variation in religious ritual performance, dietary observances, and religious holiday celebrations among Israeli Jews. (These data exclude those who define themselves as ultraorthodox or religious, for whom the presumption is that they observe these religious rituals. So these data refer only to those who define themselves as traditional or secular.) Starting with weekly Sabbath observance, the data show that half the Israelis who are traditional or secular regularly light candles on Friday night to mark the beginning of the Sabbath (92% of the *masortiim/ datiim* and 68% of the *masortiim*/not very religious) and 29% of the secular. About three-fourths of traditional Israelis start the Sabbath with a ritual blessing (kiddush), but that characterizes only 17% of the secular; almost half of the traditional/*datiim* observe travel restrictions on the Sabbath, but that characterizes only 7% of the traditional/not very religious and 2% of the secular. (Often Sabbath-day travels bring families together in leisure-time activities.) About one-third of the Israeli Jewish population (who are not classified as *haredim* or *datiim*) observe dietary regulations (but 80% of the traditional/*datiim*, 43% of the traditional/not very religious and only 10% of the secular). About half of those not classified as ultraorthodox or *datiim* observe the special Passover dietary customs, and half fast on Yom Kippur. This characterizes only (or-fully) one fourth of the secular.

In contrast, larger majorities observe some seasonal and family-based Jewish holidays (which have more often than not been redefined along nationalistic lines). Fully 79% report that they light Hanukkah candles and 88% participate in a Passover seder meal (even the secular are likely to observe these — 67% light Hanukkah candles and 82% participate in a Passover seder). At the other end of the observance distribution, only one out of ten adults prays regularly and 13% of the men put on phylacteries (t'fillin) regularly. Again these percentages are highest among the *masortiim/* religious and weakest among the secular. Few subgroups that were identified in the survey attend synagogue regularly (defined as weekly); only a small proportion of those who are not ultraorthodox or *datiim* attend the synagogue more than a few times a year, mainly at holidays or special family occasions. Hence, religious rituals that are household/family-based and are ceremonial and seasonal/occasional remain a significant way for almost all Jewish Israelis to express their religiosity (or more accurately their Jewish culture); religious rituals in the public domain and in institutions (synagogues) are observed only occasionally. Although the survey did not include details on nontraditional holiday observances, it is likely that the nationalistic interpretation of specific holidays in Israel (e.g., Passover and Hanukkah) along with new national holidays (e.g., Israel Independence Day; Jerusalem Day) are widely celebrated by all Jewish subgroups in new Israeli contexts.

The same general pattern emerges for the relative importance of maintaining religious customs associated with male circumcision (75%), celebrating bar mitzvahs (68%), weddings with rabbinical participation (64%), religious burials (64%), and sitting shiva–seven days of mourning following death (69%). Again these are levels of observance among those who are not ultraorthodox or *datiim*. In almost all these religious rituals the ethnic divide is consistent: those of Asian/African origins are more likely to observe these religious rituals while those of European origins are less likely. And recent immigrants from the former Soviet Union are least likely of all ethnic groups to observe these religious rituals and remain the conspicuous outliers. In large part they define themselves as secular and consider participation in these rituals and customs not as important. In contrast, over 90% of those who define themselves as "religious" or *dati* consider these religious rituals very important in their lives.

A set of questions that focus on the overall perception of religiosity in Israel was also included. Fully 80% of Israeli Jews of all religious orientations perceive that religion has a strong influence on life in Israel and that religion has increased its influence in recent years (63%); two-thirds think that observing the Sabbath traditionally is important, although it is unclear what they mean by this. At the same time, 57% of the Israeli Jewish population think that there should be a separation of religion and state, 62% think that civil marriages should be permitted in Israel rather than only marriages under religious auspices, as is currently the case; more than half think that the religious leadership should have a role in establishing secular policies of the state and that religious education should be an increased part of public-school education. Again variation in these overall patterns follows the expected patterns. Thus, for example, fully 88% of the recent Russian immigrants think that civil marriage should be permitted in Israel and 68% think that there should be a separation of religion and state. In contrast, the respective proportions of Israelis from Asian/African origins are less than 50%. In this context, an important point is the consistency among measures of religiosity among Jews in Israel and the fact that measures of the self-assessment of religiosity seem to be a fairly accurate and reliable single indicator of the multiple dimensions of religiosity in Israel in general. The data indirectly reveal the enormous impact of immigration since the 1990s from the former Soviet Union on national patterns of religiosity.

The continuity of secularism and religiosity over the generations suggests that, all things being equal, the contrast between secular and ultraorthodox Jews in Israel will become even sharper and the tensions between these groups associated with lifestyle will not diminish. Indeed, given the general ethnic and social-class divide among Israeli Jews, a question remains about the increasing polarization or conflict between the more religious and the less religious. The survey documented that among Israeli Jews the relationship between the religious and the secular subgroups is perceived to be "not very good" (47%) or "not at all good" (11%). Only 2% consider the relationship very good and 35% as good. Two-thirds of those who identify as nonreligious or secular describe the relationship between the religious and the secular as "not at all good," a proportion significantly higher than found among those who identify themselves as *haredim* or *datiim*. The ultraorthodox often consider themselves oppressed by the larger Israeli majority who are secular and who define the normative cultural climate. The secular see the religious and *haredim* as restricting the freedom of the majority of Jews.

Religiosity, Family, and Gender

Given Israel's history and current ethnic composition, it is not surprising that religion and religiosity have such a conspicuous role in the secular society of Israel. More unexpected is the powerful role that Judaism plays in the area of demography in general (e.g., immigration) and fertility in particular. The religious establishment has in the past defined potential immigrants as Jewish in order to determine which ones qualified for entry under the Law of Return (which specifies that all Jews outside the state have a right to immigrate to Israel): it limited qualification to those whose mothers were defined as Jewish. This power of exclusion has since been limited to the sanctioning of life-course transitions, and the state has been allowing immigrants into the country using a broader definition of who is Jewish. Over the years the Rabbinate has exercised its power to exclude some Ethiopian and Russian Jews from being a part of the Israeli Jewish community, and has excluded some Russian Jews from access to a Jewish burial because they were not halachically Jewish (because their mothers were not Jewish). The Rabbinate has also disallowed the religious conversions to Judaism of those who were converted under non-Orthodox auspices outside Israel (under Reform or Conservative Judaism) and has likewise rejected petitions to sanction Jewish marriages (Orthodox Judaism is the only recognized basis for sanctioning Jewish marriages in Israel).

In a behavioral context, religiosity is a major factor that continues to differentiate the fertility levels of young Jewish families in Israel. Parallel to earlier findings (C. Goldscheider and Friedlander 1986), recent research has shown a direct relationship between religiosity among Jewish Israelis and levels of fertility and the timing of marriage. Using four self-enumerated categories, from secular to ultraorthodox, research shows that the higher the level of religious commitments, the earlier the age of marriage and the larger the family size, even controlling for educational level. Indeed, fertility differences by religiosity are pronounced among the more educated, since there is no consistent relationship between years of education and fertility among the more religious (Kupinsky 1992; Okun 2013). These results are reinforced by systematic ecological analyses, showing the convergence of most fertility differences by ethnic origin in Israel and the decline to around two children on average, except in areas where religious Jews are residentially concentrated. The fertility levels of families living in religious areas raise the average fertility level for the Jewish population as a whole (Friedlander and Feldman 1993; Okun 2013; Bystrov 2012).

The importance of the relationship between religiosity and gender segregation is a key to understanding these family patterns. There are linkages between attitudes toward the roles of women and fertility.[4] It is not surprising that women who think that childbearing and child rearing are the most important thing in a woman's life are likely to have significantly larger families than women who look less favorably on these traditional gender-segregated roles. As a composite, the evidence suggests that women have lower fertility norms and behavior if they (1) have higher levels of education, (2) were raised by parents of Western origin, (3) are secular in orientation, (4) have a consistent work pattern outside the home, (5) share housework responsibilities with their spouses, (6) have higher family incomes and better jobs, and (7) are less positive toward the centrality of childbearing in their lives. Religiosity is the most important factor when all these variables are examined jointly (Kupinsky 1992; Okun 2013).

It is unlikely that religiosity in Judaism implies the simple connection between religious theology and fertility, since there is neither a known, simple theology/norm in Judaism on family size nor a clear-cut prohibition on the use of all forms of contraception (Friedlander and Goldscheider 1984; C. Goldscheider 1971; C. Goldscheider and Friedlander 1986). There is a clear relationship between religiosity and contraceptive usage among Jews in Israel (Yaffe 1976; Okun 2000; Okun 2013; Wilder 2000). In Israel, as elsewhere (C. Goldscheider and Mosher 1991), religiosity implies a commitment to traditional family and segregated gender roles, and particularly to the family and childbearing roles of women. For the more religious in Israel, the role of women is concentrated on family and childbearing, and is not equal to that of men. Gender segregation and inequality are likely to result in higher-fertility norms and larger families, not simply because of specific norms about birth control, but rather because of more-general norms and family/group values—and the structures that sustain them—about women's roles and family centrality (see chapters 7 and 10). Religiosity is linked to values about family and the role of women that apply to all socioeconomic contexts.[5]

One of the spheres in which women are clearly discriminated against is the politics of religion in Israel. As noted above, in addition to the formal responsibility over all religious rituals and institutions, the Orthodox religious establishment in Israel has always controlled the critical areas of marriage and divorce regulation. Religious institutions and the rabbis that control them have not been responsive to the wide range of religious and social needs of women and have normatively and legally reinforced the subordinate roles of women in their separate spheres. The emphasis on family roles (and indirectly, the priority of family over other roles) by an all-male religious hierarchy has institutionalized the disadvantaged and relative powerless position of women over the rituals of Judaism (public prayer services, religious leadership, ritual dietary supervision, and judges in religious courts) and over the role of women in marriage and family life. The religious establishment in its interpretation of Judaism and in its politics reinforces the lower and disadvantaged position of women as independent decision makers and ignores, in large part, their spiritual needs. There is no clearer illustration of these forms of gender discrimination than the restrictions placed on the full participation of women in public places of worship (e.g., in synagogues and at the Western Wall in Jerusalem's Old City). Some of these constraints are being modified in the twenty-first century among a younger generation of women who have become more educated Jewishly and active politically. The discrimination of the religious-establishment leadership against women persists.

The religious establishment in Israel, including the election of chief rabbis, is sustained by political appointments. Religious-based political parties have in the past been important coalition partners in Israel's political system (Arian 1985; Arian and Shamir 1994; Freedman 2009) and have extracted political control over "personal status"—marriage and the definition of who is Jewish, a critical dimension in a society in which Jewishness has profound political significance—as part of the political exchange and bargaining. Orthodox is the only legitimate Judaism in Israel supported and sponsored by the government. This denies formal religious representation to those who are religiously Jewish in the context of other Jewish religious denominations. As documented above, non-Orthodox religious expression and self-identification characterize the majority of the Israeli Jewish population.[6] These other Judaisms have a more-egalitarian gender theology and have been in other contexts flexible with regard to the allocation of religious and political nonfamily roles to women. They are not part of the Israeli religious establishment, in either the religious Zionist or non-Zionist (Agudah) political forms. Again this seems to be changing outside the Orthodox establishment and somewhat within some Orthodox religious communities in Israel.

The male religious establishment's control over the divorce process has severely alienated a small group of women whose husbands have refused to provide them with a divorce, thus preventing the remarriage of these women. There is no secular or civil marriage in Israel, and there is no recognition of divorce that is not a "get," a religious divorce decree. In traditional Jewish practice, men have the right to divorce their wives but not vice versa, although religious courts often exercised their power to encourage men to grant a divorce. The *agunah* status (wherein a woman is unwillingly tied to her husband either because he has refused to grant her a divorce or has disappeared, voluntarily or otherwise, and hence she cannot remarry) symbolizes in dramatic and painful ways the persistence of gender inequalities in Israel. The number of women in this state of helplessness is relatively small, but it reveals how institutions and their representatives continue to subordinate women's rights to male authority and to the controlling power of the Orthodox religious establishment.

In addition to the politics of religion, which clearly reveals the disadvantaged role of women in Israeli society, women and men have developed different relationships to the rituals and values of Judaism and different conceptions of the religious role: Israeli Jewish women tend to view religion in interpersonal terms, as in helping and caring for others; for men, religion means study and prayer. When women perform religious rituals, it is to help others in distress, the ill or the troubled. When men aid the sick or the poor, they tend to emphasize the more-ceremonial aspects of Judaism. Hence, the concepts of religion and religiosity mean different things to men and women (Sered 1993). These powerful gender differences are not captured by national survey data and public opinion polls. However, these differences reflect the separate ways that religion impinges on the lives of men and women. When these gender differences result in differential power and control, the difference becomes disadvantageous to women and reinforces gender discrimination that exists in other domains of Israeli social life (family and economy).

Religiosity among Moslem Israelis

Most of the discussions of Israeli religion have focused on Judaism, since Israel is an overwhelmingly Jewish state, dominated demographically and politically by Jews for Jews. But as we have noted, a significant minority of it residents are not Jewish. And often the non-Jews (Arabs/Palestinians) have been defined along "religious" affiliation lines for political reasons by political parties and by residential concentration. Most non-Jews live in segregated communities and face social and economic discrimination. As among Jews, there is considerable religious heterogeneity among non-Jews in Israel. The overwhelming majority of non-Jews in Israel are Moslem, but a substantial minority are either Christian or Druze. And there is an increasing number of non-Jews who are not Arab but define themselves as without religion, mainly from the former Soviet Union.

There is limited information on the religiosity of the Christian and Druze populations, and none was collected in the special survey on religiosity conducted by the government statistical bureau in 2009. One of the survey's important features was, however, the inclusion of a battery of questions on religiosity among non-Jews, the majority of whom are Moslem. Although not strictly comparable with the findings on the Jewish Israeli population, some of the main points of comparison suggest parallels

TABLE 6.2

Religious self-identity, the adult Moslem population of Israel, age 20 and over, 2009

	Very religious (%)	Religious (%)	Not very religious (%)	Not religious (%)	Total (%)
Current religiosity of respondent					
	8	45	27	21	100
Religious identity of parents' household when respondent was age 15					
	11	58	20	11	100
Respondent's religious identity by current age					
20–29	10	59	22	9	100
30–39	7	57	22	14	100
40–49	10	51	24	15	100
50+	16	63	12	9	100
Respondents' current religious identity by parents' religious identity					
Very religious/ religious	15	69	7	9	100
Not very religious/ not religious	4	41	41	14	100

Source: These data are drawn from a special social survey of the Central Bureau of Statistics, Israel, 2009, publication number 1433, 4/12/2011, especially tables 27–30.

as well as important contrasts with the Israeli Jewish population. A general note of caution in the comparison of religiosity among Moslems and Jews: Moslems who say they are "religious" do not necessarily mean the same thing as Israeli Jews, since religious requirements in Islam are different from those in Judaism. Thus, the similarity in the questions asked does not always imply that the meanings of the responses are identical between religious groups.

The major findings for Moslems, age 20 and over, are as displayed in table 6.2. About half the non-Jews (mainly Moslems) in Israel identify themselves as very religious or religious, and 48% identify themselves as not very religious or not at all religious. The proportions for Israeli Jews in the closest comparable categories are 20% very religious or religious (*haredim* and *datiim*) and 80% traditional or not at all religious. Thus, overall it appears that Jews are less self-identified religiously than are Israeli

Moslems. Similar to Jewish Israelis, a majority of Moslem Israelis are centrists religiously, neither extremely/ultra religious nor secular.

Comparing current religiosity among Moslems with the religiosity they define when they were growing up shows a clearer case of decreased religiosity generationally: 69% of religious Israeli Moslems defined their households at age 15 as very religious or religious when they were growing up compared to 53% who identify their own religiosity as religious or very religious; while 31% defined their parental households as not very or not at all religious when they were age 15 compared to 48% who define their current religiosity in that way.

Younger Moslems appear to be somewhat less religious than older Moslems. To the extent that these age-specific data reflect a trend, it appears that there are patterns of stability in religiosity among younger and older Moslems with only a slight shift toward lower levels of religious self-identification. This is also reflected in comparing the current religiosity identification of Moslems with the perceived religiosity of the households in which they were raised: 84% of Moslems who define themselves as religious or very religious grew up in households that they identified as religious or very religious; 15% of Moslems who currently identify themselves as religious or very religious grew up in households they defined as very religious. Moslems who currently are not very religious or not at all religious were raised in households that they defined as more religious than they are currently. About 55% of the Moslems reported that they had not changed their level of religiosity during their lifetime (a figure less than the proportion of Israeli Jews who so defined their religious continuity over the life course — 65%). This theme of reduction in the level of religiosity among Moslem Israelis appears more characteristic among Moslems who identify themselves currently as not very religious or not at all religious compared to those who defined their household at age 15 as not very religious or not at all religious.

Do Moslems perceive that their religiosity has changed over their life course? Four out of ten Moslems report that they have become more religious over their life course while only 4% have become less religious (and 56% did not change their religiosity self-identification over their life course). For Israeli Jews, as a comparison, 21% report that they have become more religious, 14% have become less religious, and 65% have not changed their religiosity over their life course. This comparison between the implied changes among Israeli Jews and Israeli Moslems documents the greater religious self-identification among younger Moslem Israelis than among Jewish Israelis and the greater trend among Israeli Jews toward lower levels of religiosity. Nevertheless, and most striking, neither community seems to have undergone any sharp religious transformation (by age or generational perception) toward extreme religiosity or extreme secularism in the last generation.

There is a significant gender difference among Moslem Israelis, unlike among Jewish Israelis. Moslem women over the age of 20 are more likely to identify as religious than are Moslem men and less likely to identify as not religious; about half of the Moslem women say that they have become more religious over their life course. Few Moslem men and women claim to have reduced their religiosity over their life course. In contrast, gender differences in the religiosity of Jewish Israelis are not observable.

In general, Moslems in Israel (as most Israeli Jews) consider their public religious ritual very important. Over two out of three Moslems consider circumcision, religious marriage, religious burial, and mourning customs very important. Unlike Jewish Israelis, few Moslem Israelis (17%) think that civil marriages should be allowed to take place in Israel. The comparable percentage is 62% for Jewish Israelis. In the public sphere of religiosity fully two-thirds of Moslem Israelis consider religion to have a strong influence on life in Israel and perceive that religion has strengthened in recent years in Israel; over 70% think that religion and state should be separated, a higher proportion than among Israeli Jews (57%). Yet the underlying attitudes of an overwhelming majority of Israelis is for the separation of religion from state control, which portends a future diminishing of the dominance of political control over religious issues.

Concluding Observations

The religiosity themes at the micro level of analysis are clearly one basis for the division between Israeli Jews and Moslems, although not the main source, which is political and institutional. And while the ethnic division among Israeli Jews weakens in a variety of ways by the third generation, the overlap of religiosity and ethnicity reinforces the ethnic division between Jews from the Middle East and from Europe, and particularly between the secularists and the religionists. The major source of religious friction is tied into the political system broadly conceived and the control exercised by the ultraorthodox, the small group of *haredim*, and the more-religious establishment, over public religious rituals, marriage, divorce, religious conversions, and burials—all the life-course transitions. Indirectly, religious systems have considerable impact on family systems (marriage timing and gender relationships and inequality) and the economy.

There is a considerable gap between the religious and secular among Jewish Israelis and between the more religious among Moslems and Jews in Israel. Among Jews the ethnic divide overlaps with religiosity and religious ritual observance, and hence their communities are developing in distinctive ways. Because of the political control of the more-religious Jewish Israelis over institutions of the society, an increasing gap has emerged between what Israelis observe religiously and the disproportionate power of the religious establishment over the lives of Jewish Israelis.[7]

NOTES

1. See the analysis in Spiegel 2013. She documents that the Jewish community in Palestine created enduring social, political, religious, and cultural forms through public events, such as festivals, performances, and celebrations. She finds that the physical character of this national public culture represents one of the key innovations of Zionism—embedding the importance of the corporeal into national Jewish life—and remains a significant feature of contemporary Israeli culture.

2. On the political dimensions of Israeli Judaism see several chapters in Deshen 1995, particularly chapters 5–7 and 19.

3. See the special report of the Central Bureau of Statistics. To my knowledge this is the first survey conducted by the bureau on the religious identity and religiosity of Israelis. Other sources of information include surveys by the Avi Chai Foundation using different categories and samples of Israeli Jews. See C. Goldscheider and Friedlander 1983 for an earlier review of Israeli religiosity. Unless otherwise noted the data cited in the text are from the survey of the Central Bureau of Statistics.

4. These questions have rarely, if ever, been asked of men, although men and women increasingly share in the decisions about childbearing and child rearing.

5. The efficient use of contraceptives, abortion, and the timing of marriage are more likely to be the result of fertility norms and behavior rather than their cause. Hence, my attention focuses on the factors affecting fertility, without concern at this point about the proximate or intermediate mechanisms that have been used to convert family-size norms into fertility behavior. See also chapter 7.

6. On Israeli Judaism see Deshen 1990; C. Goldscheider and Friedlander 1983; Levy, Levinsohn, and Katz 1993; Sobel and Beit-Hallahmi 1991; Deshen 1995.

7. The religious divide among Israeli Jews has major impact on the relationships between Israeli and American Jews (see chapter 11).

7 | Inequality and Changing Gender Roles

A major source of social inequality involves gender roles and statuses. Differences between men and women in access to resources and in translating resources into jobs and income are key aspects of disadvantage for women. Gender differentials in autonomy and control, in independence and decision making, are conspicuous signs of how distinctive spheres of activity become disadvantageous. The extent to which power in the workplace, within households, and in political and cultural institutions is shared equally between men and women indicates the treatment of gender as difference unattached to disadvantage.

Gender and Inequality
Theory and Mixed Expectations

Changes in gender roles have been part of the revolutionary shifts associated with the modernization of industrialized societies. Along with the transitions toward nuclear family structure and living arrangements that are not family based, there have been major transformations in the roles of women inside and outside families and the beginning of changes in the roles of men in households (among others, see F. Goldscheider and Waite 1991; F. Goldscheider, Bernhardt, and Lappegård 2014). How are gender-role changes related to the revolutionary socioeconomic developments that have characterized Israeli society? How are they linked to changes in the family, in ethnic distinctiveness, and in population processes? How are gender differences connected to social and economic inequalities and to political and religious institutions in Israel?

There are indications that greater equality between men and women is emerging in some spheres in Israel and that the empowerment of women has increased. At the same time, evidence abounds documenting the continuation of traditional gender differences in everyday life and the discrimination against women in key economic, political, and cultural institutions of the society. My focus is on the differences between women and men that can be understood as indicating gender inequality. We would expect that increased educational attainment and participation in the paid labor force would broaden the scope of women's activities, provide access to better jobs, and increase their control over their own lives. As Israel's population and economy expanded and diversified, some of the constraints on women's activities should have decreased, and new opportunities should have opened for sharing equally with men. As universalistic criteria of achievement and merit filter through the society, women should have equal access to societal rewards and compete more equally with men.

Similarly, the centrality of the nuclear family, the reduction in family size, and the control over reproduction that have come to characterize Israeli society should have led to a reduction in the domestic roles of women, creating greater access to work opportunities outside the home and thereby expanding women's roles beyond mothering, child care, and housework. With all these changes, combined with marriage at later ages and an elaborate welfare system to care for parents and older relatives, women should increasingly have time within the life course to better take advantage of outside work opportunities and convert their educational advances into well-paying jobs (i.e., equal to working men). In turn, the monetary rewards and the greater economic autonomy associated with these activities should reduce the economic dependency of women on men. In general, increasing affluence and changing domestic technology should result in lessening the time women spend on household care; life-course changes (e.g., increases in the time spent in school, marriage at later ages, and decreasing family size) should increase the time available for nonfamily roles, particularly for work in the formal economy.

Education, money, technology, and the changing opportunity structure in the labor market set the stage for alterations in women's nonfamily roles. They combine with changing values emphasizing autonomy and independence to shift the status of women away from family activities and tip the balance toward more-equal sharing between men and women. Although there has been a shift toward individualism, Israel remains a family-oriented society with high priorities placed on gender-segregated family roles. Working outside the home and having a small family do not automatically extricate women from the control of their families, husbands, or fathers. When women work in part-time jobs, in gender-segregated occupations, and retain responsibilities for household activities, working outside the home may extend gender inequality and result in a "double burden" on women, rather than their empowerment and increased independence from the control of men and from their dependency on families. This double burden may be exacerbated if women are unable to translate their years of schooling into jobs comparable to those of men and if they cannot successfully compete for employment outside traditional gender-segregated roles because they lack access to primary sources of power.

Educational attainment, occupational concentration, and economic discrimination are all part of the puzzle in understanding the role of gender in Israeli society. There are other facets related to this issue that are institutional and cultural. How do political and religious institutions deal with issues of gender? Are there forms of ideological commitments or legal discrimination against women that shape and reflect how Israeli society reinforces gender differences? Are there values and attitudes that are shared by significant sectors of the population that define women's and men's roles as different and are used to justify discrimination, inequality, and continued subordination? How have the various political transitions in nation-building and the shifts in the centrality of the military affected gender roles? The answers to these questions focus attention on the ways that specific institutional features of Israeli society may have shaped gender inequalities.

Cutting across issues of gender stratification, institutional structures related to gender, and attitudes and values about the roles of men and women is the changing ethnic and religious composition of Israeli society. This is a particular feature of Israeli society that has an important role in shaping gender issues. The differing ethnic origins of the Jewish population represent different exposures to the openness of their societies of origin to women's employment, status, and roles in society and the family. Ethnicity is connected to different levels of education and types of jobs, to resources people have, and to how they are used. Immigrants whose origins are from Western and European societies have been exposed for longer periods of time to greater gender equality and to values and attitudes that were more open to a wide range of roles for women. Israelis of Western origin were socialized in their homes and in schools with images of women who had access to the world outside families and whose commitments to gender equality and independence were valued.

In contrast, Israelis from Middle Eastern societies originated from communities characterized by high levels of gender segregation. They were more likely to have been socialized in families emphasizing the centrality of the place of women in the domestic economy, their responsibilities as mothers and wives, and their subordination to male power. In general, among Jews of Middle Eastern origin, women were more dependent on men and subordinate to them, and women's roles were located in separate spheres of activities. Ethnic divisions among Jews may be associated with gender differences in the extent of employment outside the home, in levels of education, and in different levels of commitment to family values. The critical questions are whether socialization and educational exposure in Israeli society results in greater equality between men and women in diverse spheres of activity and whether there is a tendency toward convergence in gender differences among the Israelis born of different ethnic origins.

In this chapter, I follow these mixed theoretical orientations and sketch in broad strokes the different contexts in which gender matters in Israel. I assess how changes in Israeli society have resulted in patterns of greater gender equality in different social activities. First, I review issues of education, labor force, and occupational concentration. I then turn to gender factors in military, political, and religious institutions and the role of women in contraception and abortion decisions as indicators of the relative independence of women from families and from men. Together, these pieces of the puzzle provide clues about the relative autonomy of women of various backgrounds in Israel and the trajectory of gender-role changes. These changes fit into the broader themes of demographic and ethnic changes in the context of nation-building.[1]

Three cautions need to be highlighted as a backdrop to this assessment of gender inequalities in Israel. First, the pace of change in gender relationships is expected to vary among ethnic groups and is linked to length of exposure to Israeli society. The diversity of Israel's population has implications for understanding the dynamics of change in the society as a whole. The study of the intersection of gender and ethnicity becomes critical in assessing the direction and intensity of changes. Second, the reduction and elimination of the gender gap in one area—for example, education—does not necessarily imply the absence of gender differences in other areas of social life and vice versa. Likewise, gender discrimination in one area does not necessarily mean discrimination in all areas. Each of the major areas needs to be examined directly rather than by inference. As with indicators of socioeconomic inequality, variation in the extent of gender inequality is expected among the spheres of social life. Third, the reduction in the gender gap in any area cannot always be linked directly to the emergence of new egalitarian norms. Legal and behavioral equalities between men and women do not automatically correlate with norms of gender equality or the empowerment of women. Similarly, differences between men and women do not necessarily imply structural discrimination, gender-biased state policies, or intentionality. My focus is on forms of gender differentiation and the gender dependencies that have emerged in Israel that are both legacies of the societies of origin and sustained by Israeli society.

The Narrowing Gender Gap in Education

Increases in educational attainment have been among the most powerful changes that have characterized Israeli society since the 1950s (chapter 8). Have these increases been spread equally among men and women? There is clear empirical confirmation of the narrowing of gender differences over time in educational attainment. Overall, in 2012, average (median) education of Jewish Israeli men and women was identical (13 years). The proportion with 16 or more years of education was also identical (28%), with almost similar patterns for young and older ages. The average difference between men and women had favored men by 1.5 years in 1961, by 1.3 years in 1972, and by one year in 1983 (Nahon 1987, appendix table 1; also C. Goldscheider 2002, table 7.1). Examining some of the details in 2012 shows that the percentages of men and women with 16 or more years of schooling were about the same (28% and 27%, respectively). These levels were about 10 percentage points higher than for men and women in 1999. Most of the gender differences in educational attainment are characteristic of the oldest age cohorts, with smaller gender differences for Jews than for Arabs.

Although the general level of education among Arabs in Israel is lower than among Jews, the gender gap in years of schooling among Arabs ages 15 to 35 has moved dramatically in favor of Arab women: 18% of Arab men age 25–34 in 2012 had 16 or more years of education compared to 26% of Arab women. In contrast, among those 65 years and older only 2% of Arab women had 16 or more years of education and only 5% of them age 55–64 had that level of education. Arab men had higher educational levels than Arab women among the older ages with the respective proportions 8% and 15%. In 2012, 17% of Arab men age 65 or older had no education compared to 56% of Arab women.[2] These data convey four patterns of importance: (1) all groups, men and women, Jew and Arab, have increased their level of education in the last decades; (2) Jewish men and women have increasingly become similar in educational level with women exceeding men's education in the youngest age group; (3) Jewish educational levels continue to exceed levels among Israeli Arabs; (4) the gender gap among Arab Israelis of all ages has been reduced considerably and reversed (Arab women have higher average educational levels than men) in the youngest age cohort. Inferred from the cross-sectional patterns is the different timing of the closing of the gender gap, which is earlier among Jews than among Arabs. The narrowed educational gap has been influenced in large measure by Israel's educational policy that opened schooling opportunities to both boys and girls, and for Arabs as well as Jews.

Examinations of educational changes among men and women of different ethnic-origin Jewish populations confirm these conclusions. The gender gap in years of schooling among foreign-born Jews is largely confined to and accentuated among those from Asian and African countries, but the gap has declined among them as well. By the 1980s, there was a very small gender gap among the Israeli-born Jewish population. A beginning shift toward a reduced gender gap in years of education may also be discerned among Moslems and Druze in the 1970s, consistent with the broader changes that were occurring among Moslems in that decade (see chapter 4). By the end of the twentieth century, trends are discernible toward greater similarity in numbers of years of schooling attained by young Israeli Moslem men and women.

A detailed study of cohort changes in education describes what it refers to as "the spectacular change" in educational attainment among Arab women. The research evidence documents the substantial transition to completing high school and the *bagrut* (a high school certification required for entrance to universities) and the increased participation of Arab women in postsecondary education. This reflects the opportunity structure among Arab Israelis and the large demand for teachers for the expanding Arab Israeli population of children, particularly when significant numbers of the teachers at the elementary school level are women. There has been a general reduction in gender differences in various dimensions of the educational experience among Israeli Arabs and in the transition to postsecondary education, but the levels remain relatively lower among Arab than Israeli Jewish women (Friedlander et al. 2002a, 2002b). In 1999, 23% of Arab Israeli women completed 13 or more years of education, identical to the proportion among Arab men, but this contrasts with over half of the Jewish Israelis who completed at least 13 years of education. Thus, at the same time that the gender gap in educational attainment within each of these two ethnic categories has been largely eliminated, the ethnic gap *within* gender categories has remained very wide. The level of educational attainment at the upper end of the educational distribution is more than twice as high among Jews than Arabs for both men and women.

Working Women
Juggling Part-Time Employment and Families

Are the changing gender gaps in education an indication of a reduction in gender differences in other areas, and do they point to a move toward egalitarian relationships in Israel, as in other more-industrialized nations? Tendencies toward similar educational levels by gender are likely to have implications for spheres of both work and family. Indeed, one of the direct implications of the closing gender gap in education is the connection to the labor market, in particular, how educational attainment is converted into quality of employment for men and for women. At the simplest level, we can document the increasing educational levels of employed women over time and the relative education of employed women and men. When we examine the educational level of employed persons between the 1960s and the end of the twentieth century, we note that the percentage of employed women with higher levels of education (defined as more than 13 years of schooling) increased from 15% in 1963 to 54% in 2000; the proportion with less than an eighth-grade education who were employed declined from 45% to 4%. As of the 1970s, employed Israeli women had a higher level of education than employed men, suggesting that employment may be more selective of women (the more educated) than of men. Fewer women than men who were in the labor force had low levels of education, and more had higher levels. Increased educational levels raise the quality of women's labor-force activities and pose directly the question of whether the labor-force participation rate of women has increased.

Indeed, the evidence is clear that there has been a dramatic increase in the labor-force participation of women in Israel from less than 30% overall until the 1970s to over 50% in the twenty-first century. The increase reflects the increased levels of education of women, the changing labor market structure in Israel, the changing ethnic composition of the population, and family-size changes. The increase has been most striking in the working patterns of mothers, the opening up of opportunities for part-time employment, mainly in the service sector, and the greater availability of child-care facilities. In earlier cohorts, women entered the labor force before marriage and before bearing children, withdrew as they were raising their young children, and reentered when their children grew up and were in school. Life-course employment patterns of Israeli women resembled an M-shaped pattern, with changes and variations due to the timing of marriage, childbearing, and child rearing. Replacing the M pattern was an emergent inverted U-shaped pattern—women entered and remained in the labor force through the childbearing, preschool, and schooling years of children, exiting from the labor force like men at retirement. The first sign of the transformation from an M to an inverted U was among Israelis of European and American origins; more recently, the switchover has characterized Israelis of Asian and African origins. Labor-force participation rates of Arab women remain significantly below those of Jewish women (see also the review and documentation for an earlier period in Ben-Porath 1986b).

Features of the increased labor-force participation of Israeli women over time may be summarized as follows:

1 The proportion of Israeli women in the labor force was 27% in 1955, and it increased to 47% in 1999. The increase was sharper for women ages 35 to 54, among which fully seven out of ten were in the labor force in 2010, more than 2.5 times the participation rate in 1955.

2 As the number of children age 14 and under in the household increases, the proportion of Jewish women in the labor force decreases; as their children get older, the proportion of women in the labor force increases. Over 60% of the women with their youngest child below 1 year of age worked, compared to 80% for children ages 10 to 14.

3 Israeli women of Asian and African origins are less likely to be in the labor force than those of European and American origins, reflecting differences in family formation and educational background and different priorities about the balance of family and work, particularly among mothers with young children. Israeli women of all ethnic origins with the same number of children at home and the same level of education have similar labor-force participation rates.

4 The different levels of education that characterized the women of these different Jewish ethnic groups and the resultant higher rate of labor-force participation of Israeli women of Western origin indicate that Asian- and African-origin Jewish women contribute less financially to the household. Hence, the household incomes of Israelis of Middle Eastern origin are lower than those of Western origin, even when husbands have the same occupations.

5 The more years of schooling completed, the higher the rate of labor-force participation. The differences are quite impressive: from a labor-force participation rate of 15% among married women with low educational levels to 70% among those with 13 or more years of schooling. The pattern is no less characteristic of those with and without young children at home. Among those with infants at home, 28% of the least-educated women work, compared to 71% of the most-educated women.

6 Having household help at home enhances the labor-force participation of Israeli women. Though 53% of the women without help at home work in the labor force, 66% of those with 16 or more hours of help work outside the home. Having help is a reflection both of educational level and of resources available and does not include assistance from family members. The causal direction of this association is not clear, since women work because they have access to and are able to afford child-care assistance, and women obtain child-care assistance because they work outside the home.

7 Women are considerably more likely to work part-time than are men. From the 1980s to the early 1990s, about 15% of Israel's civilian male labor force was working part-time. During the same period, the percentage of women engaged in part-time work was closer to 40%, over 2.5 times higher than that of men. There has been a trend, although not linear, toward an increase over time in the proportion of working women who work part-time, from about 30% in the 1950s and 1960s, to

35% in the 1970s, and to 40% in the 1980s and 1990s. At the same time that the percentage of women participating in the labor force has increased, the proportion working part-time has increased as well.

Occupational Concentration, Feminization, and Discrimination

The increase in the labor-force participation of Israel's women clearly documented in these official data reflects the expansion of the Israeli economy and the demand for more-educated workers, particularly in the public sector and in financial and business services.[3] At the same time that an increase in the participation of women in the formal labor force has occurred, an almost complete feminization of certain occupations had also taken place (Ben-Porath 1986a; studies cited in Azmon and Israeli 1993). This pattern appears in the detailed specific-occupation categories, not in the crude occupational distributions. This highly gender-segregated job structure can be documented in a variety of ways. In 1990, for example, three-fourths of the female labor force was employed in only 3 of the 9 major occupation categories, and one-half was concentrated in only 8 of 90 occupations (Azmon and Israeli 1993). This has changed somewhat in the twenty-first century as educational levels of women have increased and new job opportunities have opened.

There are, therefore, three interrelated dimensions of the labor discrimination against women in Israel: (1) men and women in the same job are differentially treated; that is, women with similar characteristics and skills as men are promoted less and rewarded less for similar jobs; (2) there is a concentration of women in particular jobs; that is, a process of feminization of particular occupations has occurred, in which the fringe benefits of particular jobs are less when they are occupied by women; and (3) part-time workers have significantly fewer benefits than do full-time workers, and women are more likely than men to have part-time jobs.

Even in those industries in which the criteria of promotion and salary are presumably based on merit and achievement, gender factors seem to operate. In one study of scientists in one large Israeli industry, research demonstrated that Israeli men and women experienced differential rates of promotion to the detriment of women. Although there was no direct discrimination in the wages of men and women scientists, women professional employees experienced salary discrimination. Since promotions affect wages, discrimination in promotional practices resulted in gender discrimination in wages (Shenhav and Haberfeld 1993). The number of women on a career track in academic jobs is small and concentrated in the lower echelons of the academic scale. There is little pay difference within the scale, but the different jobs of men and women result in a discriminatory pattern (see Toren 1993).

Research comparing women employed in jobs dominated by women and those more equally shared by men (and the reverse as well—men in female- and in male-dominated occupations) shows the high level of discrimination against women, measured in terms of income, particularly for women in women-dominated occupations (Moore 1993). Relative to Israeli men, Israeli women, in general, have lower-paying jobs, with lower levels of seniority and authority in occupations or industries, and are more likely to move into and out of the labor force. They are less mobile between occupations and less mobile between geographic regions than are men with comparable educational levels. Their economic networks tend to be fewer and less effective and are located in the jobs where opportunities for promotion and rewards for initiatives are fewer than those for men. When we examine the interaction of gender and ethnic origin, it is clear that Jewish Asian- and African-origin men are disadvantaged relative to European- and American-origin men, but Jewish Asian–origin and African-origin women are not disadvantaged as much relative to European- and American-origin women. Women of all ethnic origins in Israel are disadvantaged relative to men. In sum, gender is a more-powerful differentiator than is ethnicity in the occupational distribution within the Jewish population of Israel. Put more directly, ethnic disadvantage is less than gender disadvantage in the Israeli labor market (Neuman 1991; Semyonov and Kraus 1983; Hartman 1993; Rebhun 2008, 2010).

There is also some evidence that suggests an interaction effect of ethnicity and gender. Research has documented that ethnic differences in rates of labor-force participation and in the occupational prestige of women reflect differences in the educational, socioeconomic, and related demographic characteristics. There are major ethnic differences in the attitudes toward women working and concerning the balance of work and household responsibilities. These attitudes are likely to have an impact on the priorities assigned to work and to family among ethnic groups in Israel (Hartman 1993). It is likely that this has changed in the most recent decade, but the gender and ethnic gaps have not closed.

Even though discrimination on the basis of gender is not legal, there have been no affirmative-action policies in Israel. Consequently, there has been no alteration in job recruitment by gender or in job allocation, promotion, and reward. The increase in labor-force participation of women also reflects the structure of jobs that are more likely to be part-time for women and linked to family, household, and child-care needs. In addition, research has shown that women spend twice as much time in child care as men do and are much more involved in housekeeping, whether or not they are employed outside the home. Working in the formal labor force does not decrease the time women spend on child rearing or on housekeeping (Azmon and Izraeli 1993). As a result, there is a gendered division of labor in the home as well as at work. Patterns of increased labor-force participation of women, and of combining work and family activities, generate the illusion of gender equality rather than an increasing double burden placed on women. Standards of living rise, outside activities increase, household incomes improve, and there is less pressure to remark on gender inequalities and a decreased sensitivity to gender discrimination. Together, these factors explain the absence of major protests by women about the occupational inequalities between men and women.[4] Moreover, jobs are often controlled by patronage in Israel, so that networks and connections are often the primary sources of information and control (Danet 1989). In jobs controlled by the state, political considerations (often gender related) are critical. A review of labor-force activities of women notes that women remain virtually absent from positions of influence within all the major economic institutions owned by either the Labor party–dominated Histradut (the Federated Labor Union) or by the government, which together employ the majority of the labor force. The study concludes that "rather than promoting equal opportunity, current social policy tends to support a system in which the majority of women are on an often-invisible 'mommy track.' Their place in the occupational structure is paradoxical: their jobs are relatively high status, but their wages are low, and they rarely occupy the top-level positions of power and prestige" (Azmon and Izraeli 1993, 4–5). Increased labor-force participation of women has not equalized the roles of women and men inside or outside the workforce. It is unclear how much these patterns have changed by the first decade of the twenty-first century.

Women and the Military

Like working mothers, women soldiers are often portrayed as symbols of equality in Israel. And like the implications of the examination of the specific jobs that women have in civilian life, a review of studies of women in the military illustrates the ways their distinctive roles are indicators of discrimination. This is particularly the case since military service is often the basis for recruitment into higher-level positions in the civilian labor force. The military is a deeply gendered institution. The careers of men and women in the military are significantly different and have consequences for the status of women in general in the society (Azmon and Izraeli 1993). Indeed, the military institution of Israel and its segregation of women into separate jobs and different career paths is more likely to perpetuate gender inequality than to be a force for change in gender roles.

There are two ways in which the military experiences of women should be viewed as discriminatory. First, and most directly, the kinds of responsibilities that women and men have in the military are very different. The difference is not merely the absence of combat roles for women but, instead, it is that women's responsibilities are almost always subordinate to men and under male control. Promotion and reward in the military are less accessible to women. Second, and more indirectly, experience in the military is often the basis for recruitment for elite managerial and political positions in the civilian labor force. The generally lower ranks of women and their generally noncommand or nonmanagerial roles in the military reduce their ability to use the military (as men do) as a vehicle for job networking and recruitment in civilian life. Thus, in contrast to the gender-egalitarian image of the Israeli military, service in the armed forces more often than not reinforces the subordinate and less-powerful status of women in the society.

Military service is compulsory for both Jewish men and women, but, unlike men, women are excluded for reasons of marriage, parenthood, and on religious grounds. In 1990, a little over two-thirds of the cohorts of 18-year-old women were conscripted into the military, compared to 56% in the mid-1970s. Most of the increase was due to changes in the educational and socioeconomic requirements for conscription (Azmon and Izraeli

1993). The results of a detailed study of the 1954 birth cohort show that almost all the men (94%) served in the Israel Defense Force, but only one-third of the Jewish women of Middle Eastern origin and 57% of those of Western origin served. These differences are related in part to the lower ed-ucational attainments of women of Middle Eastern origin at that time and the resistance to military service among those who are from more-religious families, which are more characteristic of this ethnic-origin group. Within each educational attainment subgroup, the percentage of women serving in the Israel Defense Force was higher among Western-origin women than among Middle Eastern origin–women. This has changed as educational levels in general have increased and ethnic differences have converged. About one-third of all soldiers are women.

What are the effects of schooling and military service on subsequent occupational attainments and social participation of Israeli men and women? A pioneering study of the links between military service and ac-tual occupational attainments over the life course showed the importance of serving in the Israel armed service and the role of military rank in en-hancing subsequent occupational prestige in the civilian labor force, net of socioeconomic background and education (Matras, Noam, and Bar-Haim 1984; Matras and Noam 1987). The army experience had a positive effect on the accumulation of human capital, responsibility, and author-ity in roles; it established "connections" and networks; and it provided nonfamily (or at least semiautonomous) living experiences. Military ser-vice had a significant effect on the occupational prestige scores of women but affected jobs closest in time to that period of service, with a reduced effect over time. Ethnicity remains an important factor in women's oc-cupational prestige (unlike for men), which may reflect the role of work among Western-origin women, which is different from its role among Middle Eastern–origin women, or may indicate the use of "connections" by Western-origin women to obtain better jobs. Again, this has likely changed in the last decade in the direction of reduced ethnic differences and increased educational experience.

The argument that women's roles in the military negatively affect later traditional roles or that serving in the army is a liberating experience is an exaggeration. The effects of military service are modest at best. Many women reside at home during their military service and are likely to be engaged in gender-segregated clerical roles that are relatively powerless.

Family connections are unlikely to be fully severed by being in the Israeli military, and the liberating effects are limited as well. Taken together, the evidence seems to point to the conclusion that the military experience is more likely to reflect the society than to shape it. Service in the army is not able to help women overcome the more-entrenched and powerful effects of differential education by ethnicity and differential family background and experiences. Given the gender-segregated job allocations in the army, the closeness of army personnel to family life (as semiautonomous living), and the army's selectivity, the gender-segregated attitudes and traditional roles of the society as a whole are likely to be reinforced, rather than undermined, in this setting.

There is another aspect of the military that relates to the role of women and their place in the household. The reinforcement of traditional gender roles occurs generationally. When sons and daughters begin compulsory military service at age 18, the duties of parenting become more intense, and support roles are expected from the family.[5] As in the care of the elderly, these family-based support systems involve a disproportionate amount of the mother's rather than the father's time. Moreover, war and military activities in a conflict situation intensify the salience of primary relationships. The family and, particularly, the role of women within the family are emotional anchors, especially in such family-oriented societies as Israel. In the media and in informal settings, female roles are regularly portrayed during wars as supportive and expressive (Bar-Yosef and Padan-Eisenstark 1993).

Gender, Politics, and Religion

Discrimination against women is not limited to the formal labor force, to their concentration in specific occupations, and to their service in the military. Political and religious institutions are conspicuous in their limited representation of women and their reinforcement of the separate spheres of women's activities. We have already identified some ways in which religion and gender are interrelated and how the patriarchal elements of Judaism discriminate against women (chapter 6). Here we turn to the issues of politics and gender. Although women were formally granted equal rights by the Declaration of Israeli Independence, including the right to vote, the number of women in elected positions at all levels is small. The representation of women in the highest elected offices, as members of the Knesset, has always been small and has not increased in recent years. Over the last five decades, less than 10% of the members of the Knesset have been women. Even at the local level, less than 10% of the political officials are women, although their numbers have increased over the past decades (Azmon and Izraeli 1993, 14; see also Azmon 1990). Some research has pointed to the disadvantaged position of women in political power in Israel and the impediments that are gender related, including the fact that political power is largely controlled by men and that women are socialized into family roles (Etzioni-Halevi and Illy 1993). Women have rarely played representative roles at the local level, in party caucuses, and in the power negotiations behind the scenes. Although there have been political parties in Israel that have focused on women's rights, they have been marginal to political power.

Families and Power Abortion and Contraception

The central role of women in families in Israel is clear, and their often disadvantaged status follows from that role. In a subsequent analysis, I detail the familism that characterizes Israeli society and show the changing importance of women in perpetuating that centrality (chapter 10). Nevertheless, even in the realm of family activity, the role of women tends to be subordinate to men. Changes in fertility in Israel have facilitated the increase in female labor-force participation that I previously documented. Among younger cohorts, almost all women have been employed in the formal labor force, and this has been correlated with their decreasing family size (chapter 10; also Matras 1986). The decrease in family size should facilitate the expansion of women's work in the paid labor force.

In a related way, an examination of the sources of fertility reduction in terms of the means by which couples have planned their family size and the number and timing of births reveals again the more-powerless role of women in Israeli society. An examination of contraceptive usage and birth control points to a concentration in the past on coitus interruptus and abortion (Friedlander and Goldscheider 1984; Okun 1997; Okun 2000). These mechanisms, in large part, place women under the control of men, their husbands, and the medical establishment. Although there is a recent tendency toward greater use of the contraceptive pill for birth control, there remains a continuing pattern of male-controlled contraceptive methods or abortion.[6]

Unlike in other societies, abortion is used in Israel by married women as a last resort, after less-efficient contraception has been used and when the pressure to control family size is high. For women who married in the 1940s and were living in Israel in the early 1970s, abortion was used more by those of European origin than by those of Asian and African origin, a continuation of patterns observed in their countries of origin; among cohorts who married in the period from 1965 to 1974, no ethnic differences were evident (Yaffe 1976). It is likely that the religious factor is the major differentiator of abortion patterns, with women from more-religious families less likely to have abortions.

Official estimates from the 1980s and 1990s put the number of legal abortions close to 20,000, about one-fourth the number of live births. This appears to be a reduction in the estimated 50,000 to 60,000 abortions in the late 1960s and 1970s, which was equivalent to the number of annual Jewish births. The reduction was likely brought about by the increasing use of more-efficient contraception. About two-thirds of the total legal abortions in the 1980s were performed on married women (Sabatello and Yaffe 1988). In 1999, 60% of the legal terminations of pregnancy were administered to married women, and most of those women were over the age of 30.

What emerges from these scattered data is that the pressure for fertility control results in turning to abortion, even when illegal, as a backup to contraceptive failure. The use of more-efficient contraceptive practices and the greater access to modern contraception among Jewish women of European origin results in their lower rates of abortion. In contrast, the lower socioeconomic status of Asian- and African-origin Jewish women and their large-family-size ideals are likely to result in their wanting more children, using contraception less efficiently, having less access to abortions, and aborting less often when contraception fails. Contraceptive practices and abortion, for many Israeli women, reinforce their subordinate status to men and their traditional family roles.

Gender Equality in the Kibbutz Myth and Reality

It is not surprising that women in Israeli society have been in subordinate roles and that they have been dependent on men and the institutions men control. Israeli women share this condition with women around the world. One would have predicted that these inequalities would be more pronounced for women from gender-segregated societies and cultures and that the trajectory of change would be toward more-equal gender roles. There are some indications that changes are occurring but that institutions, particularly those controlled by men in religion and politics, reinforce the traditional separate spheres of men and women. The emphasis on family centrality and the role of women as guardians of family values constrain the shift toward greater gender equality in the society as a whole.

One would expect that egalitarian gender roles would characterize kibbutz communities in Israel.[7] Founded on an ideology of equality, with an emphasis on communal responsibilities for family and work, the kibbutz should be the ideal economic and family setting for more-equal gender roles to emerge. And there is some basis for this assessment in the division of labor among kibbutz members and the shared activities in family and labor.

Yet, it is not surprising that the kibbutz falls far from the ideal of equality. What is unexpected is that research has documented greater gender-occupational segregation in the kibbutz than in Israel as a whole. This finding contrasts sharply with the expected kibbutz environment, which should be conducive to occupational equality between men and women, given the deep ideological commitment to equality, high valuation of work, an egalitarian educational system, and collectivization of household work that allows women to develop careers. Although production is not necessarily contributed to equally by gender, equality governs the distribution of income. A striking finding of that research is that occupational segregation on gender grounds is much higher than it is on ethnic grounds—gender-occupational segregation is more than double that of ethnic segregation in the Jewish population. The occupational status of women in the kibbutz is simply inferior to that of women in the rest of Israel (Neuman 1991).

Despite the absence of salaries and income in the kibbutz, fewer women than men have access to resources. Kibbutz men have more access than women to cars and travel and occupational training. Men are, on the whole, more autonomous economically than women in the kibbutz and have a wider range of occupational choices. Hence, fewer women acquire the expertise and seniority to become heads of departments or to achieve seniority in positions in the kibbutz. Like the military and the society as whole, kibbutz life reinforces aspects of gender inequality (Agassi 1993).

Concluding Observations

In large part, gender inequalities have characterized traditional as well as modern societies for centuries. There are some signs of increased gender equality in Israel, relating to education and increased labor-force participation, in formal legal rights and in military service, and in ideological commitments to gender neutrality. Nevertheless, a systematic and careful look at these arenas of social life points to the unmistakable continuation of gender inequalities. There is little evidence that indicates that the reduced gender gap in educational attainment levels has been translated directly into occupational and labor-force equality. Powerful sources of continued gender discrimination in political, religious, and family institutions result in the disadvantaged status of women in Israel. Indeed, it is likely that these gender-segregated roles are reinforced by the educational system, so that similarity among women and men in the number of years of educational exposure does not necessarily imply similar educational experiences. As in the military, crude measures of exposure to equality in education should not be interpreted as indicators of gender equality.

The aim of the European-based society that formulated the reemergence of the state of Israel was to reorganize the family and work system and the religious and political institutions while reestablishing Jewish sovereignty. This reorganization was explicitly designed to include greater attention to equality among groups. The inclusion of large numbers of immigrants from gender-segregated societies added a continual challenge to these egalitarian tendencies. Yet, the mutable gender inequalities in Israeli society at the beginning of the twenty-first century are not simple carryovers from the past and from traditional societies outside Israel; they are Israel-created products. The role of political and religious institutions, as well as the role of the military, in reinforcing and, at a minimum, reflecting inequalities has become a powerful source of gender inequalities among third-generation Israelis.

No less revealing is the occupational segregation of women in kibbutzim, where control over the distribution of resources and of tasks is collectively managed. There, as elsewhere in Israel, some gender patterns are no less segregated (and the evidence suggests even more segregated) and unequal. Whether occupational segregation by gender is a reactionary response to the ideology of equality or a continuing gap between myth and reality, the fact is that nowhere in Israel are there important signs of gender equality in major institutions. Indeed, gender relations in Israel, as well as general family processes, point to the more-traditional basis of Israeli society relative to European and American societies but also to a more-egalitarian one relative to Third World countries. Again, Israel appears to be straddling the middle at the crossroads of change.

NOTES

1. There is an increasing social-science literature concerning gender issues in Israel, almost always defined in terms of "women's" roles. I draw on some of that research, although many of the questions that I have previously sketched require more-systematic and methodologically sophisticated studies than are currently available. For a review and collection of important materials on women in Israel, see Azmon and Izraeli 1993. Important critical assessments of gender inequalities are contained in Hazelton 1977, Rein 1979, and in Swirski and Safir 1991; in Hebrew, see Shamgar-Handelman and Bar-Yosef 1991. On the legal aspects of women's roles in Israel see Halperin-Kaddari 2003.

2. For more-detailed statistical documentation, see section 8 on education the *Statistical Abstract of Israel of 2013*.

3. I have little information about the character of the informal-employment sector. It is likely that for Jewish women the informal sector was in the past a more-prominent feature of their work outside the home. It continues to be an important feature of the Arab female population.

4. A similar pattern emerges with regard to ethnic inequalities and the absence of ethnic political protest, since social mobility has characterized all ethnic communities even as the ethnic gap in economic indicators has widened. See the discussion in chapter 8.

5. This increased parental support is in sharp contrast to the situation in the United States, where significant proportions of young adults leave home at 18 to go to college and to live away from the parental home, thereby increasing autonomy for young adults and reducing parenting responsibilities (F. Goldscheider and C. Goldscheider 1994, 1999). This has changed in the first decade of the twenty-first century in the United States with the economic downturn and increasing return of young adults in the postcollege period to the parental home.

6. On Arab family planning see Eisenbach 1986.

7. For a more-detailed description of the kibbutz as a community, see chapter 5.

8 | Education, Stratification, and Inequality

Underlying Israel's changing society in the context of nation-building are major transformations in economic development over the past several decades, including the growth in some sectors of the economy, the expansion of export markets, increased consumption, and the extension of higher levels of living to its diverse population. As Israel's economy expanded and institutions were established to maintain continuous growth, new forms of stratification and inequality emerged. These forms revolve around the transmission of social-class position and other inequalities from one generation to the next, the retention of economic resources differentially among families, and the continuing income disparities between social classes. Socioeconomic differences among ethnic groups are clear indicators of inequality, particularly when there is evidence of the generational persistence of social classes and when ethnic socioeconomic distinctiveness means economic disadvantage.

Stratification Fundamentals of Inequality

In this chapter, I address basic questions about social-class resources and the changing structure of inequality in Israel, the overlap of the social-class hierarchy with ethnicity, and the persistence of social-class differences generationally. Does the evidence point to diminishing socioeconomic differences over time? How are the sources of stratification connected to nation-building processes and immigration? Are income differences between social classes and ethnic groups changing? The answers to the persistence, convergence, and generational transmission of economic resources will help us better understand how Israeli society and its policies have altered the bases of socioethnic inequalities.

In all societies, there is an educational-occupational distribution: some groups have more education than others and are in higher-paying and more-prestigious jobs. There are differences in how economic resources and income are allocated at any point in time. When differences in socioeconomic levels and resources are transmitted generationally and reinforced institutionally, the resultant hierarchy is referred to as social stratification. Similarly, social-class differences among immigrant populations are expected, since these differences are the direct outcome of their historical circumstances in places of origin prior to coming to Israel, of the differential resources they brought with them, and of the economic context in Israel when they arrived. Are their economic circumstances transferred to their children, and are there ways that the society can break the chain of social-class inheritance? My focus is on generational changes in ethnic inequalities, in particular the transmission of social-class inequalities among those born in Israel. The analysis of stratification differences among second- and later-generation Israelis addresses key questions of the persistence of inequalities and socioeconomic convergences among ethnic groups. In turn, stratification is a core indicator of the differential quality of social life.

The Educational Dimension of Inequality

We turn first to changes over time and differentials in educational levels, a core dimension of stratification. As the state of Israel grew demographically and economically, educational levels of the population increased, networks of schools expanded, new academies were established, and opportunities for attending school were extended to (indeed, required of) all citizens. Public elementary and high schools, colleges, and universities developed to accommodate the needs of an increasing and diverse population, to educate the next generation in the political goals of the state, and to address the economic demands of an expanding and more-diversified labor market. The values placed on educational attainment and the emphases on learning in Israeli culture were expressed in the development and location of educational institutions and in the provision of resources for educational developments. Educated individuals were often highly valued in Jewish culture, and the transfer of status from "religious" to "secular" education was relatively straightforward among most Israelis who were committed to secular as well as religious values. No less important, high levels of educational attainment provided entry into better jobs and access to higher incomes and were a powerful basis for intergenerational social mobility. The expansion of educational opportunities and increases in educational levels were matched by growth in the availability of jobs demanding higher educational attainment. Job opportunities expanded, and industries developed to meet the increasing number of people participating in the labor force as well as in the broader economic goals of the state. Educational and occupational opportunities expanded in the growing metropolitan areas and developed in new geographic areas where immigrants and their families lived.

The ethnic origins of families and the ethnic composition of communities of residence are key contexts that have shaped opportunities for schooling and access to jobs. The educational and occupational backgrounds of parents and their resources are important determinants of the amount and type of schooling attained by their children. The location of educational institutions, the quality of teachers, and the orientation of their curricula are factors linked to educational levels and in turn to jobs. These sources of educational stratification are complex and involve family and personal background characteristics, institutional location, and the quality of school personnel. Their systematic analysis requires documentation of the changing levels of educational attainment, occupational achievement, and distribution of income; they point toward the exploration of changes in the education and occupation of parents, the translation of education into jobs, and the community contexts where educational and occupational opportunities vary. As a general theme, we ask: Do these broader factors translate into greater socioeconomic equality among the heterogeneous groups within Israel?

Educational attainment is a fundamental basis of social stratification. The average number of years of schooling completed provides the first clues about the complexities of ethnicity, generational change, and stratification. Three core findings emerge from an examination of the evidence on schooling in Israel. First, Israeli Jews from Western countries (European and American) have higher average levels of education than those from Asian and African countries. Among the foreign-born, the differences in education are greater than among the Israel-born as the gap has declined by the second and later generations. Second, the average educational gap has narrowed between ethnic groups because educational levels have increased for all ethnic groups. Having started at lower levels of education, the years of schooling increased more sharply for the Asian/African-origin group. The third finding makes the education story more complex because it focuses on a fuller educational distribution and shows the potential distortion when we only examine *average* levels of education. Examining the upper end of the educational distribution in the first decade of the twenty-first century (those with 13–15 years and those with 16 or more years of schooling) reveals small generational changes for both major Jewish ethnic categories and the retention of higher levels of post–high school education among the Western-origin population. Almost twice as many European/American Jews than Asian/African Jews had 13–15 years of education, and three times as many had more than a college education. These ratios are almost the same for the foreign- and Israel-born generations. At the upper levels of education, therefore, the ethnic gap at the beginning of the twenty-first century was about the same for the first and second generations.

How do these cross-sectional generational data reveal changes over time? Data organized from the 1961, 1972, and 1983 censuses of Israel (Nahon 1987) and detailed linked data from the 1983 and 1995 censuses (Friedlander et al. 2002) allow for a comprehensive examination of educational attainment among the major ethnic and religious groups of Israel. The findings reinforce the conclusion of sharp increases over time in the educational attainment of Israelis and continuing variation by ethnicity. Without exception, each religious-ethnic gender group experienced an increase in the average level of education from 1961 to 1995. Adding more-recent data from the twenty-first century shows consistent increases over five decades in the educational level of the population. In 2012, the average educational level of Jewish Israelis, men and women, and for two critical age groups (ages 25–35 and ages 45–54), was almost identical with little variation over the last decade. For Arab Israelis, the average educational level was only slightly lower than for Jewish Israelis, with a gain of one year over the last decade (cf. chapter 4 on Arab education).

Thus, one conclusion becomes clear: increases in educational attainment have not been limited to specific subpopulations and are a ubiquitous feature of Israeli society. At the same time, an ethnic hierarchy clearly emerges in these data: Jews have higher levels of education than Arabs; Jews of European ancestry have higher levels of schooling than non-European Jews; and Christians have higher educational levels than Moslems within the Arab Israeli population. Time has not eliminated but has reduced the ethnic divisions among Jews and between Jewish and Arab Israelis despite educational increases for all groups. Although full equalization in educational level among those of different ethnic origins has not occurred, educational convergences seem to be occurring on average.

The educational level of the Israeli-born of Israeli parents cannot be disentangled by ethnic origin. Given the immigration and settlement history of Israeli society, the third generation is heavily concentrated in the European-origins group (chapter 2). Their educational level is below that of Europeans of the second generation and higher than that of the Asian/Africans. These data suggest that time alone or generations of exposure to Israeli society are not the only factors that need to be considered in understanding ethnic changes in educational levels. Ethnic compositional changes within these broad ethnic groups are critical in understanding these changes in educational attainment over time in Israel.

Consistent with this series of cross-sectional findings over time is past research using the 1974 Israeli Mobility Study to examine the changing ethnic-educational connection (Shavit and Kraus 1990). Detailed data document that the overall process of educational stratification remained remarkably stable despite the profound changes in Israel during the 1950s and 1960s. In an attempt to reduce the school dropout rate among Asian- and African-origin Israelis, the government expanded vocational education at the secondary level, extended the number of years of compulsory education, and introduced compensatory education at the primary level. As a result, the effect of ethnicity on the transition from primary to secondary education declined. But there were no significant changes in the factors that governed access to higher levels of education, and ethnic origin remained a powerful differentiator for attaining and completing college-level schooling. As a growing proportion of the population completed more years of schooling, educational credentials began to lose their value as a discriminating factor in attaining jobs; new cohorts needed to attain even higher levels of education to compete for the best jobs. New job opportunities demanded high levels of educational attainment. Average educational levels for Christian Arabs increased about three years for both men and women (from 6.5 years to 9.5 years for men and 4.6 years to 7.9 years for women). At 3.2 years of schooling on average, Moslems had very low levels of education in 1961; in 1983, this figure more than doubled to 6.3 years among men and increased from 0.4 years to 3.7 years among women. The Druze pattern followed that of the Moslems, although the improvement among Druze women has been slower and their educational

TABLE 8.1

Transition of males in Israel to higher levels of education, two birth cohorts and four ethno/religious groups

	European/ American Jewish (%)	Asian Jewish (%)	African Jewish (%)	Arab (%)
1950–54 cohort				
Attained *bagrut*	62.3	26.6	23.2	24.2
Entered postsecondary school	51.2	20.2	17.5	18.5
Entered postsecondary academic program	35.3	10.8	8.7	11.5
1965–69 cohort				
Attained *bagrut*	65.0	42.9	35.7	29.0
Entered postsecondary school	50.3	28.4	23.4	16.6
Entered postsecondary academic program	36.6	15.4	12.4	10.8

Source: Adapted from Friedlander, Okun, and Goldscheider 2014.

levels lower. In 2012, the average educational level for Arab Israeli men and women was 12 years (see chapter 4).

Research based on detailed linked data from the 1995 and earlier censuses reveals that the increase in higher education among all groups has resulted in a widening gap between Jewish and Arab Israelis but a narrowing of the education gap among Jews from different ethnic origins (Okun and Friedlander 2005; Friedlander et al. 2002; Friedlander, Okun, and Goldscheider 2014). Drawing a basic summary of these changes and going beyond cross-sectional portraits, we examine transitions between grades, especially the transition to the higher levels of education (table 8.1). Two birth cohorts were examined (1950–1954, matriculating around 1970; and 1965–1969, matriculating around 1985), and changes in three transitions are presented: the attainment of the *bagrut* (a high school certification required for entrance to universities); the entrance into a postsecondary school; and the entrance into a postsecondary academic program. These cohort educational changes were then examined for European/Americans Jewish Israelis, Asian and African Jewish Israelis (separately), and for the Arab Israeli population. The results document the following:

First, European/American Jews have had and continue to have the highest transition percentages to the *bagrut*, postsecondary school, and postsecondary academic programs for both birth cohorts. This is consistent with all the available cross-sectional data. Second, the small differences in the three transitions between Asian/African Jewish and the Arab Israeli populations in the earlier cohort had increased by the 1965–1969 birth cohort. The gains over time for the Asian/African Jewish groups have been sharpest in attaining the *bagrut* and less so in the transition to higher levels of education. Both the Asian Jewish and African Jewish ethnic groups have increased their schooling levels faster than Arab Israelis. Third, the European/American Jewish group has not gained at the highest level of education; the schooling gap between this group compared to other Jewish ethnic groups has therefore been reduced over time—from three times higher than Asian/Africans (35% to 11%/9%) to little more than twice as high (37% to 15%/12%). Hence, the data show that each Jewish ethnic group has remained at high percentages or gained over time in the transition to higher educational levels. At the same time that the education gap has narrowed between European/American Jews and Asian/African Jews, it has increased between Jewish Israelis and Arab Israelis, since the transitions at the upper levels of schooling have remained relatively stable among Arab Israelis.

In short, gaps among all groups remain in the probabilities of moving from high school exposure to the *bagrut* and in the transition to higher educational levels. This comprehensive study shows stability over birth cohorts in the ranking of overall educational attainment among ethnic and religious groups in Israel. In descending rank order of educational transition are the following: the European/American Jewish group, Christian Arabs, Jews of Asian origin, Jews of African origin, Druze, and Moslems (Friedlander et al. 2002). Furthermore, detailed data (not presented in tabular form here) document a sharp increase by age in the proportion of men and women of all ethnic origins with higher academic degrees and the significantly higher levels of education among European- and American-origin Jews than among other groups. Differences between those socialized in Israel and those immigrating to Israel at age 17 or over (i.e., receiving their education in countries of origin) are striking. Immigrants arriving after age 17 have higher levels of education than their age cohorts and gender counterparts socialized in Israel (partly reflecting the influx of highly educated immigrants from the former Soviet Union). Significantly lower proportions of Asian/Africans socialized in Israel have attained advanced academic degrees than those who migrated to Israel after age 17, but the latter's numbers are lower than those of European/Americans, whether socialized in Israel or immigrating as adults. The proportion of younger Asian/African Jewish males socialized in Israel who have advanced academic degrees is significantly below that of Christians in Israel and even below that of Moslems.

These results are a powerful test of the ethnic convergence issue, since they reflect the educational inequalities that have been generated and reinforced by the expansion of schooling opportunities for Jews of different ethnic origins in Israel. The expansion of educational opportunities increased the average level of education for all groups. In part, this reflects the enactment and implementation of government policies mandating education for all. Only Arab women have not experienced the full impact of the law, and only among Moslem and Druze women. The educational increase has reduced major intragroup variations among some groups (women, Arabs, and Jews of Asian/African origins). Asian/African Jews who were socialized in Israel have moved toward a high school level of education; the educational level of the European/American Jews has increased to a post–high school level. At the same time, these changes have not eliminated the educational gap among different ethnic-origin populations. Educational inequalities have persisted in the face of the Israeli policy committed to reduce (if not eliminate) interethnic educational gaps. Again, data from the 1995 census confirm these patterns at the upper end of the educational distribution.

It should be noted that in the absence of an educational policy to reduce inequalities among Jews and between Jews and Arabs, the educational gaps would likely have been substantially greater. The question of educational inequality must be considered not only relative to an ideal of perfect equality but also relative to an alternative of no policy or a weaker policy. The measure of comparison must take into account as well the initial educational differences among immigrants in places of origin and levels of education among minority populations when the state was established.[1]

Hence, the focus here has been on the experience of the Israeli-born second generation, whose educational experience has been in Israel.

Another set of issues relates to the nature of the categorization of ethnic populations in Israel. The construction of ethnic groups into two major categories (European/American and Asian/African origins) appears somewhat artificial, since there are dozens of specific countries of origin that make up these groups, and there appear to be wide cultural and social-demographic differences within these ethnic categories (chapter 2). One way to investigate whether the ethnic dichotomy so often used in Israel to characterize Jewish ethnic origins captures the complexity of ethnic divisions is to examine empirically the educational transformation of each of the detailed subgroups.

Studies have documented that sharper educational differentiation between the broad groups designated as Asian/African and European/American has emerged over time that has altered the degree of educational variation within each of these Israeli-created ethnic groups (C. Goldscheider 1996). Using 1983 census information, research has shown that there was significant educational variation within the older (ages 60–64) Asian/African group born abroad. An examination of three countries illustrates the range: Older Israeli Jews born in Egypt had an average of 10 years of formal education; those born in Iraq had 8.5 years; and those born in Yemen had only 4.0 years. Thus, some Asian/African immigrants (e.g., those from Egypt) had levels of education as high as some immigrants born in Europe (e.g., Poland and Romania).

The second generation from these specific countries of origin (those ages 30–34, who were raised in Israel) had almost identical educational levels. Israelis of Egyptian origin had 11.3 years of education; Israelis of Iraqi origin had 10.8 years, and those of Yemenite origins had 11.0 years. Thus, the educational levels of younger cohorts of Israelis of Asian/African origin, when divided by specific countries of origin, were much more similar to each other than to those of their parents, who were educated outside Israel. More important, their educational levels had become increasingly different from those of the second generation of Jews of European origin. Although the children of Romanians and Poles attained levels of education similar to those of the better-educated European/Americans, the children of better-educated Asian/African immigrants attained levels similar to those of the less-educated Asian/Africans. Ethnic polarization in the educational level of the dichotomous ethnic groups (European/Americans and Asian/Africans) emerges in the second generation, and differences among specific country-of-origin subgroups of an earlier generation have been reduced to insignificance.[2] While the gap in the average level of educational attainment among ethnic Jewish groups has been reduced, the rank order of ethnic differentiation at higher levels of education remains among the second and third generations.

One conclusion we can draw from this exercise is that an examination of the educational patterns of the socially constructed dichotomous ethnic categories is fully justifiable. Analytically, these findings are consistent with the argument that ethnic differences among the second and later generations are not simply a carryover from places of origin but are the result of an Israeli-generated stratification system, reinforced by a complex combination of people and institutions—schools, teachers, family, and neighbors. The ethnic groups designated "Asian/Africans" and "European/Americans" are Israeli ethnic constructions, based on the ethnic origins of groups but reflecting the contexts of Israeli society. The evidence available is clearly not consistent with the view that the continuing educational and other distinctions among ethnic groups are primarily the result of cultural distinctiveness and proximity to the cultures of places of origin (see Goldberg 1977; Morag-Talmon 1989).

What factors account for the emerging dichotomy among Jewish ethnic groups? One part of the explanation for the growing similarity in the educational level attained by the diverse ethnic-origin subgroups within the Asian/African group relates to their treatment in educational and related institutions. These diverse groups were often lumped together by the European-dominated systems as if they were an undifferentiated and a socioeconomically deprived segment. This "labeling" occurred despite the wide range of levels of educational attainment in countries of origin and the negative socioeconomic selectivity of immigration to Israel.[3] Children of Asian/African-origin Jewish immigrants tended to be labeled *t'unei tepuach*, educationally deprived children requiring remedial assistance. In addition, the larger-than-average family size of Jews from Asia and Africa generally reduced the available capital they needed to invest in the education of their children (particularly at upper levels of education). Ethnic discrimination in the school setting, combined with larger family size, contrasts with the greater economic control and more-extensive networks of veteran European-origin Jewish populations, whose family size was smaller and socioeconomic resources greater.

Another part of the complex story relates to the continuing educational disadvantage of the population living in development towns (chapter 5). Jewish residents of development towns are characterized by the lowest levels of educational attainment. This is the case for all ethnic groups, men and women. For example Asian- and African-origin groups residing in development towns succeeded least in attaining the *bagrut* (matriculation certificate). Most of the educational systems located in development towns are vocational rather than academic. One conspicuous ethnic difference in educational levels therefore connects to the role of place of residence, which implies a complex of factors (Friedlander et al. 2000a, 2002b). Jews living in development towns are the most disadvantaged educationally and have been the least successful in completing high school and going beyond. In turn, this has led to the continuing generational socioeconomic disadvantage of the population living in development towns. The concentration of the Asian/African-origin population in development towns results in the continuation of the ethnic gap in education among third-generation Israelis.

In a more-detailed examination of the "quality" of the matriculation diploma (not only its attainment)[4] and the transitions between educational levels, the evidence becomes sharper: estimates based on research in the twenty-first century suggest that out of a birth cohort of 1,000, 179 Jews of European origins will attain a high-quality matriculation diploma while only 66 Jews of Asian/African ancestry and 26 of Arab ethnicity will do so. Social class and ethnicity combine with family background to shape the educational attainments of Israelis.

An additional part of the educational picture in Israel relates to the type of school attended by members of these ethnic groups: Asian/African-origin Jews had been more concentrated in vocational schools, European/American-origin Jews are in academic schools, and Arabs are almost all enrolled in academic schools since there are few vocational schools accessible to them (Nahon 1987; Shavit 1984, 1989, 1990, 1993). Research using the 1954 cohort of young Israeli men shows that there is a higher dropout rate in vocational schools. Most of the vocational schools do not encourage or allow the attainment of a *bagrut*; this thereby prevents or discourages the attainment of a college- or university-level education. Again, these patterns have changed somewhat during the 1990s, but significant ethnic differences remain in the shift to academic-oriented high schools and to post–high school education.

There are also economic constraints that affect the high school dropout rate among Asian/Africans, such as direct costs of continuing in school and wages lost through delayed employment, particularly among those with lower educational levels (see the studies by Shavit 1984, 1989, 1990, 1993). These findings may not apply to more-recent groups, who have been exposed to greater schooling-continuation rates among those attending vocational schools. However, the role of the economic crunch following the intifada in the late 1980s, the increase in tuition costs, and the deterioration of general educational quality that seems to have occurred at that time (see Ben-Yehuda 1989), along with the increased competition from the large number of Eastern European immigrants in the early 1990s, do not point in the direction of greater equalization of educational outcomes among ethnic groups.

These tracking patterns reinforce the observation that the educational system and its institutions have shaped the ethnic educational distinctiveness of the 1990s generation, beyond differences among ethnic-origin groups in "ability" and family background. Moreover, normative expectations result in greater tracking of Israelis of Asian/African origins into non-academic institutions and their continued educational distinctiveness. This educational distinctiveness is translated into socioeconomic disadvantage. Administrators and teachers are likely to play important roles in continuing this type of tracking. There is some indication that they tend to reinforce the lower expectations of Asian/African-origin Jewish students (Nahon 1987). Over time, therefore, as the educational system in Israel expanded, ethnic differences were reinforced and reestablished even as overall levels of education increased.[5]

Occupational Inequality

One of the consequences of reinforced educational distinctiveness among ethnic groups relates to the linkages between schooling and jobs. Educational experiences are intimately related to access to jobs and, in turn, to socioeconomic status and its correlates. As educational levels on the whole increase and as the labor market continues to demand higher levels of education to carry out more technically based jobs, the rarity

TABLE 8.2

Proportions of employed men in high-level occupations
by population groups, Israel, 1972–2011

		Portion of Israeli-born Jewish		
Year	Portion of total Jewish population (%)	Father born in Europe/America (%)	Father born in Asia/Africa (%)	Portion of total Arab population (%)
1972	18.6	34.8	7.6	6.0
1983	26.2	43.3	3.4	11.0
1995	30.7	47.7	18.8	11.9
2011	42.0	54.3	26.0	15.5

Note: People in high-level occupations include academic and associate professionals, technicians, and managers.
Source: *Statistical Abstract of Israel*, various years. Adapted from Friedlander, Okun, and Goldscheider 2014.

(in the statistical sense) of completing higher levels of education gets transformed into a new normative expectation. Ethnic educational distinctiveness leads to occupational distinctiveness and, in turn, to ethnic inequalities in occupations.

What are the occupational distribution patterns among ethnic groups? Occupational differences among ethnic-origin groups remained significant through the end of the 1990s. About one out of four Jewish males are in jobs classified as academic or professional. Among foreign-born European/American-origin Jews, the proportion working in these types of occupations is 31%; the level is even higher among immigrants from Europe who arrived during the years 1975–1989 (47%). In sharp contrast, only 16% of the foreign-born Asian/African Jews are in these two types of high-level jobs.

A summary of changes in several of the top-ranked occupations combined reveals the sharp increase among Israeli Jews in these occupations, from 19% in 1972 to 42% in 2011 (table 8.2). An examination of Jewish ethnic-group variation documents, as expected, large proportions in high-status occupations among European/Americans, increasing from 35% in 1972 to 54% in 2011. The proportion working in jobs at the same high-status occupational levels among those of Asian/African origin increased as well, from 8% to 26%. Thus, while the relative occupational ranking (in terms of which ethnic group had a larger proportion in higher-level jobs) remained the same between the two Jewish ethnic populations, the gap between them has narrowed. In contrast, the proportion of Israeli Arabs in the higher occupational levels has also increased but not as significantly as among Jewish Israelis. As a result the gap between Jewish and Arab Israelis has widened from 1972 to 2011, and the gap between Arab Israelis and Jews from Asian and African countries has increased as well. The occupational gap clearly does not reflect a simple case in which no changes have occurred for one group while significant changes have occurred for the other group. Rather, changes have occurred for all groups, but the pace of changes has been more intense among Jewish groups than among Arab Israelis. Given the closing gap in educational attainment among these same groups, it becomes reasonable to suggest that the clear translation of educational attainment to higher-levels jobs has occurred less among Arab Israelis than among Jewish Israelis.

There are also large ethnic differences in the age profile of participation in the labor force. Jews of Asian/African ethnicity enter and retire from the labor force earlier than do European/American-origin Jews, reflecting differences in length of time spent in school and variations in labor-market opportunities, as well as the effects of public and family support systems. As with education, ethnic differences reflect the educational and occupational conditions of Jews in countries of origin and the selectivity of immigration to Israel. The critical question about ethnic-group occupational distinctiveness is the extent to which there is a carryover beyond initial occupational differentiation to stratification in the younger generation raised and educated in Israel.

About one-third of the Israeli-born of European-origin males can be classified as working in high-level white-collar jobs, a slight increase from their parents' generation. In sharp contrast, only 18% of the Israelis of Asian/African origins are in these high-level jobs. An examination of the lower end of the occupational distribution confirms the generational transmission of occupational level among ethnic groups. Among the foreign-born, 33% of the European/American-origin Jews and 36% of the Asian/African origin work in jobs classified as skilled laborers. By the next generation, the proportion of Israeli-born Jews of European origin that held these lower-level occupations dropped to 19%, but the level among Asian/African-origin Israelis remained about the same (37%).

In my review of the changing occupational distinctiveness of ethnic groups in Israel, I underlined the occupational concentration of ethnic groups in particular sectors of the economy and the links between jobs and schooling. The expansion of the occupational structure in Israel in the 1980s and 1990s reduced the opportunities for those with only a high school education who were more likely to obtain blue-collar work. The great expansion of educational opportunities for Asian/Africans and their attainment of high school levels of education did not in the aggregate improve their access to the expanding occupational structure. Their vocational training was more likely to lead to blue-collar work. Comparing the older and younger generations of Asian/African-origin Jews shows that despite the increase in the number of years of schooling among the younger generation, their occupational structure reproduced that of their parents' generation. These ethnic-group generational contrasts result in an increase in the occupational gap between the younger Israeli-born generation of Asian/African and European/American Jews. The continued concentration of second-generation Israelis of Asian/African origins in blue-collar jobs, combined with the decline in the status of these jobs, has meant that generational occupational stability has been translated into the declining occupational status of the less-advantaged group.

In contrast to Asian/African-origin Jews, Arabs with higher levels of education have better jobs and even better opportunities to move into white-collar, particularly high-level white-collar, jobs in their own communities. As the rate of higher education increased among Arab Israelis, and did so with less expansion of the high-level white-collar job opportunities in the Arab sector, the more-educated Arabs have had to seek job opportunities in the Jewish sector and compete with better-educated Jews. It is reasonable to assume that, in this competition, Arabs are not likely to be the advantaged or the equal group (see chapter 4). At the end of the twentieth century, the Arab population was significantly more concentrated than Jewish Israelis at the lower end of the occupational structure.

Occupational Prestige

Another view of the occupational distribution emphasizes the relative prestige of detailed occupations, modeling the factors determining rank. There has been a long and distinguished history of using occupational differences as an indicator of "prestige" in Israel (see Kraus and Hodge 1990).

Most of the occupational studies of Israeli society have argued that occupational-prestige differences among the various ethnic groups reflect differences in educational attainment. The first studies of the stratification process focused on a period of time after the establishment of the country, the economic absorption of mass immigration, rapid economic growth, and the crystallization of economic, social, and political institutions. The major changes in the stratification system identified in these studies have been the social mobility associated with increasing educational attainment, particularly the expansion of postelementary and post–high school education, increases in the occupational skill levels of the Israeli-born population, and the development of alternative avenues of social mobility that were not necessarily based on formal education (Kraus and Hodge 1990; Nahon 1987, 1989; Shavit 1990; Yuchtman-Yaar 1986).

Hence, the major transformation has been from stratification based on ethnic origin toward one based more on universalism and achievement. It is generally argued that the critical factor in the lower occupational prestige of Asian/African Jews is their lower educational attainment and, only indirectly, their socioeconomic origins. At similar educational levels, it is argued, Asian/African-origin Israelis are able to convert their education into status and income (Kraus and Hodge 1990). But as I have documented, educational inequalities among ethnic groups have persisted through the beginning of the twenty-first century.

Part of the increasing merit-based (educationally driven) stratification system has been the policy of the state to generate greater ethnic equality through equal access to educational institutions. As in Western nations, the commitment to the expansion of the educational enterprise as a basis for reducing ethnic inequality has been only partly successful in Israel. Too often the expansion of the educational system has resulted in the "reproduction" of the existing class structure and its legitimation. Indeed, the expansion of educational and occupational opportunities in Israel seems to have duplicated the ethnic gap and moved it from lower to higher levels. Increasing the educational levels reduces the value of average educational attainment as a basis for particular openings, because when everybody must obtain a high-level education to qualify for a job, other criteria must be invoked for job selection. The dominant group (European/American-origin Jews) tends to be favored when educational levels are equalized; networks and connections are invoked as deciding factors in employment. Even in the merit-based system, it is often who you know—that is, the connections and networks that you have—rather than your credentials that determines the occupational returns to your investment in higher education.

Together, these factors have resulted in the differential exploitation of job opportunities among the different ethnic groups in Israel. Occupational inequalities have been retained among the Israeli-born in conjunction with educational expansion, since the educational and occupational systems carry their own institutional biases toward European/American Jews. These biases combine with differences in parental resources to invest in the next generation, the negative labeling of Asian/African Jews, and the more-valuable economic networks of European Jews.

The disadvantageous occupational patterns and educational levels of the younger generation of Asian/African Jews are exacerbated by location and ecological factors. Geography combines with government policy to set limits on where job opportunities are located and where related institutions were developed to promote educational mobility. Both job and educational opportunities have been more concentrated in the urban centers of Israel and not in the periphery. Government policy defined where resources were allocated and where investments were made geographically. Initially, these policies attempted to redirect industries and people away from concentrated and densely settled urban centers toward development towns and then toward territories administered by Israel, where Jews were settling. These subsidized economic activities encouraged selective immigrant streams to move toward these areas and, over time, resulted in the reinforcement of economically disadvantaged ethnic populations. Ethnic origin often interacts with location to increase ethnic economic inequalities (see chapter 5 for a review of these communities).

Self-Employment in Israel

Are there alternative paths to social mobility that are less reliant on educational attainment beyond high school or on an achievement-based hierarchy? Are there social-mobility tracks that circumvent the educational disadvantages of ethnic groups? One such path for ethnic social mobility may be by way of ethnic economic networks that operate through self-employment or family-based economic connections. There are important aspects of self-employment that connect to ethnic continuity. First, self-employment means greater direct control over one's own job and, indirectly, greater reliance on family for resources and connections. Working in a family business or being self-employed may also involve power over resources to be distributed to others and, where appropriate, to co-ethnics. It often implies the formation of networks and contacts with others in similar positions. Are there ethnic differences in self-employment, and does working for oneself (or more broadly for one's family) serve as an alternative avenue for social mobility that is less connected to educational attainment? Self-employment would be a form of ethnic entrepreneurship that reinforces ethnic distinctiveness and at the same time reduces ethnic economic disadvantage.

In Israel, there is a small proportion of the employed who work for themselves; they have a higher rate of income than those who work for others but have lower levels of education (see Shavit and Yuchtman-Yaar 2001). Given that the income returns to self-employment are greater than those obtained by working for others and that educational levels of the self-employed are lower, self-employment appears to be a potential source of social mobility for some ethnic communities that functions outside the educational system. Since a major source of the lower socioeconomic position of Israelis of Asian and African origins is their continuing lower level of education and the occupation gap, the question of substitute paths to social mobility, circumventing the educational system, takes on particular importance.

As in other countries, there have been steady declines over time in self employment in Israel. While the proportion of self-employed declined among Jewish men of European/American origin, self-employment has remained relatively steady among Asian/African-origin Jewish men. Indeed, the percentage of self-employment among men age 25 and over in 1983 was about the same for European/American Jews, Asian/African Jews, and Arabs (Nahon 1989). Overall, there is not a clear European/American and Asian/African dichotomy, since the proportion of self-employed among Iranian and Iraqi Jews is significantly higher than among Yemenite and Moroccan Jews but is closer to that among Russian and Bulgarian-Greek Jews. A more-detailed look at the self-employed who are employers splits more dichotomously into the two broader ethnic groups, with greater homogeneity within these two broad groups than between them (Nahon 1989, appendix table 3).

Self-employment patterns need to be further refined by categorizing occupational levels, since the different meaning of self-employment for carpenters and for physicians is substantial. This is particularly the case when we focus on the social mobility and stratification implications of self-employment. In the 1980s, with only minor exceptions, Asian/African-origin Jewish males had higher self-employment levels than did European/American-origin Jewish males in every job category that was blue-collar, and they had lower levels of self-employment in every high-level white-collar job category. Thus, the occupational inequality between ethnic groups in overall occupational distribution extends to job concentration and self-employment. Most importantly, ethnic-group occupational inequality characterizes the youngest age groups of the Israeli-born. These patterns have changed in the twenty-first century as ethnic differences in self-employment have converged. This reflects both compositional changes in the Israeli labor force and the effects of changes in the occupational distribution. Thus, the influence of Russian immigration and its impact on the occupational differences among ethnic groups and the increases in self-employment associated with the growth of the technology sector of the economy have altered the implications of ethnic differences and of self-employment in the twenty-first century and have made comparisons with previous periods more complex (Shavit and Yuchtman-Yaar 2001).

When the linkage between education and occupation is added to the self-employment equation, the evidence becomes even sharper: the correlation between educational level and occupation is weaker among the self-employed than among those employed by others. Although education remains an important factor among the determinants of occupation even among the self-employed, it is less significant than among those who work for others. The ethnic gap in self-employment increased between 1961 and 1983 and among those young adults socialized in Israel, but somewhat less so than among those who work for others (Nahon 1989).

An intergenerational finding of importance documents that the economic success of the Jews of Asian/African origins who are self-employed is translated into the educational achievement of their children. There is some intergenerational inheritance of self-employment, for both Asian/Africans and European/Americans. Research carried out in the late 1980s showed that Asian/African-origin Jews who were self-employed in partnership with others were more likely than European/American-origin

Jews to prefer to be partners with their brothers, even after controlling for the number of brothers (Nahon 1989). Thus, self-employed European/American-origin Jews exhibit a wider economic network that is nonfamilial than do self-employed Asian/African-origin Jews. The connection between education and self-employment appears to be weaker at the individual level but stronger intergenerationally—educational attainment does not appear to strongly affect the likelihood of higher education of the next generation. As the labor-force structure of Israel's economy changes and self-employment levels are reduced even further, the major impact of self-employment as an avenue for ethnic social mobility has to be through the educational system.

When one examines the economic mobility patterns of Asian/African- and European/American-origin Jews, it is clear that those who came from European countries started with an initial advantage with their concentration in professional, managerial, and clerical occupations. Evaluated by relative earnings, the Jews of European/American origin and their children continued their economic advantage over those of Asian/African origin (Ben-Porath 1986a). As a result of the exposure to Israeli society, Asian/African Jews were transformed twice: First, they were directed into agriculture, and the relative earnings gap between Asian/African and European/American Jews became larger in Israel than in their countries of origin. Second, in the 1960s and 1970s the exit of Asian/African Jews from agriculture and entry into blue-collar and some white-collar occupations occurred, but European/American Jews entered into white-collar occupations, abandoning all others. The economic gap in the second generation grew even larger than that of their parents, so that upward mobility was more marked in the group that was more advanced to begin with (Ben-Porath 1986a).

A review of earnings and income differentials by ethnic origin, based on an income survey conducted by the Central Bureau of Statistics, shows that ethnic-origin-related income differences have narrowed over time (Ben-Porath 1986b). Income differences by country of origin appeared in the late 1960s to stem almost entirely from educational differences (Ginor 1979). These reflected the background of immigrants and the differential exposure of the second generation to educational opportunities in Israel. But the continuing ethnic-group educational differences among the Israeli-born Jews have implications for perpetuating the economic disadvantages of Asian/African-origin Jews, even as some pro-portion may circumvent the education-occupation connection through self-employment. The process of finding alternative avenues to the edu-cational system as a means of increasing income will result in a reinforce-ment of ethnic distinctiveness, although not necessarily in conspicuous earnings differences or in standards of living. We should expect continued ethnic differences in lifestyles and values.[6]

With the influx of Russian immigrants and the developments in tech-nological industries, it has become clear that the path to income and oc-cupational success has primarily been through educational attainment, particularly at the highest levels. Those without educational attainment at the highest levels are likely to be left behind in the technological world of occupations in the twenty-first century.

According to Central Bureau of Statistics information, income gaps be-tween the highest and lowest levels of the distribution have increased. In 2008, the average income after taxes for the wealthiest 20% of Israelis was 7.5 times higher than for the poorest 20%. And this income gap has in-creased significantly from ten years earlier. Income inequality is greater in Israel than in any of the 27 countries in the European Union. The number of Israelis who risk falling below the poverty line has increased, because of the proportionately larger Arab Israeli and ultraorthodox Jewish families, the two poorest communities in Israel. Both communities for different reasons have high rates of unemployment and do not have the necessary schooling to compete in the expanding arenas of high technology. The in-creasing inequality in income and the continuing gaps in education and occupation among native-born Israeli Jews are in sharp contrast to the ideology and vision of the founders of Israeli society, who aimed for so-cioeconomic equality and the breakdown of generational social-class persistence.

Concluding Observations

Intergenerational mobility has not fully closed the educational or occu-pational gaps between immigrant Jewish ethnic groups and their children. Although every ethnic group has been characterized by social mobility, the ethnic gap has not fully diminished and, at times, has even widened. Thus, inequalities have persisted, even with rapid development and eco-nomic growth and the development of new opportunities in a relatively open stratification system. This has intensified in the quarter of a century since the 1990s. Ethnic differences in economic, social, cultural, and political spheres extend to the second and third generations born in Israel. Social inequality can be only partly explained by the different socioeconomic backgrounds of these ethnic groups. Exposure to Israeli society has led to social mobility but has also reinforced disadvantage among some as the economy has changed and the demands for a more-educated labor force have increased. The economic integration of immigrant populations in Israel resulted in continuing forms of ethnic distinctiveness; social mobility did not necessarily result in greater equality or in the elimination of the socioeconomic gap between groups. Ethnic residential concentration among communities and within large metropolitan areas is central to the perpetuation of Israel as an ethnically divided society. This conclusion applies to the ethnic divisions among the Jewish population and clearly characterizes the Arab-Jewish distinction. The arrival of a large number of Russian immigrants in the 1990s with high levels of education and occupational experience has resulted in the perpetuation of the ethnic gap that disadvantages those from Asian and African origins. This may be particularly the case among the children of the Russian immigrants, who are likely to attain higher levels of education and become more prepared for Israel's expanding technological sectors.

Socioeconomic differences are not the only manifestations of ethnic inequality. In the next chapter, I consider questions of ethnic differences in mortality and health to examine how some socioeconomic differences are translated into "life chances." Moreover, ethnicity and gender are often intertwined and form an additional basis of inequality. In the Israeli context, gender differences interact with ethnic origin and reinforce ethnic distinctiveness at the family-household levels. I turn to a consideration of these forms of inequality in chapter 10 with a review of family themes and connect them to gender questions that we outlined in chapter 7.

NOTES

1. I make a similar argument in chapter 9, in the context of inequality as indicated by mortality levels among ethnic populations in Israel.

2. For more detailed statistical evidence, see Nahon 1987, table 4. Compare similar patterns for mortality and fertility differentials by ethnic origin and generations in chapters 9 and 10.

3. See Inbar and Adler 1977 on the higher levels of educational attainment of Moroccan brothers who immigrated to France compared with those who immigrated to Israel.

4. See Friedlander, Okun, and Goldscheider 2014.

5. Among Asian/African-origin girls, the rate of enrollment in academic institutions is twice as high as that of boys (Shavit 1984). This gender difference has implications for ethnic intermarriages and the nature of the marriage market for Asian/African Jewish women (see chapter 10).

6. For a dissenting view of inequality based largely on income data for both Arabs and Jews see Plaut 2014.

9 | Inequality and Mortality Decline

The changing quality of life in society is often revealed by the changing pattern of death. Societies with high rates of mortality, a heavy concentration of death among infants and children, causes of death that reflect conditions of poor public health and sanitation, and an absence of adequate medical and preventive care are likely to be those where economic development is low, where medical care and access to it are minimal, and where knowledge of disease prevention is limited. Therefore, mortality conditions have often been viewed as indicators of the economic and health contexts of a society and of its quality of life (C. Goldscheider 1971).

In similar ways, societies in which differential mortality rates characterize subpopulations or regions are likely to have other forms of inequality as well. There are no examples of societies with high mortality levels and systematic differential mortality rates that are not at the same time characterized by social and economic inequalities. But the reverse is not necessarily the case: similar mortality levels do not always imply equality among groups, and high levels of economic development cannot be inferred from low mortality levels. The transfer of death-control and health-care technology among countries and within countries to disadvantaged groups may obscure inequalities and distort mortality as a measure of development levels.[1] In this chapter, I examine mortality patterns in Israeli society as a whole, with an emphasis on the dramatic reduction in death rates over time and the narrowing of mortality differences among population subgroups. I show how changes and fluctuations in death rates offer conspicuous clues about the changing quality of Israeli life. Using mortality differences as indicators of inequality allows me to specify which types of inequality have characterized the society as a whole.

Mortality levels and differentials reflect how resources in countries are mobilized and used to control the health and welfare of populations. The use and application of resources for the regulation of health and death are, in part, dependent on their availability, but are also influenced in powerful ways by the policies and programs that distribute those resources and use them to improve the welfare of people. Into the twenty-first century, extensive technical knowledge about health and death control is available and can be transferred between countries. This knowledge can also be organized to be distributed within a country in a way that increases equality. The availability of major forms of death control, and the ways governments and their institutions deploy resources to improve the quality of life of their populations, determine whether mortality levels are low, particularly among infants and children who are most vulnerable. Public health and medical technology, its development and transfer (internally and internationally)—not economic development alone—have become key factors in the reduction of mortality around the world. Ironically, as public-health technology becomes increasingly transferable between places, politics, not technology, emerges as a major source of variation in mortality levels among and within countries.

The links between political and economic development and levels of mortality are manifest in reductions over time in mortality and in the distribution of welfare and health services to the diverse populations in a country. Differences in levels of mortality by social class, economic category, and residence (rural and urban) and among ethnic and racial groups have diminished over time in most pluralistic, Western, more economically developed areas of the world. The greater the variation in mortality among ecological, economic, and ethnic-group divisions in countries, the more likely that these differences reflect the unequal distribution of resources and the priorities of government investments. Hence, differential mortality rates are reflections of both the inequalities in social life and the values of the political system. In these ways, differential mortality rates are systematic, not random; they are group characteristics and are less likely to be primarily biological or individualistic in origin. Mortality variations are mainly the result of social processes and do not reflect the "tastes" or preferences of populations.

At the most general societal level, mortality rates are an intrinsic part of the population-growth process of a country—levels of mortality, together with levels of fertility, shape the "internal" growth of the population (with net immigration rates affecting population size through "external" processes). Here I emphasize the long-term trends in mortality in Israel and connect changes in death rates to immigration and political and economic developments since the establishment of the state. I also examine changes in the distribution of health and medical care reflected by differential rates of death and dying. Hence, mortality trends and their variation among subgroups offer another context to evaluate the changing inequalities in Israeli society.

Mortality Levels and Changes

I begin by documenting the contemporary mortality pattern in Israel, describing some of the common statistical measures of mortality, particularly those sensitive to the health and welfare of children. What were the patterns of mortality in Israel at the beginning of the twenty-first century? Levels of life expectancy for Israeli society as a whole are comparable to those of the most economically advanced countries of the world. In 2012, life expectancy was 80 years for Israeli men and 84 years for Israeli women; infant mortality rates were 3.5 per 1,000 births. These levels reflect the widespread availability of medical care and public-health services for adults, children, and infants, and an extensive welfare system that protects against the debilitating effects of economic hardship, poverty, and malnutrition.

Most persons who die in Israel do so at older ages, largely from cancer and heart disease. In 2012, there were about 42,000 deaths recorded in Israel, a crude death rate of 5.3 deaths per 1,000 population. Most of these deaths were of older persons—79% of all deaths in Israel were of persons age 65 or over. Improvements in mortality, in general, have been quite dramatic since the 1950s in Israel, particularly among infants and children before their first birthday. Have mortality levels decreased proportionately for all groups? Have inequalities in death levels among Jews and between Jews and Arabs narrowed with changing levels of mortality? Are there continuing sources of variation in inequality in contemporary Israeli society that would identify groups or areas where differential death rates have been more persistent? Have government policies been supportive, in design and in implementation, of improving the health and welfare of the diverse populations in Israel and thereby narrowing the mortality gaps among groups?

The decline in mortality in Palestine and in the state of Israel has been well documented (Friedlander and Goldscheider 1979; C. Goldscheider 2002). Life expectancy at birth increased for the Jewish population from about 60 years in the 1930s to 65 years in the 1940s to over 70 years by the late 1950s. By the end of the first decade of the twenty-first century, life expectancy among Jewish Israeli men was over 80 years and 84 years for

Jewish women, among the highest in the world. Life expectancy among the Arab population had been 35 to 38 years during the 1920s and 1930s, but it increased to about 50 years during the 1940s (and among Christian Arabs, the increase was from less than 50 years in the 1930s to 60 years in the 1940s). Life expectancy in 2012 was 77 years for the Arab male population of Israel and 81 for Arab women. Thus, Jewish and Arab levels of mortality have improved over time with a remaining mortality gap of about three years on average between them.

The infant mortality rate (the number of deaths of infants less than 1 year old per 1,000 births) is the measure of mortality that tends to be most sensitive to health and economic conditions as well as governmental policies concerned with the welfare of mothers and children. Data show the patterns of infant mortality reduction for both the Jewish and Moslem sectors, from the 1920s in Palestine to the end of the twentieth century in Israel. There were dramatic declines for both populations. For Jews there was a systematic decline, from 133 infants per 1,000 births in 1925 to about 32 deaths per 1,000 births when the state was established and the population was largely European, declining to less than 10 deaths per 1,000 births beginning in the mid-1980s. The infant mortality level shifted to 2.7 per 1,000 births in the 2010–2012 period. These declines occurred despite major shifts in the ethnic origin of the Jewish population and the arrival of a large number of Jewish immigrants from countries characterized by significantly higher levels of mortality than Israel.

Equally impressive declines in infant mortality may be observed for the Moslem population in Israel. Starting from a higher level than that of Jews (about 18% of all children born to Moslem women in the 1920s did not survive their first year), the proportion of Moslem babies not surviving their first year of life decreased to below 10% in the mid-1940s, to less than 5% in the 1960s. The Arab infant mortality rate was 6.9 per 1,000 births in 2012.[2] A similar reduction in infant mortality characterizes both the Christian and Druze subpopulations, with the Druze pattern closer to the infant (and adult) mortality levels of Moslems and the Christian pattern closer to the patterns of the Jewish population.

Consistent with these infant mortality rates are the simple data on the numbers of infants who die before their first birthday. These numbers reveal that infant deaths impact not only families but also communities and the society as a whole. There has been a decline of 50% in the number of infant deaths in Israel as a whole, from 2,000 infant deaths annually in the 1950s to fewer than 800 in the late 1990s. The number of Jewish infants who died in their first year of life declined even more sharply, from 1,700 in 1951 to only 334 in 2012. These changes point to the shifts from being a more-common occurrence among the youngest and most vulnerable members of families toward becoming a rare event for infants and a more-common pattern among the older age segments of society.

In Israeli society, young adult males have emerged as a new vulnerable age group. They have been exposed to military activities and to wars that have substantially increased their risk of dying. The costs of the Israeli-Arab conflict are reflected in these young-adult deaths and in some conspicuous health and disability patterns, as well as in the time spent away from other activities—economic, educational, and family—that active military duty entails. The military obligation in Israel extends beyond the few years of full-time active service for most males (and substantial, if lower, proportions of the unmarried female Jewish population) to include weeks of commitment annually for significant years of the life course. The role of politics in shaping the mortality curve by age is nowhere more obvious. As death control from some ages is reduced by the politics of public health and welfare, the increases in deaths (and disabilities) among young adults and the costs of increases in widowhood among the young are directly affected by the politics of war and military conflicts.

The overall dramatic mortality reduction over time reflects the commitment of the government in Israel to provide extensive health and medical care. Mortality levels in Israel are low and reflect well on the general quality of life, the values placed on the health and welfare of children and adults, and the general high level of socioeconomic development and political organization of the society. Nevertheless, it is also clear that the gap between the mortality levels of Jews and Arabs in Israel remains large. Infant mortality data for 2012 show that rates among Moslems in Israel are about two and a half times as high as among Jewish Israelis, despite the major declines in mortality rates in both populations. The Jewish-Moslem infant mortality gap is greater in the twenty-first century than it was during the 1920s, when the levels for both populations were much higher. Thus, comparing the current mortality level of each population with its own past reveals impressive mortality declines; comparing long-term infant mortality rates between the Jewish and Moslem populations reveals a continuing health-mortality gap between them that has not decreased over time.

Immigration and Mortality Differentials

The documentation of the mortality gap between Jews and Arabs, along with mortality reductions over time, raises the question whether there are other sources of mortality variation that may also indicate social inequalities. We turn first to ethnic variation in mortality among Israeli Jews (see the excellent collection of essays in Schellekens and Anson 2007).

Immigration and subsequent ethnic compositional shifts in Israel have had a major impact on mortality trends over time, as well as on the types of differentials in mortality that remain among the second and later generations. Immigrants arrived in Israel from areas characterized by widely varying levels of health and socioeconomic development: some immigrants came from European countries with low and controlled mortality, but others came from Middle Eastern countries characterized by high, uncontrolled mortality. Moreover, the position of Jews in these societies ranged from middle to lower classes. Hence, there is every reason to expect that immigrants to Israel would be characterized by levels of health and mortality that would reflect the conditions in their countries of origin — in the double sense that Jews came to Israel from areas that had varying health and mortality levels and that the Jewish immigrants from these countries had significantly different socioeconomic backgrounds and exposure to modern medicine than longer-term Jewish residents. These contexts should result in a great diversity in mortality patterns among first-generation immigrants in Israeli society. The key analytic question is directed to the Israeli experience of these immigrant groups: What happened to the mortality levels of these diverse immigrant groups on arrival and subsequently? Do social forces in the society reinforce mortality variations by ethnic origin or do they facilitate their reduction? Have mortality levels converged among second-generation Israelis of different ethnic origins?

The data to answer these questions consistently point to the conclusion that the decline in mortality for all Jewish ethnic groups over time is one of the clearest ethnic demographic convergences in Israel. Research shows that the initial differential mortality by ethnic origin of Jewish immigrants in Israel largely reflected the range of mortality levels among their places of origin. In turn, mortality variation reflected the level of health and social development of these places of origin (the countries themselves and the place of Jews within them). A simple but revealing illustration is immigrant Jews from Yemen. Upon entering Israeli society, Yemenite Jews had rates of mortality that were similar to those in less-developed countries of the 1950s, with life expectancies of less than 40 years and infant mortality rates that translated into the death of about one-third of the babies during their first year of life. In contrast, the European immigrants to Palestine and to Israel had levels of mortality that were more like the Western mortality model, with average rates of life expectancy of 60 years and infant mortality rates of 3% of births when the state of Israel was established (Bachi 1977; Peritz 1986).

With the improvement in the level of health and its extension to the variety of ethnic immigrant groups in the country, there was an almost immediate decline in the mortality levels of Jewish immigrants from Asian and African countries. Upon entry into Israeli society, they were exposed to new and better health conditions. The life expectancy calculated from vital statistics in Israel for the Middle Eastern–origin Jewish population was 35 to 40 years in 1948; by the end of the twentieth century the life expectancy of Jews in Israel was 78 years, with almost no variation by ethnic origin. The beginning of the mortality decline was almost immediate upon arrival and fully affected the first generation of immigrants of all origins. To the extent that mortality levels were the only indicator of immigrant integration, one would conclude that the integration of Jews from countries with diverse mortality levels and with varying socioeconomic backgrounds was in the direction of the rapid reduction of the mortality gaps (and therefore by inference the inequality) among ethnic groups (Friedlander and Goldscheider 1979).

The decline in mortality and the convergence process among Jewish ethnic groups can, in large part, be attributed to changes in the basic patterns of the health infrastructure, the control over environmental conditions, and the increased access to health resources among all the Jewish immigrant origin groups. These changes were part of the development of an entitlement system associated with an emerging welfare state in Israel, which resulted in the spread of health clinics and medical personnel, maximizing the accessibility of these resources to the Jewish population. Health and welfare institutions were developing in the society as a whole;

they were distributed among communities and in neighborhoods where immigrant Jews settled, in an attempt to integrate them into the new society and to increase their health and welfare (see Doron and Kramer 1991 on Israel's welfare system; see articles on mortality variation in Schellekens and Anson 2007).

Since the initial ethnic differences in mortality reflected conditions in the migrants' countries of origin, the observed ethnic inequalities in mortality were not an Israeli-created product. Instead, mortality and health patterns were the consequence of the "baggage" that immigrants brought with them—their own characteristics and their societal origins. The explanation of residual mortality variation in Israel cannot be assessed simply as the product of a system of inequality relative to the ideal of perfect equality. More appropriately, the residual ethnic mortality differences should be contrasted with what the alternative mortality rates would have been had there been no system of entitlement and no attempt to reduce the health-welfare gap among immigrant groups from diverse places of origin. Even though it is likely that ethnic mortality differences would have declined over several decades, the speed of the decline and the clear-cut trend toward convergence in ethnic mortality levels can only be understood as a political (in the sense of policy) attempt to build the society on the basis of health and welfare accessible to all Jews, regardless of ethnic origin and timing of immigration.

One implication of this argument is that there is no evidence of institutional discrimination in health care against immigrant Jews or against those of a particular ethnic origin that extends beyond socioeconomic factors.[3] Had there been institutional sources of discrimination in this area of social life, ethnic mortality differences would have been sharper, the declines of mortality levels among the less-advantaged Middle Eastern–origin population would have been slower, and convergences with the dominant European-origin population would have taken significantly longer. To the extent, therefore, that there are pockets of higher mortality among Israeli Jews that are ethnically based, the source of the ethnic difference should be explored as a secondary consequence of socioeconomic or geographic patterns associated with ethnic origin. The system of entitlements that was designed to overcome the liability of ethnic origin for the Jewish immigrant population and to provide equal health treatment to all persons in Israel is not perfect. Two types of contemporary differences in mortality can be examined with research data that isolate some of the sources of contemporary variation in Israel: areal and socioeconomic differences in mortality. On these bases, contemporary ethnic differentials in mortality can be assessed.

Areal and Socioeconomic Variation

Changes in mortality differences among geographic locations within Israel are associated with the impact of the location of health services and medical personnel on the health and welfare of the population. Indirectly, location variation in mortality reflects the role of resources—occupation, education, and money—to purchase access to health care to reduce mortality gaps. Part of the contemporary ethnic differential in mortality may be reflected in the concentration of disadvantaged groups in selected locations in the country.

Overall the evidence points to a general convergence in areal mortality differences over time. One can selectively examine some broadly defined urban places and a few areas that are located geographically and socially on the periphery of Israeli society. Over time, the areal variation in mortality diminished significantly, although some small differences remained. The early areal variation in general levels of mortality in Israel in 1960 had moved toward lower levels by the 1980s, as all areas had experienced improved health care. An even smaller range in infant mortality rates characterized areas by the early twenty-first century.

Residual areal differences reflect conditions in specific places and the differential distribution of resources among populations, as well as the fluctuations associated with small numbers of infant deaths. More-distant development towns have fewer means of access to health services and are less able to purchase them. Disadvantaged populations in development towns and those more distant from the main population resource centers, therefore, are likely to be characterized by lower levels of health. It is also likely that there is some health and mortality variation among neighborhoods in the larger urban areas, although systematic evidence is not available to confirm this. Populations living in areas of poorer economic circumstances are less likely to have equal access to medical care or to receive equal care than populations in areas with better socioeconomic resources. Some areas have fewer public-health institutions and, often, the facilities they do have are of lower quality. Populations located in these poorer areas have not been as successful economically and are more likely to be of Middle Eastern rather than of European origins. In these ways, ethnic variation in health care and in mortality levels in cities seems to be primarily a reflection of economic and geographic circumstances and the overlap of ethnic origin and residential concentration. It is difficult to know how much of these areal differentials in mortality simply reflect socioeconomic variation, without more-precise data than are currently available.

Contemporary Ethnic Differences

What do these differences in mortality by geographic locations and by social class imply for the second and later ethnic-group generations? Preliminary analysis of combined ethnic and socioeconomic variation in mortality based on the linkage of census (1983) and mortality records (1983–1986) shows that differential mortality levels (and also official causes of death) by ethnic origin in Israel remain: African-origin Jews have higher mortality (and from causes of death that are more directly controllable) than those of European or Asian origin (Eisenbach et al. 1989; Friedlander, Ben-Moshe, and Schellekens 1989). Part of these ethnic-origin differences reflects variations in socioeconomic level between these populations. Standard mortality ratios by education and ethnic origin, along with three categories of cause of death, confirm the inverse relationship between educational levels and death rates that appear by age, sex, and ethnic origin, as well as by cause of death; differential mortality rates by ethnic origin narrow considerably when educational levels are neutralized. There are no final data on the residual ethnic variation controlling for education, age, and sex, but based on cumulative research, one would expect it to be minimal.

An exploration of areal variation in ethnic mortality differentials with socioeconomic and religiosity variation confirms the importance of these three factors explaining interlocational differences in old-age mortality, with socioeconomic status the most important factor. Changes between 1972 and 1983 point to a reduction of the differences in the old-age mortality of the Asian-origin Jewish population in Israel but not fully for the African-origin Jewish population. Between these dates, social inequality as measured by areal socioeconomic data on old-age mortality in Israel increased (Friedlander, Ben-Moshe, and Schellekens 1989). Linking census records with records of subsequent death (the Israel Longitudinal Mortality Study) and focusing on women has documented that mortality differentials were higher for women who were poorer, less educated, nonmarried, childless, not in the labor force, and those of North African origin. The latter again was found to be due to differences in socioeconomic levels (Manor et al. 2007). Higher mortality characterizes those who are less "protected" and more vulnerable; socioeconomic factors seem in large part to reduce or eliminate ethnic variation and inequalities among Israel's Jewish population.

An early examination of specific ethnic-group differences in mortality (Peritz 1986) sharpens the analysis and points to the fact that North African Jews in Israel (the largest and most disadvantaged immigrant population in economic terms in the mid-1980s) had a distinctly higher mortality rate than Jews from European or Asian communities; the foreign-born had higher levels than the Israeli born. These patterns characterize both men and women among those born in Libya, Morocco, Tunisia, and Algeria. The importance of socioeconomic factors in accounting for these findings is clear, but the details by cause of death suggest that other factors may also be at work that are not only economic. Some have suggested that cultural factors appear to be operative, but these are not yet understood and have rarely been measured directly. Clearly, there are areal and socioeconomic factors that operate jointly to affect ethnic mortality differentials, and they are more important for the second and later generations than for the immigrant generation. The bottom line: there is no systematic evidence available that significantly higher mortality levels characterize Jewish Asian- or African-origin populations of the second generation that are not in large part accounted for by socioeconomic factors and geographic concentration.

A set of studies also examined part of the impact of religiosity on mortality rates among Jews in Israel. Research comparing religious and secular kibbutzim concludes that there was a distinctly lower mortality rate in religious kibbutzim than in secular kibbutzim for both men and women and at all ages (Kark et al. 1996). Controlling for several possible confounding factors, the research suggests an effect of religiosity. Others suggest that lower death rates characterized the observance of the Sabbath, which is not only a day of rest but a time devoted to social gatherings and family solidarity (Anson and Anson 2001). Again it is not religious ideology that is operative but the social significance of religious behavior. A similar argument has been made with regard to the role of religiosity on fertility (chapter 6; C. Goldscheider 2006).

What about the Jewish-Arab mortality gap? Are there any indications that the political and socioeconomic disadvantages of the Arab Israeli population are associated with higher mortality levels? There is evidence that location—in particular, the high level of Arab residential segregation—is associated with lower government investments in the economic and health infrastructure of the Arab community (Al Haj and Rosenfeld 1990). These structural features are likely to be the key to understanding the continuing mortality gaps between Jews and Arabs in Israel and the inferred discrimination that results.

What about socioeconomic factors among Israeli Arabs? Recent research has attempted to examine the relative importance of socioeconomic factors in Arab and Jewish mortality, linking individual death-record data with the socioeconomic characteristics of the areas. This is a particularly promising avenue of research on mortality, since rich areal data are collected and are available, as are vital-statistics data by area. Although the links between areal and individual data always suffer from the methodological limitations of the "ecological fallacy" (i.e., attributing group characteristics to individuals), the extent of bias is largely a function of the degree of overlap among characteristics. At least for the examination of Jewish and Arab mortality differentials, the areal approach appears relatively unbiased.

Results of recent areal analyses connecting mortality and standard of living for Arabs and Jews in Israel are revealing (Anson 1992; see also Friedlander et al. 1990). The results show the expected positive association between standard of living and life expectancy for the total Israeli population. But this correlation is not characteristic of all subpopulations in Israel. Using a series of areal indicators—including economic measures, quality of housing, labor force, and consumer goods—life-expectancy rates were calculated for both the Jewish and Arab populations, separately for men and women (Anson 1992; Schellekens and Anson 2007). The most intriguing findings of this exercise show that life expectancy among Jews increases as the standard of living improves—that is, the better the economic living conditions, the lower the rate of mortality. Among Arab males, however, life expectancy declines somewhat as the standard of living rises; for Arab women, there is no relationship between life expectancy and measures of the standard of living. In short, the relationship between standard of living and life expectancy is positive for Jews and negative or nonexistent for Arabs.[4]

These findings on mortality point to the health and welfare costs of the areal concentration of the Arab population. Residential segregation of Arabs from Jewish populations is a form of structural discrimination that results in these different levels of mortality. The data suggest that mortality differences between Jewish and Arab populations are unlikely to converge when socioeconomic differences between the populations decrease. There are other factors that need to be considered, probably those specifically associated with the lower niche and disadvantaged position that the Arab population occupies within the stratification system in Israel. Combined with the evidence on the sustained infant and adult mortality gap between Jews and Arabs, these detailed areal data point to the need to consider more directly the geographic segregation of the Arab population in Israel as a key manifestation of the structural inequalities between Jews and Arabs. And by inference, we need to explore the types of structural discrimination experienced by Arab Israelis.

Concluding Observations

Several conclusions and inferences can be drawn from this broad overview of mortality trends and variation in Israeli society. First, the major declines in mortality rates in Israel reflect the concerted policies of bringing public-health practices and medical care to the wide range of persons who were populating Israeli society. These policies were extremely successful in the process of nation-building, particularly when judged by how swiftly and how extensively mortality rates declined. Second, the mortality reductions affected all groups, but not equally or instantaneously, since groups of immigrants brought with them differential health practices and exposures to disease from countries of origin. They also brought with them different resources that provided initial access to the emerging and burdened health system in the early period of mass immigration. The national health and welfare system that was developing led to the rapid reduction of mortality rates of those whose mortality levels were high by Western standards, whose resources were not sufficient to purchase medical care, and whose living circumstances were less conducive to the prevention of illness. As a result, the wide discrepancies in infant, child, and adult mortality rates that characterized the society at the early stages of its development have diminished.

Third, contemporary cross-sectional differences in the mortality patterns of the Jewish population tend to be locational and contextual and, to some extent, socioeconomic. Hence, these differences in mortality levels are unlikely to be the direct effects of discriminatory inequalities of the first order but are the indirect effects of geographic and social-class characteristics of groups, which have consequences for mortality variation. The overlap of ethnicity and location (and, to a lesser extent, socioeconomic status) appears to be salient for an understanding of ethnic differences in mortality rates among Jews.

Fourth, the two patterns for Jewish Israelis—ethnic convergences and minimum residual differences that are not socioeconomic and locational—are not characteristic of the Arab-Jewish comparison. Moslems and Druze in Israel continue to have significantly higher levels of infant and adult mortality and have less access to health systems, quality health care, and prevention than do Israeli Jews. The higher Arab than Jewish mortality and morbidity rates reflect the costs of locational constraints (i.e., segregation). Arab mortality levels do not improve systematically with improvement of their socioeconomic environment. Hence, the analysis of Arab Israeli mortality cannot be understood in the same framework used to understand mortality changes among Jewish ethnic groups. The Jewish-Arab mortality gap has remained wide, despite reductions in mortality rates over time, and the socioeconomic environment has a different impact on Jewish and Arab populations in Israel.

The continuing differential mortality patterns between Jews and Arabs have consequences for differences in population growth. The higher Moslem than Jewish mortality rates in the past have led to much more rapid differential population growth among Jews than would have occurred had mortality levels been similar. The transition from high to low mortality levels and the mortality convergences among ethnic groups have removed mortality from being a major factor in the different demographic profiles of ethnic populations in Israel. But mortality variations have much broader social significance than demographic growth rates.

Mortality changes over time in Israel have resulted in its classification as among the most demographically developed countries of the world. This is surprising only because Israel has incorporated within its population a wide range of Jewish immigrants from diverse countries of origin, many of them from areas characterized as places of high mortality. The low level of mortality among European-origin Jews is expected, given their origins; the low mortality characteristic of Israel as a whole when it was established is also not particularly striking, given that 85% of the Jewish population at that time originated from European countries. What is surprising is the rapid mortality reduction among immigrants from high-mortality areas. They were integrated demographically upon arrival in Israel, and their mortality levels declined rapidly and dramatically. It is likely that, within a relatively short period of time, the immigrants from Ethiopia who arrived in Israel in the 1990s with higher levels of morbidity and relatively low life expectancies compared to the Israeli population will begin to approach the long life expectancies and low levels of infant mortality characteristic of the rest of Israel's population.

Although some differential mortality patterns remain in the Jewish population of Israel, they are relatively minor and revolve around levels that are genuinely low, comparatively and historically. To the extent that one examines the efficacy of government policy, it becomes clear that the health and welfare system in Israel along with its entitlements has had a major positive impact on the trend toward an equalization of health and welfare among the various segments of the Israeli Jewish population.

At the same time, it is likely that the geographic separation of Arabs in Israel resulted in their continued higher levels of infant and adult mortality. Government policy was designed to bring about a demographic transformation for all the citizens of the state and to provide equal access to health and welfare for all segments. But other policies that were designed for a variety of political and social objectives have affected the health and mortality patterns of Arab Israelis. As a result, mortality levels of Arabs in Israel have not been reduced to the same extent as the Jewish levels, and the mortality gap between these populations has remained significant. Had there been no policy to bring modern health care to Arab Israelis, their levels of infant and adult mortality would have been much higher; had there been equal treatment of Arabs and Jews and greater residential integration and fuller availability of health services, differential mortality between Jews and Arabs would have diminished even more quickly.

Mortality reduction has improved the quality of Israeli life, and death has become a rare event, concentrated among older persons. Casualties among young adults in the armed forces, however, remain a powerful symbol in Israel and have directly affected a significant number of Israeli families and neighborhoods. War and continuous army service take their toll on the lives of Jews. Among the younger adult population, the major causes of death are war-related or involve accidents on the road.

The significance of mortality reduction on population growth is straightforward. Its importance extends to family structure, fertility, and migration. In particular, reductions in mortality are likely to be among the factors that have influenced fertility changes in Israel, as the rising survival rates of infants have placed an economic burden on large families. In turn, the resulting reduction in fertility may have increased the likelihood of survival of children and women. The influence of mortality on family patterns, on relationships between parents and children, and on the norms associated with the household roles of men, women, and children require extensive study. The impact of mortality on the structure of households and their changing composition requires new and challenging research.

NOTES

1. The relationship between mortality levels and economic development is a classic illustration of asymmetry. All areas with high levels of development have low mortality levels, but all areas of low mortality do not have high levels of development. The key to the paradox is the transferability of public health and technology between areas and its direct impact on mortality.

2. These overall data for Moslems in the Palestine and Israeli periods are conservative estimates because of the high rate of out-migration of the Moslem middle classes from Palestine around 1948 and the retention in Israel of the less-advantaged Moslem population. See the discussion of these selective out-migration patterns in chapter 5. For somewhat different estimates of the general pattern of mortality decline during the early period, see Bachi 1977; Friedlander, Eisenbach, and Goldscheider 1979.

3. This lack of evidence of institutional discrimination against Jews of different ethnic groups does not mean that there are no differences in the quality of health care or in health-care attitudes and practices. Instead, it is argued that these ethnic differences do not result in mortality differences that extend beyond socioeconomic and locational factors. Concerning general health patterns in Israel, see Shuval 1992; Schellekens and Anson 2007.

4. Even a casual examination of infant mortality rates by area points in the same direction. There is a considerable areal variation in Arab infant mortality rates in Israel, with Arab rates higher in rural areas. In contrast, there is almost no systematic areal variation in infant mortality among Jews. Indeed, rural Jewish populations tend to have the lowest infant mortality rates. Areal variation, in this case, reflects both differential availability of medical and health services and differential access to areas nearby that have such services.

10 | Family Formation and Generational Continuities

Families are the building blocks of social organization. In obvious ways, families reproduce and socialize the next generation in the values and lifestyles of the community. They are sources of both comfort and conflict, of generational continuity and change, of financial support and the transmission of values; and they are the basis of the social and economic networks that adults share. Family life places the next generation in adult roles, educates children about assuming responsibilities in the community, and fosters family and socially related obligations. Families provide support and networks that are economic and political, as well as social and personal.

The formation of new families is among the most significant transitions young adults make in becoming fuller members of their community. These transitions are marked by ceremonies and rituals, providing public and social recognition of new families in the community. Newly separated from their families of origin and independent of the full constraints of their parents and their parents' household, new families are nevertheless linked to the past and form family-based connections. These transitions may be viewed as linkages among families in which new relationships develop for the couple, for their parents and relatives, for broader family networks, and, in turn, for the community. Because these linkages are often economic and social, cultural and political, they redefine the integration of the individuals within the community. In these ways, family patterns reflect the broader societies of which they are a part and shape those societies as new generations develop and new families are formed.

Marriage and Family

Like families elsewhere, Israeli families are characterized by family transitions that are consistent with the changing contexts of society. The mixture of persons in Israel from very different societies, with concomitantly different family backgrounds, sets up the basis for family transformations consistent with these new social, economic, political, and cultural contexts. The radical societal changes that Israel has experienced since the 1950s, along with the integration of immigrants from diverse countries of origin and the continuing differentiation in Israel of ethnic communities, raise two questions about family change and continuity. First, how have social, demographic, economic, and cultural changes influenced Israeli family patterns? Second, how are family changes linked to the integration of ethnic groups and the narrowing of family differences among those coming from diverse families of origin?

The family life course from birth to death is experienced very differently by persons of different social and cultural backgrounds who are exposed to a rapidly changing society. The overall dramatic shifts in mortality and the fertility experienced by Israeli society imply that more adults in Israel grow up with surviving parents and grandparents, with the possibility of more-extensive generational relationships, vertically and horizontally. The reduction in fertility results in fewer siblings in smaller families, placing greater individual responsibilities on children to care for the older generation and creating a very different milieu in the parental household. Given the same general investments, smaller families mean more attention to individual children, and, at the same time, there are fewer years in which the household contains parents and children.

These changes also place strains on marriages. The reduction in mortality implies that marriages have the potential of lasting more years and involving more-intensive relationships, which in turn may lead to strains and possible dissolution. The shorter span of the life course when there are young children living in the household is likely to have an impact on the economic roles of men and women. As the state replaces the family in providing some of the care for older and less-healthy persons while also fulfilling some of their social obligations, the welfare system also replaces some family responsibility for the education and socialization of children. With the extension of life, the reduction of family size, and the myriad structural changes that ensue, critical questions emerge: What happens to family values? Do these radical social and demographic changes carry with them the cost of greater emphasis on the individual to the detriment of the family? Do the benefits accompanying structural changes in the extension of life and the reduction of family size outweigh the costs to the family?

Changes in family structure have an impact on the decisions about whether, when, and whom to marry. In some ways, marriage is often the step toward independence from the family of origin but also is likely to be the basis of forming new family linkages, with both the family of origin and the spouse's family. Moreover, the timing of marriage is linked to education and work roles and to other sources of independence. Who one marries is important as it relates to connections to family extensions and to networks for the couple as well as for their children. A focus on independence from family and on family extensions connects to broader issues of communities and their cohesiveness.

There are two revolutions confronting the family at the end of the twentieth century (F. Goldscheider and Waite 1991). The first is internal to the family and involves a change in gender roles, increasing the participation of women in the paid labor force outside the home and challenging the traditional separation of male and female activities. The second revolution involves reductions in family living and increases in living alone and in settings where individual worth and dignity are not associated with family roles. This chapter assesses changes in the marriage and childbearing regimes and alternatives as expressed in living arrangements among young adults. Marriage across ethnic boundaries informs us further about the social integration of families and the family networks that are established and reinforced, hence about the relative assimilation of ethnic groups. As part of our analysis, we explore a firmer answer to the question of how familistic Israelis are and infer how important family connections are in the changes that have enveloped the society over time.

Family Formation Extent and Timing

At what age do Israeli men and women start new families? Are there major ethnic differences in these family formation patterns among Jews and between Jews and Arabs? The available data portray almost universal exposure to marriage. Over 85% of the women and over 80% of the men in Israel have been married by ages 35–39, and most by age 30. Men marry at later ages than women, but almost everyone (95% of the population) has been or will be married at least once during his or her lifetime. Marriage is thus the normative life-course experience in Israel, with but minor exceptions.

When the data in 2011 are reviewed in a life-course perspective, they display the movement from almost universal singlehood in the 15–19 age group to almost universal marriage by later adulthood. Marriage rates increase slowly among those ages 20–24, more for women than for men, toward a gradual equalization of levels among men and women. There is little teenage marriage among all groups in Israel; fully 90% of Moslem women ages 15–19 have not yet married. By ages 20–24, 49% of the Moslem women had never married compared to 78% of Jewish women. While 64% of the Jewish Israeli men were single at ages 25–29, only 45% of the Moslem men were still single.

The evidence supports the conclusion that family-formation patterns have changed substantially toward the later timing of marriage, but they have changed little in terms of eventual family formation. During five decades of major demographic change (1961–2011), the proportion of young Jewish adults ages 20–24 who are single has increased. In 1961, 34% of the women and 74% of the men in their early twenties were single; by 2011, the proportions had increased to almost 80% of the women and 90% of the men. The postponement of marriage has been more dramatic for women than for men and, hence, the gender gap in singlehood has narrowed considerably. These changes over time for the Jewish population are consistent with the increase in schooling and military obligations, both extending young-adult dependency on parents further into adulthood. Nevertheless among those ages 30–34 in the first decade of the twenty-first century, 80% of the Jewish women and over 70% of the Jewish men in Israel have been married.

These patterns of singlehood are reflected in the changing median age at marriage, which has increased among Jewish women and Jewish men since 1970 as Israelis participated in the baby and marriage booms characteristic of Western societies.[1] In 2005–2011 the median age at marriage was 28 for Jewish grooms and 26 for Jewish brides. Three decades earlier in 1980 the median age of marriage for Jewish grooms was 25 and 22 for Jewish brides. Over time, groups from all ethnic origins have moved toward a new "Israeli" pattern of marriage timing and a considerable narrowing of Jewish ethnic differences in this regard.

The ages of marriage of Moslem Israeli men and women have also become later, although more slowly and at earlier ages than among Jews. Christian Arab women marry on average much later than do Moslems; Christian men marry significantly later than either Moslem or Jewish men. The pattern of Druze women and men is very similar to that of Israeli

Moslems: There is a five-year age gap between brides and grooms of the three non-Jewish Israeli groups, twice as high as the age gap between Jewish brides and grooms.

Most Israeli Jews (56%) report that the ideal age to start a family is between 25–29 for men, and almost as many say the same for Jewish women (49%); most Israeli Arabs (63%) agree that the ideal age for men to start a family is 25–29 but 20–24 for women (62%). Religiosity is a key differentiator of the ideal age to start a family among Israeli Jews: 88% of the *haredim* (the ultraorthodox) consider the ideal age for men to start a family is before 25 compared to 42% of the *datim* (religious), 10% of the *mesortim* (traditional), and 5% of the *helonim* (secular).[2] Fully one-third of the secular see the ideal age for starting a family as 30 or older, compared to less than a quarter of those defined as traditional and almost none of the religious. The ideal age for a Jewish woman to marry follows the same pattern by religiosity but at somewhat younger ages.[3]

Familism, Divorce, and Living Arrangements

Taken together, data on the extent and timing of marriage suggest the normative condition of marriage and, indirectly, the family centeredness of Israeli society. Clearly, new families are being formed in Israel almost universally, even as the timing of marriage is changing. As marriage timing extends later into the adult life course, there is an increased potential for dependence on parents for a longer period of time and an increase in time available for living in a nonfamily context. Getting married may be viewed as one indicator of the value placed on families; the changing level of divorce and the extent of nonfamily living arrangements are two additional indicators that support this assessment:

Divorce. Although the divorce rate in Israel is relatively low by U.S. standards, an increase in divorce is well documented. Since the mid-1950s, the number of divorces has increased in Israel from about 2,100 per year to 3,100 in the mid-1970s and to over 13,000 in 2011 (over 10,000 of which are among Jewish Israelis). The increasing numbers reveal the spread of the divorce experience among larger numbers of persons but do not indicate the relative rate per population. A calculation of crude divorce rates per 1,000 population also shows an increase, from an average of 1.0 to 1.7 per 1,000 over the five-decade period to 2011. There has been a doubling of the divorce rate from 1961 to 2011 among Jewish men and women ages

17 to 49. Since the early 1970s, the rate of divorce among Moslem men and women has also more than doubled, and the number of divorces among non-Moslem Arabs in Israel is very low. Thus, although divorce is increasing in Israel, the low level further supports the argument of the continued family centeredness of Israeli society.[4]

Living Arrangements. Two indicators of strong family ties—the high levels of marriage and low rates of divorce—are consistent with an assessment of changing living-arrangement patterns in Israel. Most unmarried persons live in family settings, with marriage marking the transition from one family setting to the next, and with the incorporation of a widowed parent into a family-based household. The extension of life and the increase in age at marriage have not resulted in large proportions of people living independently. Compared to the United States and to other Western countries, there has not been a conspicuous growth of nonfamily living in Israel.[5] In the last decades these patterns have begun to slowly change. The percentage of cohabiting Jewish couples that were unmarried doubled from 2.5% in 2000 to 5% in 2011, and a large majority (69%) of the unmarried couples living together are childless.

Recent research on cohabitation in the twenty-first century documents the increasing level of unmarried cohabitation among Jewish Israelis who define themselves as secular or traditional. This is particularly the case as a prelude to marriage. Over three-fourths of the secular-identified Jews support cohabitation among the unmarried and 83% support premarital cohabitation. Only about one-fourth of the *datiim* (religiously identified) are supportive of cohabitation among the unmarried and few among the ultraorthodox are supportive. Religious women are less likely to postpone marriage or experience alternative nonfamily living arrangements. Moslem women in Israel closely resemble the ultraorthodox in this regard (Bystrov 2012, table 2).

There has been a slow increase in the proportion of households containing only one person: only 10% of the Jewish households in 1960 were one-person households, and this percentage doubled in 50 years. There has been little or no increase among Arabs. Clearly, the Israeli level of nonfamily living is below that of Western European countries (where it is about 25% of all households) but above that of many other parts of the world (see F. Goldscheider and C. Goldscheider 1989, 1994). In the early 1970s, most unmarried adults in Israel lived with their families until they were married, and marriage was the major passage to independence. But this has been changing over time. At the other end of the life course, there were 753,000 Israeli Jews over age 65 living in households in 2011. Of these, 24.4% were living alone; 14% of the older Arab population were living alone (Okun 2013).

Research has shown that there is some ethnic variation in living arrangements in Israel. Moslems are least likely to live in nonfamily households, Jews of Asian and African origins are next, and those of European/ American origins are most likely to live in nonfamily households. This ethnic pattern does not appear to be the result of education, life cycle, or the marital status factors that differentiate these communities. There were no generational differences within the ethnic categories, suggesting that the length of stay or experience in Israeli society had little effect on this dimension of ethnic differences in family and kinship ties. Differences among ethnic categories are therefore not due to differences in economic resources or life-cycle factors that differentiate these communities (F. Goldscheider and Fisher 1989); they are consistent with ethnic differences in familism and the association of living alone with greater independence and individualism. This too seems to be changing, and ethnic differences seems to be narrowing among the second and third generations.

Families and Assimilation
Ethnic Families and Intermarriages

The familistic context of Israeli society implies the importance of family-based networks for social and economic activities. One source of these family networks is the ties that are formed within communities through marriage. An examination of changes over time in who marries whom in Israel helps us to understand the family connections associated with marriage choices and, in particular, changes in the extent of marriages within ethnic communities.

Intermarriage across ethnic lines may be understood in terms of two interrelated themes. First, and most obviously, marrying across ethnic communities reflects the assimilation and integration of populations of different ethnic origins. Isolated ethnic communities that do not have social contacts with each other are unlikely to experience high rates of intermarriage. A second theme emphasizes the linkages through marriage of two different extended families. Interethnic marriage may be viewed as the breakdown of the ethnic family based on networks and an increase in broader community and national allegiances. Increasing levels of interethnic marriages imply greater independence and autonomy of couples from their family origins. Intermarriage rates have often been interpreted as a prime indicator of the breakdown of the family, or increases in individual decision making toward the maximization of personal choice.

Intermarriage among ethnic groups counterbalances tendencies toward ethnic particularism and the reinforcement of ethnic communities. Marriage patterns are structural dimensions of social life that most clearly and directly appear to be linked to ethnic continuity. The incidence of interethnic and intraethnic marriages reflects and affects ethnic continuity. In a system of choices, persons who interact are likely to develop a relationship that may result in marriage. Hence, the greater the isolation of ethnic groups, the greater the barriers to social interaction across ethnic groups and the lower likelihood that interethnic marriages will occur. The higher the rate of interethnic marriages, the more likely that the family networks of ethnic groups will be reduced, leading generationally to further interethnic marriages. Indeed, intermarriage has often been viewed as the quintessential indicator of ethnic assimilation; at the group level, it is associated with the path to the ethnic melting pot.

By implication, ethnic communities are not able to sustain social and cultural continuity in the face of high levels of interethnic marriage. The argument has been made that by the third or fourth generation of ethnic intermarriages the identity and the culture, the in-group interaction and the networks, have become so mixed that ethnic origin no longer is salient.

Although the power of intermarriage to dilute and diminish ethnicity is clear, we should be cautious about overinterpreting intermarriage rates and their changes over time. First, individuals can move into and out of ethnic communities, reducing the salience of ethnicity for them as individuals, even as the community as a whole retains a core with greater commitment to ethnic continuity. The selective out-marriage of those who are more marginal to the ethnic group may result in a core remnant of ethnic-group members who are even more ethnically committed. Although it may seem counterintuitive, intermarriage may actually strengthen ethnic communities over time if those who leave are the most marginal ethnically and if those who remain are core sources of social and cultural continuity.

A second caution relates to the assumption that the intermarriage rate itself is an indicator of the total assimilation of groups (as viewed by Gordon 1963; Alba 1990; Alba and Nee 2005; and many others who have studied ethnic assimilation). The key question left unspecified is how the children of interethnically married persons view themselves and how they are viewed by the various communities with which they identify. If children of the intermarried identify themselves in terms of the ethnic group of one of their parents, then the ethnic identity of that group is not diminished. There is, of course, the possibility that interethnic marriage would result in strengthening neither origin group but rather the formation of a new ethnic group—broader than the original groups but containing some of the elements of both. Some interethnic marriages in Israel have resulted in the formation (and perhaps the reinforcement) of new ethnic divisions among Jews, the result of some types of marriages and not others. Marriages between Jews of Russian and Argentine origins in Israel or between those of Yemenite and Moroccan origins would fit the newly formed categories of "European-American" and of "Asian-African" that have emerged (see chapter 2).

A third caution is the assumption that increases in the rate of intermarriage mean the growth of individual choice over family preferences. The emphasis on choices that individuals make often excludes consideration of the constraints on the options available. Often there are limits on the availability of potential spouses within the market of eligible spouses. The selection of spouses from an ethnic group is based first and foremost on availability. If there are few potential spouses to choose from, then spouses can be selected from a different ethnic origin, if they are defined within the field of eligible partners. To the extent that markets of eligible spouses contract and expand with waves of immigration and with the age, gender, and marital-status composition of specific ethnic communities, marriage markets are likely to change rapidly. For example, if there are very few immigrants from Argentina in Israel of the appropriate age, gender, and marital status, the choice of an Argentine marriage partner will be severely constrained, unless the field of eligible spouses is expanded to include a wider range of potential partners from other Latin American countries or from other ethnic origins. The interethnic-marriage issue, then, involves not only whether young adults "choose" persons from other ethnic origins but also whether there are persons available from similar origins to select from.

Another option for those who cannot find a spouse within their own ethnic group and who do not widen the range of eligible spouses is to remain unmarried. If judged by the marriage patterns in Israel, this more-radical alternative (nonmarriage) has been selected by few. Indeed, Israelis faced with a narrowing market of potential spouses of their own ethnic origins have almost always chosen to expand the pool of eligible spouses to include those of other ethnic origins.[6] This ethnic-marital choice has been reinforced by the Zionist Israeli ideology, which challenges the legitimacy of ethnic origins among the Israeli-born (see chapter 2). Marriages between those of different ethnic origins have been actively encouraged by the national ideology in Israel (Rosen 1982). Interethnic marriage in Israel may be viewed under some circumstances as a trade-off between familism and ethnic continuity. In the clash between the values placed on ethnic community (with marriage-market constraints) and family formation, the overwhelming majority of Israelis appear to select family values.[7]

The Increase in Interethnic Marriages

Overall rates of ethnic out-marriages show clear increases over time. By the end of the 1980s, about 20% of the Jewish marriages in Israel were between those of different ethnic origins. The level has remained relatively steady over the past several decades (Okun 2013). Census data on first- and second-generation couples married in Israel who were in their first marriage (Eisenbach 1989) show an increase in intermarriage by marriage cohort; interethnic marriages increased from 8% in the 1949–1953 period to 22% in the 1979–1983 period. In part, this increase reflects changes in the composition of the population—the increase in the proportion of Asian/ Africans in the marriageable age group from about 36% in the early 1950s to about 62% in the 1980s. This compositional shift accounts for increases (from the 1960s to the 1980s) in the proportion marrying out among European/Americans (from 16% to 32%). The proportions marrying out remained at a rather steady level among Asian/Africans (about 16%). In the 1949–1953 marriage cohort, 80% of women of African origin married men from Africa; 81% of Asian women married men from Asia; and 95% of European women married European men. In the 1979–1983 cohort, these figures were 59%, 57%, and 73%, respectively (Eisenbach 1992, table A.2).

Viewed another way, the proportion out-married of those married in Israel (defined dichotomously as Asian/African and European/American) was 5% until 1945, increasing to 9% from 1946 to 1955, to 13% from 1956 to 1961, to 18% from 1964 to 1973, and to 21% from 1974 to 1983 (Schmelz et al. 1990). In each cohort, and for both husbands and wives, the Israeli born have a higher ethnic out-marriage rate than the foreign born. However, there is a great deal of specific country-of-origin variation in the extent of ethnic homogamy. Thus, for those marrying in the period from 1974 to 1983, higher rates of in-marriage characterize Jews from Yemen, India, Morocco, and the USSR, compared to Turkey, Egypt, Germany, and Austria. These differences reflect the size of the marriage market and the recency of immigration, as well as the strength of the communal-ethnic ties and cultural-family relationships that have characterized some groups (C. Goldscheider 1983; Schmelz, Dellapergola, and Avner 1990).

An interesting exploration of these patterns of ethnic homogamy can be organized by examining data on the ethnic origins of Israeli couples in 2012. Using broad continent-of-origin definitions of ethnicity, about half of the men whose continent of origin was Africa were living with women whose continent of origin was Africa (and another 20% were living with women from Asian countries). Over 70% of men of European origin were living with women of European origin. In this context, the majority of Israel's population lived in ethnically homogamous households in 2012. This is a minimum measure since part of the difficulty with these data is the category "Israel" as a continent of origin where ancestry or ethnic origin has not been specified. Thus, while 40% of the American-origin households are homogamous, adding European-origin households increases the homogamy to 74%. Of the women not in European/American homogamously defined households, most are in households with third-generation "Israeli" men. It is likely that the overwhelming majority of these are from European origins.

The major conclusion from these data is a clear pattern of ethnic homogamy, redefined by broad continents of origin rather than specific countries and recategorized into Israeli-defined groups. Research in general shows a modest increase in interethnic marriages but the retention of broadly defined ethnic homogamy. When each ethnic group's total number of homogamous married couples is compared with those who were married since 1996 (and living in Israel in 2012), the evidence shows that African homogamous households declined from 55 to 43%; the Asian from 52 to 27%, and the European from 71 to 60%. Again the decline in homogamous households is evident, with the retention of homogamy for broad ethnic groups in Israel.

The increasing level of intermarriage across ethnic groups directs our attention to the question of the characteristics of those who marry within their own ethnic group compared to those who out-marry. One of the most fascinating results of recent analyses of interethnic marriages in Israel is the educational selectivity of the intermarried among different ethnic-origin groups. These ethnic-education trade-offs are quite complex. The notion that intermarriage between those from different ethnic origins results in an ethnic melting pot is grossly oversimplified without taking into account these trade-offs. And, unfortunately, the available evidence is weakest when intergenerational questions are raised. Even with weak evidence, there is a reasonable case to be made that some ethnic inter-marriages in Israel result in the strengthening of ethnic communities. Children of mixed ethnic origin can primarily select the ethnic group of one of the parents, adopt neutrality with regard to ethnic origin, remain committed to both ethnic sides of the family, or vary ethnic identity with context and with changes over the life cycle. These choices mean that only if ethnicity loses its salience in the family and community senses can we expect ethnic intermarriages to result in the reduced significance of eth-nic origins generationally. There are indications at the community and socioeconomic levels that such a diminution of ethnic salience is un-likely, at least for the next generation in Israel (cf. Okun 2004; Okun and Khait-Marelly 2008).

What does the limited evidence reveal about these trade-offs? The most significant finding is that interethnic marriages are more likely among the Middle Eastern–origin ethnic populations with higher educational levels, but are more likely among Western-origin groups with lower educational levels. The proportion out-marrying in the Middle Eastern–origin group increases with education, and it declines with education in the West-ern-origin group (Eisenbach 1992; Schmelz, Dellapergola, and Avner 1990; C. Goldscheider 2002).

No less important, the decline of place-of-origin endogamy also re-flects the erosion of ethnicity as a central axis of social organization in the Jewish population (Matras 1986, 32, 38). Others have made a similar argument that "the high rate of ethnic intermarriage reflects ethnic con-vergences and at the same time contributes to further integration in the future" (Peres and Katz 1991, 30). Using a special file that linked records from the 1995 and the 1983 censuses of Israel, Okun has explored for the first time the marriage behavior of persons of mixed ethnic ancestries. She finds that persons of mixed ethnic ancestry are less ethnically endogamous than other groups, which contributes to ethnic blending and to the blurring of ethnic boundaries. Using a complex statistical model examining ethnic-educational trade-offs, she suggests that ethnic distinctiveness is reinforced in these marriages. In particular, marriage patterns of those of mixed ancestry increase the association between low socioeconomic status and Asian/African identity (Okun 2004).

Some supportive evidence among high school students in Israel reinforces the notion of specific ethnic-origin preferences among those who will marry in the next generation. Israeli-born Jewish young adults of Israeli-born parents raised with egalitarian and liberal attitudes toward ethnicity express very ethnic-based attitudes about their own ethnic preferences in spouse selection and have fairly strong negative views about specific ethnic origins. Those of Middle Eastern origin are more likely to view others of Middle Eastern origin (not necessarily of their specific country of origin but the Israeli-constructed category of "Oriental") as preferable potential spouses and partners over "Europeans" or Westerners (Shahar 1991).

There is every basis for arguing the continuing salience of ethnicity in the next generations because of the overlap of ethnic residential patterns and education and occupational patterns with ethnic origin, along with implications for socialization and politics. Ethnicity in Israel is not simply the reflection of closeness to cultural roots; it is the lack of socioeconomic equalization among groups that has characterized Jewish ethnic subpopulations. Family, economic, and religious networks have served to reinforce family ties and ethnic communities based on family ties. The shape ethnicity will take in the long term will depend in large part on the continuing overlap of ethnicity and social class, residence, and culture in the next generation. Religiosity, which has served as a major dividing line among Israeli Jews, may reinforce ethnic variation as well (chapter 6).

A general review of the evidence in Israel suggests two conclusions. First, interethnic marriages have increased over time; and second, higher interethnic-marriage rates among Jews do not, in and of themselves, imply the demise of ethnic communities. These conclusions parallel those pertaining to the narrowing of ethnic differences in other areas of Israeli social life. While increases in interethnic marriages in Israel do not indicate total ethnic-group assimilation, they are consistent with the changing definition of Jewish ethnicity. Ethnic differences that primarily reflected past origins diminished as Israeli institutions and Israeli contexts shaped immigrant groups and their children. Institutions, such as the army and the system of ethnically integrated schooling, operated to reinforce national allegiances and collectively shared culture. However, family centrality helped sustain ethnic continuity and reinforced ethnic communities based on residential patterns. Stable rates of intermarriage and the educational and ethnic trade-offs, along with uncertainty of how children of mixed ethnic origins will select their own ethnic communities over their life course, point to the continuing salience of ethnicity for several generations.

The ethnic options available to the next generation of the interethnically married may help to solve the ethnic-origin dilemma of these children. Their generational choices are to select an ethnic origin of one of the parents or retain the combined mixture of Western and Middle Eastern origins. The latter combination is possible, but the evidence suggests that it is not a viable alternative (Okun 2004).

The second generation of mixed ethnic origins could become "just" Israeli and treat ethnicity as irrelevant. Those of mixed origins might select this option while retaining some relationship to grandparents or other extended relatives who are ethnically identified. Members of the mixed third generation are most likely to respond to a question about their ethnic identity by identifying themselves as "Israeli," but that may not be sufficiently clear as a basis for networking or for identity in all circumstances, even though it solves the confusion of the moment. Networks based on ethnicity are not simply the result of the social psychology of personal identity. The option of individuals identifying themselves only as "Israeli" is most likely to occur when ethnicity at the group level loses its family and social-class importance.

The revolutions in family patterns in Israel are surprising—not because of the changes that have occurred but because of the continuities in family centrality despite major changes. Family has remained normative for almost everyone in Israel. Radical demographic and social changes have not moved persons toward nonfamily alternatives, either nonmarriage or extensive nonfamily living arrangements. Delayed marriage, which is responsive to the social, economic, educational, and political contexts among all ethnic origin groups in Israeli society, becomes marriage postponed but not forgone. Changes both in the proportion married and in the age at which persons marry reveal important ethnic convergences and join the converging ethnic differences in other areas as powerful indications of some forms of the national integration of ethnic groups.

Family connections must serve economic needs, provide comfort and support of children and grandchildren, and provide social and political connections in order to be sustained in the face of the major demographic and social upheavals Israel has experienced. It is the structural connections to families, not the "value" placed on the family, that have shaped these types of family continuities. Family continuities in Israel are one basis of continuities in ethnic communities. Ethnicity and family issues revolve around generations and around the transmission of community and culture, of rights and obligations, and of continuity and social networks. Together families and ethnicity provide the building blocks for the next generation of Israeli families.

The Transition to Small Family Size
The Fertility Revolution and Ethnic Convergences

One of the revolutions associated with the modernization of Western societies has been the transition from large to small family size. This transition has been linked to the changing roles of women, to the increasing investment parents make in their children, and to the higher costs of raising them. It has also been related to the greater ability of couples to implement their reproductive decisions. Indeed, the revolutionary changes in fertility levels are one manifestation of the increasing range of choices that accompanies modernization and the higher value placed on individual rather than family goals (C. Goldscheider 1992, 2006). An examination of changing fertility levels in Israel provides insight into the linkages among our themes of inequality, familism, and ethnicity.

Fertility levels, in conjunction with mortality, are primary sources of population growth; with the decline in mortality in Israel, fertility levels have shaped rates of overall population growth and have become sources of differential ethnic-population growth rates. Given the importance of population growth for economic planning and development, govern-

ments have often fostered policies to enhance fertility control and to provide maternal and child-welfare services to emphasize the quality of life
over the number of children. Fertility-control policies in Israel have often
clashed with pro-natalist Zionist ideologies and Israeli norms, which valued the increase of Jewish population through diverse means—primarily
by way of immigration but also through sustained large family size (see the
historical review in Friedlander and Goldscheider 1979).

Powerful linkages between immigration and the differential fertility of
ethnic-origin populations raise questions about the demographic assimilation of groups among Jews and between Jews and Arabs as well. Through
the combined effects of immigration and differential fertility, the ethnic
composition of Israel has been transformed. Generational continuity of
ethnic communities is dependent on childbearing and intraethnic marriages. The study of the transition to smaller family size is therefore important for its demographic relevance, for what it implies about individual
gender and family roles, and for its relevance to the structure and composition of communities over time. Because of the links between family size,
generational replacement, and social mobility, the decline in fertility level
has been used as a prime indicator of the advantage (or continuing disadvantage) of subpopulations and of the relative integration of immigrant
groups from different fertility backgrounds.

Similar to other countries, Israel has experienced fertility reductions
over time and the transition to small family size; fertility changes have
occurred in more-compressed time periods in Israel than elsewhere and
without direct government intervention. Moreover, significant fertility
variation has characterized major ethnic subgroups in Israel in the past
and is likely to continue to have implications for social, economic, political, and demographic processes into the next decades.

Changing Fertility Patterns over Time

What have been the major changes in fertility and family size in Israel?
A careful and detailed look at fertility patterns in Israel since the 1950s reveals several major revolutions, not one simple pattern. The fertility level
of Israelis of European/American origins has fluctuated, though it has remained near lower levels, with slight increases over time. In contrast, there
has been a steady decline in Christian Arab fertility levels over more than
a half century and a significant reduction in the Moslem Israeli fertility

level since the 1970s. Major fertility reductions have characterized Jewish immigrants from Asian and African countries and their Israeli-born children, dropping by 50% from the 1950s to the 1980s.

Thus, the first fertility pattern that emerges clearly is a reduction in family size over time, fluctuating around low levels of controlled fertility in the new millennium. There has been a decline in the crude birthrate among Jews from 34 per 1,000 population in the 1920s to below 30 per 1,000 in the mid-1950s, to around 20 per 1,000 starting in the late 1980s and continuing through the first decade of the twenty-first century. This rather steady overall decline was, in fact, much sharper than what may appear at first glance, since the decline incorporates immigrant Jewish families arriving in the 1950s from Middle Eastern countries, who were characterized by higher fertility than that of the European-origin Jewish population in Israel.

A second pattern evident in these data is the consistently higher levels of fertility among Moslems than among Jews throughout these seven decades. The Moslem fertility level, overall, has also been high relative to world fertility levels, although the current level is among the lowest of Arab populations in the Middle East. The crude birthrate of Moslems in Palestine was over 50 per 1,000 population in the 1920s, and it continued to fluctuate at high levels until the mid-1970s, when a noticeable decline in Moslem fertility began. The Moslem crude birthrate in Israel in the 1990s averaged 37 per 1,000 population, a level characteristic of the Jewish population in Palestine in the 1920s and comparable to that of many countries in Asia and Africa. In 2012 the crude birthrate of Moslem Israelis was around 28 per 1,000.

The declining fertility over time and the higher Moslem than Jewish fertility level raise the question of the changing gap between these populations in Israel. The crude birthrate gap between Jews and Moslems in Palestine and in Israel increased significantly until the end of the 1960s, and from an 18-point gap (per 1,000) to a 26-point gap in the early 1970s. The increasing differences between Moslem and Jewish birthrates reflect the relative stability of the Moslem level and sharp declines in the crude birthrate among Jews. Since the mid-1970s, the gap between these populations has narrowed considerably as the crude birthrate among Moslems declined and the Jewish rate declined only slightly during the same period.

These three patterns—general fertility-rate declines, higher Moslem than Jewish fertility levels, and the changing fertility gap between those two populations—are derived from simple measures, relating births to total Jewish and Moslem populations rather than to women in their childbearing period. A more-refined measure of fertility (and one that has more-intuitive meaning) is the total fertility rate: the cumulative age-specific pattern of births to women in the childbearing ages.[8] Changes in these rates over time and in other direct fertility measures reveal clearly the overall decline of one child per woman among Israeli families from the mid-1950s until the 1980s, from a total fertility rate of 4 children per woman until 1970 to 3 children per woman during the decades of the 1980s, 1990s, and up to 2010. This decline was quite pronounced among women with larger numbers of births. The proportion of women with 5 or more births declined in Israel from about 25% before 1970 to about 15% in the 1990s. Examining the total fertility rate shows a Moslem fertility decline from over 5 children in the 1980s to around 4.5 children in the 1990s, to 3.6 in the period 2005–2009 (Okun 2013, table A1).

These measures of changing fertility levels over time reinforce the conclusions derived from the crude birthrate data and add details and refinements. For the Jewish population as a whole, there was a decline of 1 child per woman on average (from 3.6 to 2.7 children) during the period from 1955 to the 1990s; the proportion of Jewish women having 5 or more births fell by half, from 24% in 1960 to 13% in the 1990s (the proportion actually dipped below 10% in the 1980s). Impressive fertility shifts occurred among ethnic groups in the Jewish population. Among Israeli Jews born in Asian and African countries, the total fertility rate dropped steadily and dramatically in 40 years—from a total fertility rate of 5.7 children per woman in 1955 to 3.2 in the 1990s. The fertility level of European/American-origin women has been lower and declined only modestly, from 2.6 children per woman in 1955 to 2.3 in the 1990s, having increased to 2.8 children during the 1970s and 1980s.

Fertility convergences among Jewish women of different ethnic origins (and with different fertility histories) have occurred in Israel, even as women of Asian and African origin have retained a somewhat higher level than those of Western or European origin. Convergences mean narrower gaps over time, not necessarily the full closure of differential fertility among all groups.

Fertility Transitions, Immigration, and Jewish Cohorts

The fertility changes that I have described direct attention to the reasons underlying these changes and to the factors that need to be taken into account for their explanation. Research addressing these issues provides the basis for understanding the connections between fertility and social-demographic, economic, and political changes and the changing roles of women and families in the Jewish population.[9] The country of origin of immigrants is associated with their particular socioeconomic backgrounds. European-origin groups have had, and continue to have, low levels of fertility. Jewish immigrants from European countries arriving before the establishment of the state had, on average, 2.3 children over several cohorts, with no fertility differences among people from different places of origin within Europe. Jewish immigrants from Europe who arrived after the establishment of the state had even lower fertility levels, reflecting the effects of the extremely harsh circumstances of World War II on women's reproductive patterns. Recent cohorts of European-origin groups in Israel have experienced about a 10% upswing in fertility (a mini–baby boom), averaging around 2.5 children per married woman. The small increase in fertility characterized all European-origin groups and has resulted in higher levels than that in Western industrialized countries.

Immigration from Asian countries was concentrated in the earlier periods of nation-building. Immigrants from North African countries arrived later and were spread over a large number of years (see chapter 3). Initial levels of fertility among both groups were high—about 6.5 births among those who married in the 1930s (most of whom were married and had children before immigrating to Israel), declining to an average of 3 children among marriage cohorts of the 1950s (most of whom were married and having children in Israel). Fertility levels were almost halved between cohorts 25 years apart, and large family size has been replaced by medium-to-small families. Jewish immigrants from North African countries had higher levels of initial fertility than did Asian immigrants, about 7.5 children per woman. Sharp and early fertility reductions took place for these immigrants upon exposure to Israeli society. These reductions occurred quite soon after arrival in Israel and converged with the patterns for Asian immigrants.

The fertility differences between Asian and African immigrants and among specific country-of-origin groups within these populations reflect differences in the timing of immigration and length of exposure to Israeli society, not cultural differences among groups. As length of exposure to Israeli society increased, these country-of-origin differences in fertility disappeared. Fertility convergences in Israel have occurred within and between Jewish ethnic groups. Israeli-born Jews of Western origin have somewhat higher fertility than their parents' generation; the second generation of Middle Eastern origin has lower fertility than their parents' generation. Cohort fertility patterns are thus converging between Israelis of Western and of Middle Eastern origins.

One puzzling feature of these changes is that the fertility convergences of the second and later generations of Israelis have stabilized at higher levels when compared to those of Western countries generally. Explanations for these higher fertility levels relate to specific economic and military conditions in Israel. The economic conditions in Israel have improved considerably for the Jewish population in the post-1967 period, following the Six Day War. Because of the improvements, births, which had been delayed or postponed because of the socioeconomic hardships of earlier periods (among the children of European immigrants) increased, as did the desire for a third child. But why should the Israeli-born want and have three and not two children on average? It may reflect what demographers have referred to as an "insurance" effect, motivated by Israel's flow of military casualties (Friedlander and Goldscheider 1978). This means that people decide on an additional child as insurance against the risk that war or military action will result in the premature death of one child. Higher fertility levels may thus be a result of the willingness of Israeli Jewish families to allocate more resources, compared to people in Western countries, toward raising a somewhat larger family. The economic circumstances of the late 1960s and 1970s transformed that potential into childbearing. This would account for the fertility increase among all Jewish ethnic groups (and none of the Arab populations) and their fertility convergences.

Other explanations emphasize the familistic orientation of Israeli society and the continuing segregated roles of Israeli women. Unlike in some Western industrialized nations, the employment of women in Israel does not seem to conflict with their family-size goals, nor does it lead to their increased autonomy and status within the family (chapter 7; Kupinsky 1992). The greater familism in Israeli society is thus associated with higher fertility levels in Israel than in Western countries.

Clearly, the contemporary Israeli pattern involves fluctuations around low fertility levels, and there is no indication of a return to larger family size. Most interesting, but less fully documented, are the unfolding fertility patterns among the recent immigrant groups from the former Soviet Union, who have had very low fertility, and immigrants from Ethiopia, who have had higher fertility and mortality. How these groups will develop in Israel will be the social-demographic stories of the twenty-first century (cf. Nahmias 2004).

With increased levels of education among all Jewish ethnic groups, fertility differentials are converging and are likely to converge even further. Indeed, ethnic-origin differences in fertility levels tend to be minimal in the most recent marriage cohorts. As length of exposure to the norms and values of Israeli society and to the institutions that shape the lives of those married and educated in Israel increases, fertility patterns lose their ethnic distinctiveness (Eisenbach 1992). In the past, the convergence in ethnic fertility has often been attributed to the changes and improvements in the level of schooling, the negative association between number of children and investment in children, the increase in interethnic marriages, and a likely convergence of human-capital endowments (Ben-Porath 1986a).

Interesting and important insights into fertility have been derived from Israel's Social Surveys 1979–2009 with links to questions on religiosity (Okun 2013; see chapter 6). Among Jews, religiosity is a significant differentiator of family size. In 2007–2009, the total fertility rate among ultraorthodox women was 6.5 (having declined from over 7 children in the late 1980s through 2005); among the "religious" the total fertility rate was 4.2; the rate among Jews who defined themselves as traditional was less than 2.5, and among secular Jews the rate was just under 2.1 (actually an increase in the rate among the secular from the 1990s). In short there is a direct relationship between religiosity and fertility among Jewish Israelis in each of the time periods considered over a period of three decades. Some have argued that the somewhat higher fertility in Israel compared to other Western countries is primarily the effect of the larger family size of the religious Jewish population (Friedlander and Feldman 1993).

The similar experiences of Israeli young adults and their shared communications in a variety of settings are likely to result in the growing similarity of their family-building and family-size patterns. Commonalities in terms of women's roles, the army, and educational experiences; the smallness of the country; and the national welfare-entitlement system yield some uniform family-formation patterns and shared generational family-size goals. Access to information about controlling family size among the diverse segments of the population influences ethnic fertility convergences over time and helps to explain the family-size decline converging toward a new Israeli norm. Familism, gender-role segregation, and traditional pressures from both Judaism and secular Zionism result in levels of fertility higher than in Western countries in general.

Moslem and Christian Fertility Changes in Israel

In general the fertility of Moslem women declined from around 6 children in the late 1970s to 3.6 in the 2005–2009 period. But the relationship between religiosity and Moslem fertility within each of the five-year periods considered is somewhat erratic and no singular pattern emerges, although there is an unmistakable family-size decline among Moslem women in all religiosity categories. The crude birthrate data documents the slowness of the Moslem fertility reduction and the changes that began to occur in the 1970s. More-detailed data show important variations between the fertility of Moslems and Christians in Israel. Fertility levels among Moslems fell from a high of over 9 children per woman on average in the 1960s to 4.7 children per woman in the 1990s; 50% of the Moslem women had 5 or more births through the 1970s, declining by 50% in the late 1990s. Moslem fertility levels continue to be higher than those among Jews but have clearly moved toward lower levels in recent generations. Processes of Moslem-Jewish fertility convergences are therefore clearly evident.

The Arab population in Israel is clearly not homogeneous in terms of fertility processes. Both the level of fertility and the pace of its reduction differentiate Christian from Moslem Israelis; in turn, the fertility patterns of both populations are different in pace and level from the Jewish ethnic patterns that we described. Nevertheless, convergence toward small family size has become ubiquitous among all groups. The Arab Christian fertility levels are more comparable to the Jewish levels (indeed, their fertility levels have often been below the overall Jewish levels in the 1980s and 1990s). The fertility decline has been more regular among the Christian population, and there are indications that it began among the urban and more-educated women as early as the marriage cohort of the 1920s (see Friedlander, Eisenbach, and Goldscheider 1979). In 1998, the total fertility rate among Arab Christians was 2.6 children per woman (lower than among Asian and African Jewish immigrants, higher than among European/Americans, and slightly below the overall Jewish level of 2.7) compared to 4.8 per woman among Moslems and 3.1 per woman among Druze. Very sharp declines in childbearing among younger Christian Arab women may be noted, as well as the stopping of childbearing at higher parities.

A study of ideal family size by marriage cohort (as viewed in the 1970s) has documented the changing attitudinal and normative expectations of Arab women (C. Goldscheider and Friedlander 1986). Christian women who were married before 1955 had an ideal family size of about 6 children, but the cohort married in the post-1967 period had an average ideal family size of 4 children. Moslem women of the older cohort had an ideal family size of about 8 children, declining among those married in the 1970s to 5 children. In contrast to the Jewish pattern, most of the Moslem women controlled family size after long marriage durations, using contraception for stopping childbearing but not for the spacing of births. In the period since 1975, fertility reductions occurred even among Moslem women at shorter marriage durations and have included all socioeconomic segments of the Arab population, even the less educated (Eisenbach 1989). The total fertility rate for the 1990s (4.7) is similar to the number of children considered ideal by the cohorts of Moslem women married in the late 1960s and early 1970s.

The general factors associated with lower Arab fertility patterns include the continuing declines and low levels of mortality (life expectancy increased to about 73 for both sexes; infant mortality declined from 60 deaths per 1,000 births at the end of the 1950s, to 41 deaths per 1,000 births in 1975, to 15 in 1989, and to 9 in 1999—see chapter 9). In addition, there has been a continuing increase in the educational attainment of Moslem women: those who benefited from the mandatory education act in Israel reached their childbearing period only in the 1970s. Thus, among those women who were married between 1974 and 1978, only 8% had 9 or more years of education, compared to 31% among those who married from 1979 to 1983. The labor-force pattern of Israeli Moslems has also changed. The formal participation of Moslem women in the paid labor force remains lower than that of Christian and Jewish women—but the more-educated Moslem women (13 years or more of schooling) participate in the labor force as much as the Christian Arab women (Eisenbach 1989; Grossbard-Shechtman and Neuman 1998).

Other factors influencing Moslem fertility connect Moslem families to the communities in which they live. There has been a shift in the kind of male employment, tied to the economic "integration" of Arabs in the Jewish economy (chapter 4). Moslem Israelis have left agriculture and commute to jobs in the Jewish sector (in 1983 only 7% of Moslem men worked in agriculture, compared to 18% in 1972 and 35% in 1961; fully half of the Moslem men worked outside their residential areas in the 1980s). The proportion of men working in white-collar jobs was 14% in 1983, double that of a decade earlier. Part, but not all, of the move toward white-collar jobs was facilitated by the entrance into Israel of Arab day laborers from the administered territories, pushing the Israeli Moslems upward socioeconomically. Standards of living have increased in real terms: between 1972 and 1983, the income of Moslem laborers in cities increased by 50%, a 5% per capita increase per year. Consumption has increased as well (Eisenbach 1989; see also chapter 8).

Increases in the standard of living and in education, along with the benefits from the welfare state and the increase in the opportunity structure, suggest that the power of the extended family and the *hamula* has declined,[10] particularly among younger couples whose economic futures are less under the control of their extended families. Thus, from the point of view of the Arab community, fertility is a feature of intergenerational family and economic connections and is an important reflection of the ways Arab Israeli communities are organized. Changes in the decade beginning in the 1970s put pressures on this connection and, combined with socioeconomic increases, led to the beginning of the transition to small family size.

Have state policies been involved in the changing pattern of Arab fertility? The state has provided the opportunity to increase the educational level of the population; the provision of social security organized at the national level has increased the expectations for higher levels of living. Moreover, the state supports families through subsidies and tax benefits; welfare payments through the national insurance system may, in the early years, have prevented an earlier and even sharper fertility decline (see Friedlander, Eisenbach, and Goldscheider 1979). The shift toward smaller families in conjunction with economic trends has steadily eroded the control that the *hamula* exercised over women and the value of children and large family size. These changes have broken the powerful linkage between place of residence, *hamula*, and fertility (Al Haj 1987).

There has been a slight increase in the average age that Moslem women marry, from 19.7 years in 1960 to 20.6 in the 1980s and 1990s. In the period from 1964 to 1968, 34% of those who married were under age 18, compared to 18% among those married from 1979 to 1983. It is estimated that about one-third of the decline in the fertility of Moslem women between 1972 and 1983 can be accounted for by the decline in early marriage (Eisenbach 1989). The relationship between education of women and their age at marriage is U-shaped among Moslems. Both the least educated and the most educated marry later, in part because of the arranged-marriage system wherein women with education are less desirable spouses and women with more education are more likely to delay marriage until after school and some work experience. Thus, when the average age of marriage of Moslem women was 20.6 years, it was 21.7 for those with 0 to 4 years of education and 22.8 years for those with 13 or more years of schooling. Later age at marriage characterizes the Moslem population in the recent period and for each of the levels of education (Eisenbach 1989). The declining Moslem fertility among the younger generation has occurred primarily through the use of contraception to control births within marriage.

Changes in marriage and in the control of fertility within marriage are clearly linked to the major demographic and socioeconomic transitions that have characterized the Moslem Israeli population in the last three decades, and these changes gained momentum in the 1970s and 1980s. Large family size contradicts the emerging tastes associated with higher standards of living and increased education.

The importance of higher Arab than Jewish fertility for differential population growth is unmistakable. The emerging ethnic convergence in fertility levels indicates the end of the sharp fertility gap that has characterized these populations for a century. High fertility rates reflect the traditional family roles of Moslem women, their segregation, lower status, and less power in the society. High fertility has been costly for Arab women and families; it has affected the availability of socioeconomic opportunities for the next generation. In large part, the traditional role of Arab women has almost always been treated as one of the determinants of sustained high fertility levels. The argument has been that unless the status of women changes to nonchildbearing roles, there is little likelihood of a significant change in fertility rates. As a result of this perspective, the theoretical challenge became to understand why the role of Arab Israeli women did not change with the first indication of economic development and why large family size was reinforced by the absence of migration and by state welfare policies (Friedlander, Eisenbach, and Goldscheider 1979; chapter 4).

But gender and family roles are not only causes but also consequences of the size of families. Large family size reinforces the traditional ties of women to households and families and enhances their segregated roles. It takes sustained economic, political, and social-demographic changes to break the cycle so that women (and men) are able to move toward the small-family-size model. Often this sustained break comes with migration (or immigration), when the family is no longer the source of economic reward and family members become less dependent on traditional economic supports. The break between family and economic resources is often facilitated by geographic and social mobility. In the case of Moslem Israelis, the state reinforced the family and economic connection as it sustained a dependency of Arab Israelis on the Jewish economic sector. The absence of Arab geographic mobility resulted in higher levels of dependency at a time when economic and social characteristics would have led to the expectation of greater mobility. Only after sustained changes could the cycle be broken. The longer-term disadvantages of high fertility levels for mobility is clearly emerging for Israeli Arabs, and the role of large family size in sustaining the family-oriented roles of women is clearly weakening.

The Nature and Impact of Fertility Policies

There is no reason to postulate (as some have in the past—see Bachi 1977 and the extensive evaluation in Friedlander and Goldscheider 1979) that Israel will face a demographic "crisis" from the differential population-growth implications of the low fertility levels of Jewish Israelis and the high fertility levels of Arab Israelis. The differential fertility of Jews and Arabs does not translate into differential population-growth rates that result in a "demographic threat" from Arab Israelis or from zero population growth among the Jewish population. The higher-than-average level of Jewish fertility (even not taking into account the powerful and continuous demographic role of Jewish immigration to Israel) and the declining rate of Moslem fertility (even not taking into account their small proportion of the total population) make the Israeli concern over a demographic crisis unrealistic. Indeed, the continual fears expressed about the potential "decline" in the Jewish population in Israel is a demographic myth, reinforced by the lower fertility levels of Jews in communities outside Israel and by the threat that is invoked by the Holocaust and the continuous Palestinian-Israeli conflict.

Without an empirical basis to identify a problem, it is difficult to consider seriously fertility-stimulating policies. Nevertheless, there is a demographic policy center attached to the prime minister's office in Israel that has, over the years, espoused policies to increase Jewish fertility in Israel. Myths are often powerful when they are reinforced by a broader ideology, regardless of the evidence about the reality. A central tenet of Zionism is the need to "repopulate" the Jewish nation-state and rebuild it culturally as the center of world Jewry since, it is postulated, Jewish communities outside the state are not likely to survive demographically and culturally. On these grounds, the higher fertility level of the Israeli Arab population and the lower-than-average Jewish fertility level in communities outside Israel reinforce these myths of a Jewish demographic crisis in Israel.

Fertility policies in the Israeli context have in the past been pro-natalist in ideology and have been addressed to the Jewish population (Friedlander and Goldscheider 1979, 1984).[11] Official fertility policies have never been effectively implemented, however, and have had marginal or no impact on increasing fertility levels. Indeed, as I have reviewed, the major feature of fertility in Israel has been its remarkable decline, particularly among Middle Eastern immigrants and their children. This transition from the larger to the small family occurred without direct government intervention and primarily through the use of nonmechanical contraceptive means, withdrawal, abortion—not always legal—and delayed marriage. No fertility policy has been designed for the Arab population in Israel, although it has been influenced indirectly by health- and welfare-entitlement programs designed for the Jewish population. Modern contraception has become more readily available from the public-health clinics that serve the majority of Israel's population, Jewish and Arab.

Given the heterogeneity of Israel's population and the fertility levels characteristic of the various communities, religious and ethnic, a comprehensive fertility policy would have to be differential. By this I mean that policy measures directed at reducing fertility for some communities (e.g., rural Moslems) would not be applicable to others (e.g., Israelis of European origin) (see C. Goldscheider and Friedlander 1986). If, for ideological or political reasons, the state of Israel wants to increase the fertility level of the Jewish population as part of a grander Zionist design to increase the population of Jews, such pro-natalism would hardly be appropriate for Israeli Arabs. It is difficult to construct a national pro-natalist policy that does not apply to all the various segments of the population that is not at the same time coercive or discriminatory. The tensions between the democratic base of Israeli society and its ethnic particularism are clearly reflected in these concerns.

There are fertility policies that are direct in that they are specific to fertility issues; other policies have primarily socioeconomic or welfare goals that have important, albeit indirect, consequences for families and fertility. Policies relate to both the normative climate of reproduction and the provision of efficient means of fertility control. Data on fertility norms collected in the mid-1970s and reinforced by survey data in the 1980s point unmistakably to the normative changes that have already occurred for the high-fertility populations of Israel. The difficult task of restructuring norms toward smaller family size has already occurred, in large part as a result of the transformations in socioeconomic conditions, families, and women's roles.

The provision of a full range of contraceptive information and family-planning strategies will reduce the reliance on abortion as a last resort for unplanned late births and the reliance on less-effective birth-control methods. Unlike in other countries, a significant proportion of abortions in Israel are obtained by married women with several children (Okun 1997; Wilder 2000). The introduction of new contraceptives would provide women with greater autonomy and control over their lives and would reduce their dependency on male-controlled contraceptives. Current contraceptive patterns often result in the use of inefficient contraception and in unplanned pregnancy (among older as well as younger women). The provision of contraceptives to all communities would enhance greater demographic equality among religious and ethnic communities. Policies that expand these family-planning services can rely on the existing public-health institutions and mother-child clinics, which have already played an important role in bringing medical care to the population and which have reduced significantly the differential accessibility of that care to the more economically disadvantaged sectors.

The major reasons that a more-equitable policy of family-planning information and access has not been implemented are related to the coincidence of political-family-ideological-religious interests. The religious and socially conservative argument emphasizes the traditional sanctity and importance of the family, the retention of traditional roles for women within the family, and limiting the role of sexual activity to marriage. Normally, these forces would be on the decline in a modernizing country that is governed by a secular polity. Two features upset these processes in Israel. First, religious institutions and political parties have played an important part in recent years in coalition politics. The price of the religion-and-politics connection has been the disproportionate power of religious institutions in reinforcing limited contraceptive access. In turn, this connection has been reinforced by the Zionist ideological commitment (among some but not all secular Zionists) to increase the Jewish population of the state, either through immigration of Jews from outside Israel or through the retention of a larger family size. The external conditions of the Arab-Israel conflict and the concern expressed by some Israeli policymakers about the large Arab populations that surround the state of Israel or the growing Palestinian population living in the West Bank further strengthen this ideological concern about Jewish population size.

So Israel has not and is unlikely to adopt a policy that more democratically educates the population in the planning of family size and in the use of efficient contraception. This does not mean that fertility will increase or that contraception will not be used. Instead, it means that the pressure to limit family size, derived from economic, housing, employment, and lifestyle contexts, will more often than not result in limiting childbearing through later marriage, abortion, and less-effective means of birth control. It means, as well, that those who can afford to purchase birth-control information and obtain family-planning materials and contraceptives in the private market will do so. The absence of a more-democratic policy will reinforce the existing social-class and, in turn, the ethnic and religious gaps that exist in Israel's population. No less important, and often overlooked, is the leverage these patterns exert for the perpetuation of inequalities in women's roles and the lack of control women are likely to continue to have over their family and social status. These are high costs indeed for a democratic society.

Concluding Observations

The first general lesson to be learned from studying fertility patterns in Israel is the importance of the variety of transitions. Some populations have experienced fertility decline, baby boom, and recovery, but there have been continuous declines in fertility for other populations; the pace of fertility change has varied among the various groups in Israel. An examination of national data only on fertility levels would have neutralized these variations and would have led to a chaos of explanations, since the ethnic-compositional shifts of the society as a whole have been enormous. Communities defined in real terms of ethnic origin or religious divisions are the more-appropriate unit for fertility analysis.

A second lesson derived from an analysis of fertility in Israel is the importance of family, in the context of roles of women and the connection of the family to the community. The key linkages have been those that connect family processes to the economy and that emphasize social class and political and family networks. A focus on family and household units is the most direct way of approximating the links between the individual and the community. Limiting fertility studies to women often misses family and community connections.

Studies have demonstrated the different ways in which family and economic changes have brought about pressure to reduce family size for communities faced with different circumstances. The response of Christian Arabs has been to delay marriage; withdrawal and abortion have been used efficiently among Asian- and African-origin Jews; increased use of contraceptive pills has characterized young Israelis. The important point is that there have been a variety of responses to the pressures to reduce family size. The state has played an important role in the process of fertility reduction, but not in the sense of direct birth control or anti-natal family-planning policies. Instead, Israel has developed an extensive welfare-entitlement system, along with health and educational programs, that has had important indirect effects providing incentives to reduce family size. These incentives in the past have had the reverse effect on the Arab population, slowing the pace of fertility reduction by relieving the pressures from the family. This is all the more remarkable (and ironic) since the formal policy of the government and the official ideology were pro-natalist for the Jewish population (which witnessed the most impressive voluntary decline in fertility recorded); they were unintentionally pro-natalist for the Arab population. The state can have a powerful role in altering fertility patterns, even when policies are not fertility-specific and regardless of the policies' "intention."

One of the lessons that one can derive from studying Israeli fertility patterns is that changes in fertility are connected to other issues of demographic importance. Clearly, the relationship of fertility to immigration is well documented and, along with the decline in mortality, lies at the heart of issues of demographic and ethnic changes. But it is less well appreciated how migration and location have shaped fertility responses. The residential stability (nonmigration) of the Moslem Israeli population, the selective migration of the Middle Eastern–origin Jewish population, the links between migration and schooling, jobs, and generational continuity are powerful in the migration-family-fertility connection.

In the end, the analysis points us in the direction of community, focusing on family and gender roles, migration, social class, and the use and distribution of resources. The demographic assimilation of Jewish ethnic groups in Israel does not necessarily imply the broader pattern of total ethnic assimilation. A similar conclusion emerges from the understanding of changes in the Israeli Arab community, where the powerful effects of their continuing geographic concentration and segregation have been noted. These ethnic-related patterns appear as ethnic distinctiveness in the context of assimilation in some, but not all, dimensions of social life, and in the context of the continuing importance of family and ethnic networks in fostering generational continuity at the community level.

Ethnic continuity confronts the question of national-community developments in Israel. Indeed, the ideological and political question raised in the nineteenth and early twentieth centuries in Europe of the role of ethnic communities in the development of the nation-state is again raised by Israeli patterns, as it is being addressed by other multicultural and pluralistic societies around the world. The "Jewish question" raised by Karl Marx in 1843 about the place of the Jewish minority in the emergent nationalism and capitalism of Europe has become Israel's ethnic question. The place of Jewish and Arab ethnic groups in Israel's changing society becomes the question in the beginning of the twenty-first century.

NOTES

1. Age-at-marriage data for women and men are from the registry of marriages and therefore do not take into account the whole population, that is, those that do not marry. Hence, these data complement but do not substitute for population-based data.

2. See chapter 6 for the definition of these categories of religious identity.

3. See chapter 6 and the special survey of the Central Bureau of Statistics in 2009, table 46.

4. Divorces are available in Israel, but the religious establishment controls the procedures of divorce and the granting of formal divorce decrees. There is no civil divorce in Israel, as there are no civil marriages.

5. For a review and an analysis of American data among young adults and older persons see F. Goldscheider and C. Goldscheider 1994 and 1999 and the references cited therein.

6. The marriage market for Jews in Israel has never included the Arab populations. Arabs in Israel are not acceptable as spouses for Jewish Israelis (and vice versa), on political and institutional grounds as well as for religious considerations from the perspective of both communities. The few-in-number Jewish-Arab couples in Israel tend to live on the margins of both communities. Intermarriages across "religious" national lines are not legally permitted in Israel without religious conversion.

7. Many of the first social studies of Israeli society treated intermarriage between ethnic groups as one of the powerful indicators of national integration, and scholars expected this form of ethnic assimilation to occur by the third generation. See for example, Bachi 1977; Bar-Yosef 1971; Ben-David 1970; Eisenstadt 1954, 1969.

8. The total fertility rate of a given year indicates the average number of births per woman if all women were to live through their childbearing years and have births at the same rate as women of those ages who actually gave birth in that year. It is an artificial construct that may be viewed as an estimate of eventual family size over the life course, derived from cross-sectional, age-specific patterns. It is particularly unreliable as an estimate of actual family size when age-specific fertility patterns are changing.

9. These questions and the detailed data needed to examine them form the basis of research that appears in Friedlander and Goldscheider 1978, and Friedlander, Eisenbach, and C. Goldscheider 1979, 1980. We draw on past research for the retrospective reconstruction of cohort ethnic changes in fertility, adding more recent data for the 1980s, 1990s, and 2000s.

10. The *hamula* is a patrilineal descent group that involves kin rights and ob-

ligations and establishes kinship relationships. See Al Haj 1987; Rosenfeld 1968; chapter 4.

11. Official pronouncements and ideological exhortations to the Jewish population about "internal" immigration—having more children—have been associated most prominently with Israel's first prime minister, David Ben-Gurion. He was quoted as saying, "Any Jewish woman who, as far as it depends on her, does not bring into the world at least four healthy children is shirking her duty to the nation, like a soldier who evades military service. . . . Every family (should) have at least four sons and daughters, the more the better" (Rein 1979, 65; see also the discussion in Friedlander and Goldscheider 1979).

11 | Emergent Israeli Society
Nation-Building, Inequalities, and Continuities

My primary focus has been on the formation of Israeli society and its development. I have identified some of the central threads of its social, economic, political, and cultural transformations and have explored the changing significance of ethnicity, religion, community, and family. In the process, I have analyzed the impact of Israeli-created conditions of social inequality and assimilation in the context of group experiences prior to arrival in Israel.

Yet, internal developments do not occur in an international or regional vacuum. As a new state, Israel has political and economic linkages to countries and people in and out of the region. As a Jewish state, it has important social and cultural relationships with Jewish communities around the world, those that represent potential sources of immigration and that are primarily sources of social, political, and economic support, as well as those that have received significant numbers of Israeli emigrants and visitors. Ethnic and religious divisions among Jews in Israel are strongly influenced by events occurring outside the state. As a state with a significant Arab population that is under its administrative control and a state that occupies a territory that has been claimed by some former residents, Israel has been centrally positioned in the aspirations of Palestinians for political autonomy.[1]

My goal in this chapter is to review some of the externals to enhance the understanding of internal developments in Israel's changing society. I focus on three questions. First, what is the relationship between Jewish communities outside the state of Israel to developments in Israeli society? I shall refer to this as the "Jewish diaspora" question. Second, what has been the relationship of the state of Israel to the territories it administers (referred to as Judea and Samaria, or the West Bank, or Palestine by persons of different political-ideological orientations)? I shall refer to this as the "Palestinian" question. Third, what are the prospects for Jewish ethnic assimilation in Israel, and what is the role of the Arab or Palestinian citizens living in the state in the context of both the Palestinian and Jewish diaspora questions? I shall refer to this as the "ethnic-national" question. I identify how these three sets of "external" considerations have conditioned developments in the state and, in particular, how they have influenced nation-building.[2]

The Jewish Diaspora and Israeli Society

The background for understanding the emergence of Israel includes the links between the state and what it defines as the *golah*, or the Jewish diaspora, that is, Jewish communities outside the state. Most directly, these links are important because these Jewish communities have been the sources of immigration to Israel. Hence, they have had a powerful influence on the changing Jewish ethnic composition in Israel and its population growth. Moreover, these Jewish communities have been Israel's financial and political backbone, supporting domestic programs and providing important aid for defense purposes and political legitimacy in the international arena. Jews outside Israel have been partners in formulating the intellectual and ideological basis of Israeli society and have provided the political rationale for its reemergence. What occurs in Jewish diaspora communities has important consequences for developments in the state; what happens in Israel has implications for Jewish communities outside Israel. Although a systematic analysis of the impact of Israeli society on Jewish communities outside Israel moves this work beyond its primary focus, some aspects of the organization and functioning of Israeli society are conditioned by the relationship of the "center" of Israel to its defined Jewish "periphery."[3]

Three brief examples illustrate some of the more-obvious interdependencies between Israel and Jewish communities outside Israel. First, changing immigration rates and shifts in the composition of immigrant streams to Israel have been strongly influenced by changes in the number of potential Jewish immigrants in communities around the world. The size of particular Jewish communities and the pool of potential Jewish immigrants have varied since the 1950s, in part in relation to the rate of immigration to Israel. The end of Jewish emigration from Yemen or Iraq, for example, can only be understood against the background of the demographic demise of those Jewish communities. The commitment of American Jews to remain in the United States has a major impact on the relationships between Israel and the American Jewish community and the U.S. government. Shifts in the cohesion of the Soviet Union and its breakup, along with implications of these changes for the Jewish populations living there, were the most immediate cause of the large-scale immigration of Russian Jews to Israel in the 1990s, as was the shifting immigration policy of the U.S. government in regard to accepting Russian immigrants. Thus, an examination of the impact of the timing and rate of Jewish immigration from various countries of origin to Israel must be understood in the context of these Jewish communities.

A second example relates to the ways that events in Israel affect Jewish communities in the world. The 1967 Six Day War between Israel and its Arab neighbors had a major impact on economic and political developments within the state and deeply affected the relationship of Israeli Jews to Palestinians and to the Arab populations of the region. The effect of the war extended well beyond the border of the state, increasing the financial and political support of Israel by Jewish communities around the world and more firmly anchoring their ethnic identities in Israel's development. As the very survival of Israel was perceived to be threatened, the post-Holocaust generation of Jews outside Israel responded in a variety of ways to link itself to the future of the Jewish state. After 1967, Israel symbolized the political "redemption" of the Jewish people and redirected issues around its role in the continuity of Jewish communities. These developments, in turn, led to new and more-conspicuous dependencies between Israel and Jewish communities, often involving Israel's acknowledging the legitimacy of some forms of Jewish "ethnic" identity in communities outside Israel in exchange for the political and financial support of these diaspora communities.

A third illustration relates to the continuous terrorist attacks directed at Jews in Israel. These have always generated political responses and concerns among Jews outside Israel; attacks on Jewish communities in North and South America, in Europe, and in Asia and Africa have, in turn, generated responses from the Israeli government. Israel views itself as the guardian of the Jewish people; Jewish communities outside Israel are defined as part of the history and culture of Israeli Jews. An attack on Jews anywhere is treated as an attack on Jews everywhere, promoting a mutual, unwritten pact of normative responsibilities and obligations. Often this takes the form of political action; at times, economic exchanges or military actions are generated as well, reinforcing the bonds between Israel and Jewish communities around the world.

These simple illustrations can be multiplied. The major point is that there are important linkages between internal developments in Israel and Jewish communities outside Israel that require analysis if the goal is to understand the dynamics of Israel's changing society.

Who Is Jewish in Israel and in the Jewish Diaspora?

Since Israel defines itself as the center of the Jewish people, an elementary question about the "ethnic" relationships between Israeli and non-Israeli Jews is, Who is included as a member of the Jewish people? The sociological response for voluntary communities is that membership is by self-definition, along with the normative consensus of the community. Political criteria (such as citizenship) or some other formal status (such as temporary resident status) are used for states.[4] The definitional question of "Who is a Jew?" in the state of Israel symbolizes the connections, and the gap, between the two largest Jewish communities in the world: Israel and the United States.[5]

The definition of who is to be included in the category "Jewish" falls under the Law of Return in the state of Israel (the law that grants every Jew in the world the right to immigrate to Israel and thereby become a citizen of the state). The state formally grants citizenship rights to all those who are Jewish by ethnic criteria, while the Israeli Rabbinate in Israel limits the definition to religious and legal (halachic) criteria (birth to a Jewish mother or conversion to Judaism by a recognized Orthodox rabbi). At the beginning of the twenty-first century, having one grandparent who was defined as Jewish allowed for entry into Israel under the Law of Return. But the Rabbinate would not recognize such a person as Jewish for purposes of life-cycle transitions. Occasionally, these formal definitions are problematic. Discussion about the criteria used to define Jewish in Israel often occurs in the context of coalition politics involving "religious" political parties that exercise power over the definition at the junctures of political transitions (i.e., citizenship in the context of immigration) or life-course transitions (e.g., marriage, divorce, or death). Israeli Jews are rarely affected by these coalition bargaining tactics, and the issue is marginal to their lives, except as it reveals the political nature of Israeli Judaism. In contrast, when these tactics are enforced and publicly debated in Israel, the vast majority of Jews living in the United States become concerned.

The issue of defining who is Jewish is not new historically nor is it particular to the state of Israel. All societies struggle with defining membership and citizenship. In Israel, the definition had in the past been decided by Israel's parliament, the Knesset, on "religious" grounds and has been implemented by the Jewish religious authorities of the state, that is, by Orthodox rabbis and their institutions. The paradox is that American Jews are concerned about the legalities of citizenship in a Jewish country thousands of miles away that many have never visited and in which most have no intention of applying for such citizenship and are unlikely to test whether they would ever fit those criteria. The subgroup of American Jews who are most likely to immigrate to Israel would be defined as Jewish in the overwhelming majority of cases.

To understand this elementary issue from the point of view of Israeli society, we can unravel the Israeli view of the core issue of Jewish life in the aftermath of European modernization: the integration and assimilation of Jews in modern, secular, open, pluralistic societies. In its most simple form, the Israeli argument about the assimilation of diaspora Jews is as follows. In modern, open, pluralistic societies, for example in America, Jews are assimilating. Assimilation, they argue, means the erosion of Jewish life in the process of becoming like non-Jews. Intermarriage is the most conspicuous indicator of such erosions, because when Jews intermarry with non-Jews, they are distancing themselves from their "traditional" roots, rejecting their Jewishness and their Judaism together with their links to the Jewish people, community, history, and culture. Such intermarriages are unlikely to occur in Israel (in large part because of the boundaries between Jews and Arabs); "assimilation," therefore, is only a problem when Jews are a minority community. Since American Jews are assimilating, the Israelis argue, it is particularly unclear why they should be concerned about the way Jews are being defined in the state of Israel. Assimilating Jews should be particularly indifferent to formal issues about the Judaism of the Jews. Why should American Jews care about the way rabbis, from another culture and with very different values from theirs, jockey for political power and make legal and political pronouncements that are irrelevant to their lives and their Jewishness? Shouldn't Jewish Americans, who are committed to the American political values of separation of church and state (not necessarily Jewish or Israeli political values), be indifferent to religious-political parties in Israel?

The answer to these questions relates to changes in Judaism in the process of modernization. Over the past century, Jews have become less-observant religiously, their institutions have become secular, and their Judaism has been re-formed. At the same time that traditional religious practices and institutions were declining, new ways of expressing Judaism were emerging, and new forms of Jewishness were substituting for religion. Just as secular Zionists developed new ideological and cultural Jewish expressions, rejecting the traditional Judaism and the "diaspora" Jewish culture of the past, so American Jews found new ways to express their Jewishness and Judaism. They redefined their religious commitments into new denominational forms and developed new Jewish institutions and ideologies.

These expressions of Jewishness took shape through secular-based social and communal institutions, emphasizing Jewish peoplehood and American versions of Zionism. As American Jews became less religiously and ritually observant, moving away from Orthodox toward Conservative and Reform Judaisms, the state of Israel became a major basis of communal consensus, reinforcing Jewish continuity as part of ethnic activities, in other words, Jewish peoplehood. Thus, religious changes did not imply the end of their commitments as Jews within their families and their communities or as part of the Jewish people everywhere and over time. "Ethnic" Jewishness, and especially its Israel-centered component, emerged for many to replace the Judaisms of ritual and belief.

Most American Jews, then, define Israel as a very important part of their lives and central to the education of their children. Substantial proportions of American Jews have visited Israel, have relatives and friends living in Israel, and financially contribute to Israeli-related projects. Israel's survival is bound up with the ethnic lives of American Jews since they consider themselves part of the Jewish people. The state of Israel has become a psychological anchor for many American Jews and is the sociocultural foundation of their Jewishness and a source of communal cohesion. American Jewish identity is defined by its pro-Israelism. How Jewishness is defined in Israel, therefore, seriously matters to most Jewish Americans.

The centrality of Israel in the Jewishness of American Jews is one side of the story; Americanness is the other side of Jewishness. Clearly, Jews living in the United States have assimilated, changing and adapting to the society in which they live. However, assimilation and integration have not, by and large, led to the total loss of community. After decades of integration into American society, the Jewish community has powerful anchors of social, religious, and family life (see C. Goldscheider 1986a, 1986b, 2002). Family, communal, political, economic, and associational networks are the key indicators of ethnic continuity in Jewish communities as it is in the Jewish state. Most American and Israeli Jews would not be very Jewish if religious observances were the only criteria (on the religiosity of Israeli Jews, see Deshen 1990; C. Goldscheider and Friedlander 1983; Levy, Levinsohn, and Katz 1993; Sobel and Beit-Hallahmi 1991; chapter 6).

Although there have been increases in the rates of intermarriage between Jews and non-Jews in the United States, there is no simple association between intermarriage and alienation from the Jewish community. The relative rates of generational continuity of the intermarried in the Jewish community (i.e., how many children raised in households where one or more persons was not born Jewish remain Jewish as they form their own families) have changed over the past decades as the levels of intermarriage and conversions have increased and as the levels of acceptance of the intermarried in the community have increased.[6] In many intermarriages, the Jewish partner remains attached to the Jewish community through family, friends, and organizational ties; often the non-Jewish-born spouse becomes attached to the Jewish community, as do many of the children of the intermarried. Most of their friends are Jewish, many support Israel, and most identify themselves as Jews. Some proportion formally convert to Judaism; many are converted by religious procedures under the direction of Orthodox and Conservative rabbis, but more are converted to Judaism by Reform rabbis using nontraditional religious criteria.

Taken together, the research evidence shows that the intermarried, certainly the formally converted (by whatever denomination and by whatever criteria) cannot be written off as lost to the Jewish community. Their families, rabbis, and Jewish organizations have not excluded them, and they have not excluded themselves. Can a citizenship law in the state of Israel write them off as Jewish people without creating concern among the intermarried, their families, their rabbis, their community, their institutions, and particularly their children?

The increasing rate of intermarriage means erosion of the Jewish community primarily through the prism of the segregated Orthodox, who reject the Jewishness of non-Orthodox Jews, and from the perspective of Israeli Jews who reject the possibility of Jewish continuity in the diaspora. High intermarriage rates mean that the wide networks of Jews are affected by the intermarriage issue and that these networks are larger than the percentage who are currently intermarrying. There is hardly a Jewish household in America that has not experienced the taste of intermarriage among family members, neighbors, or friends. Even American Jews who have not been affected directly by intermarriage are concerned about the political resolution of a formal "Who is a Jew?" question in the state of Israel. American Jews are concerned when the secular Israeli Jewish government declares that their Jewish friends, neighbors, and family are not "Jewish" based on a definition shaped by the interests of coalition politics and political bargaining in Israel.

These issues come to a head when large numbers of temporary non-Jewish immigrants are working in Israel (about 250,000 in the twenty-first century). These workers are in large part replacing the Palestinians who are blocked from working in Israel because of the Palestinian-Israeli conflict. They add to the significant number of non-Jewish immigrants from the former Soviet Union who have joined family members who are Jewish and have been granted the rights of citizenship. An estimated half of the immigrants from the former Soviet Union entering Israel during the last two decades have been defined as not Jewish on their own and by Orthodox religious criteria. These two groups of immigrants, the temporary foreign workers and non-Jewish immigrants, are again raising the Jewish and the Zionist questions in the state of Israel.

Even though immigration to Israel is not part of the agenda of most American Jews, their identity as Jews is intertwined in complex and profound ways with their associations with Israel. At the same time, about 85% of American Jews reject Orthodox Judaism as their form of religious expression, and most have developed religious alternatives; their legitimacy as Jews is unquestioned in America. Although, in large part, they have rejected the version of Zionism that insists on their immigration as the only legitimate solution to the Jewish condition in the diaspora, they have developed alternative versions of Zionism that allow them to have strong bonds to the state of Israel. Pro-Israelism has been their commitment without the ideological imperative of immigration, which would mean rejection of the continuation of American Jewish life (see S. Cohen 1983; Liebman and Cohen 1990).

American Jews are comfortable as Jews where they live and display their Jewishness openly and legitimately. Anchoring their Jewish identity in the Jewish state, which calls into question their legitimacy as Jews, their children's legitimacy, and that of their religious leaders, becomes untenable. For some time, Orthodox rabbis have called into question the Jewishness of those who have become Jews by choice or who practice their Judaism differently from Orthodox Judaism. American Jews have, in large part, ignored these Orthodox rabbis and have been indifferent to their values. Orthodox Judaism in Israel, in its political form, has become more intolerant of Jewish diversity, at the same time that American Jews have embraced pluralism in Judaism. By recognizing only one of the several variants of Judaism, Israel calls into question the ethnic legitimacy of the overwhelming majority of American Jews. Recognizing that the American Jewish community is a viable and concerned Jewish- and Israeli-oriented community would raise fundamental questions about the premises of some forms of Zionism.

The United States and Israel represent different strategies of Jewish survival in the modern world. The state of Israel is a major source of Jewish culture, experience, identity, and history for American Jews, since it is their link to Jewish peoplehood, the quintessential form of political ethnicity. Israel is not their "national origin" in the geographic sense. In its constructed ideological form, Israel is no less powerful as a symbol of ethnicity for Jewish communities. For many Israeli Jews, however, the American Jewish community is the paradigm of erosion and decay and the lack of Jewish viability and continuity, yet a source of potential immigration.

Gaps Between Jewries Are Relationships Changing?

The different constructions by Israeli politics and American Jewries of "Who is a Jew?" reveal broader political and cultural differences between these communities. American Jews view their Jewishness in the context of individual choices and communal consent; Israeli Jews have a major political component attached to their assigned status. How have these relationships changed over time? Have Jews inside and outside Israel moved closer or further apart? The "peoplehood" paradigm has a component that emphasizes "oneness" across contexts, which has been emphasized by both Israeli and non-Israeli Jewish institutions. It is symbolized by the public-relations slogan "We are one," used in the past by national and international Jewish organizations. There is some basis for this view in the long history of Jews and in Judaism, often in response to how others define Jews as part of one people and as being distinctive.[7] Only in the past century have Jews formulated a separation of Judaism and Jewishness—a postulation that being religious and being part of the Jewish community are not necessarily the same, although the integration of religious and ethnic forms continues to be the defining quality of community and cultural forms of Jewishness.

Oneness does not necessarily imply similarities in every cultural and communal sphere; obligations and responsibilities do not mean uniformity of identity and singularity of goals and objectives or sameness of values. Indeed, there are increasing indications that Israeli Jews and Jews in communities outside Israel are moving apart from each other. Although the state of Israel has become the center of Jewish peoplehood, large, cohesive, and powerful Jewish communities have emerged in modern pluralistic societies. These are legitimate and accepted ethnic-religious communities, with long-term roots in these societies, as well as strong linkages to Israel. Whereas most of the Jews outside Israel are committed to the state, in their view and in their behavior they are not in "exile" or in diaspora. Their home is where they live, where they expect to continue living, and where they are raising the next generation to live. Mutual dependencies have developed between Israel and the Jewish communities outside Israel. These dependencies have changed over time as these communities have responded to each other and as technology has brought geographically spread persons into new forms of communication to exchange ideas, cultures, and people. The exchanges have flowed in both directions.

In the past, there were major commonalities of background and experience between Israeli and American Jews. Both groups were heavily influenced by their European origins, and many Jews were raised in families where Yiddish was spoken and were rooted in Yiddish culture. Many struggled with second-generation status; in other words, they were raised by parents who were not native to the country in which they were living. Many shared the cultural and social disruptions of secularization and assimilation; the struggles of economic depression, war, and Holocaust in Europe; and the rebuilding of the lives of Jewish refugees. They shared in the most tangible and dramatic ways the establishment and the rebuilding of the state of Israel. Jews in both Israeli and non-Israeli Jewish communities had limited exposure to formal Jewish/religious education, rejected traditional Jewish ritual observances as reflections of their discarded past, and developed ethnic-national Jewish rituals as substitutes. Israeli Jews became less traditional by becoming attached nationally to their new country; American Jews became less traditionally oriented by becoming American. In short, there was a shared sense of origins, experiences, and objectives in the past, although each group was living in a different society and building a new community with an appropriate set of institutions.

New generations have emerged in Israel and in the United States that are more distant from Europe and from the commonalities of language. For them, the European Holocaust is history, and immigration origins are far away, as are the struggles of pioneering in Israel and upward generational mobility in the United States. The different experiences of Israel and the United States as societies have shaped the lives, lifestyles, institutions, and values of the people of these communities. Not only have past commonalities declined, but also new gaps have emerged. A key example is the role of women in both societies. American Jewish women have been in the forefront of social changes in their increasing independence from traditional gender roles and family relationships. Their high levels of education, career orientations, small family sizes, and high aspirations for themselves and their children have been truly revolutionary. Many American men have shared and adjusted to these changes in the workplace and in families. In contrast, Israeli men and women tend to have much more traditional segregated family and social roles. Family relationships are more patriarchal, work patterns for women are less tied to careers, and Israeli women lack the autonomy of American women. So this particular gap, with its implications for work and family, has grown in recent years. But it is slowly changing in Israel toward a more-egalitarian model at least among the more secular.

A second, related shift involves the growing demographic, political, and cultural importance of Asian/African-origin Jews in Israel. This compositional change has created new gaps at the leadership and community levels between Israelis of non-European origin and American Jews. Language barriers have increased, and limited communication occurs between these communities. Diverse social-class backgrounds and lifestyles

exacerbate these differences. Jews in the United States have become concentrated in high-level educational, occupational, and income categories.
College-educated, white-collar professionals are less common among Israeli Jews, and particularly among women. So, social-class, ethnicity, and
gender differences reinforce gaps between Jews in Israel and the United
States. Note that the immigration of Jews from the former Soviet Union to
Israel and to the United States has created new selective bonds of connections and networks. Global connections of economy and culture have also
been potential sources of connections between Jews in both countries.

Religion is the most-serious manifestation of the gap between Israel
and Jewish communities external to Israel. Judaism has been highly po-
liticized in Israel, with control over religious institutions exercised by one
segment of Judaism (the Orthodox). Religious leaders of Israel and of communities outside Israel have so little in common that there is virtually no
communication between them. Although the Jewish populations in both
societies have similar levels of secularization, the gap in religious leadership is total.[8] Add in the religious role of women in American Judaisms and
one sees that there is a stark contrast between the dominance of American
Reform and Conservative rabbis (men and women) as religious leaders
outside Israel and the general lack of legitimacy of non-Orthodox rabbis
in Israel. Yet that too may be changing slowly among the more-modern Orthodox, but it appears to have a long way to go before converging with the
more liberal American Judaic ideologies.

The commitment of American Jews to the separation of religion and
politics contrasts sharply with the clear interrelationship of religion and
politics in Israel, although almost six out of ten Israelis desire the separation of religion from the state (chapter 6). Religious pluralism characterizes Jewish communities outside Israel, and multiple expressions of
Judaism are normatively accepted and valued; "orthodox" is the only Judaism defined as legitimate in Israeli society, although there are two chief
ultraorthodox rabbis defined along ethnic lines. Israel and its leaders are
not committed to ethnic or religious pluralism in the same way that is
characteristic of American Jewry, at least not in practice. The trajectories
of changes in these two communities are moving in the direction of strain-
ing the relationships between them, not in closing the gap. As each is moving through its own developments, each is moving away from the other. In
the short run, at least for another generation, differences between Jews in

Israel and elsewhere are likely to be accentuated, despite increasing flows of money, culture, and people between these communities.

The Palestinian Diaspora

How have the external conflicts with Arab Palestinians reshaped and affected the changes within the state? How have they influenced the way Israeli society relates to its Arab minority and to the broader Arab-Israeli conflict? What is the situation of the Palestinians who are residents of the areas that have been administered and occupied by the state of Israel since the 1967 war? Through the end of the 1970s, these territories were referred to officially as administered territories and incorporated the West Bank and Gaza (the latter and Jericho came under Palestinian administration in mid-1994). They became officially known by their biblical names, Judea, Samaria, and Gaza—reflecting the ascendancy of the Likud government in 1977 and its more-nationalistic policies with regard to these territories. The political symbolism of this name switch is of profound importance in understanding the relationship of the Israeli government to these areas,[9] which encompassed almost 350,000 Jewish settlers and over 2.7 million Arab Palestinians at the beginning of the second decade of the twenty-first century. The Jewish population living in Judea and Samaria (the settlements on the West Bank) has been the fastest-growing geographic-area subpopulation in Israel. Starting from 1,500 in 1972, the Jewish population increased to 275,000 by 2008 and to 334,000 in 2012. Significant proportions of migrants to the West Bank define themselves as religious.

The Israeli administration of these territories since 1967 has influenced population, socioeconomic development, and ethnicity in all of Israel through the territories' impact on the economy, their connection to the Israeli Arab community, and their influence on stratification and inequalities in Israeli society. The Jewish commitment to live in these areas is often couched in religious (if not messianic) language. Religious institutions—schools and synagogues—connect suburban-like housing to form vibrant and cohesive communities.

The Israeli government has never officially incorporated into Israel the Arab Palestinian population living in these territories, except for East Jerusalem in 1967. The political rights of citizenship accorded to Arab Israelis were not extended to those living in the West Bank and Gaza. The incorporation of the large Arab population within "Greater Israel" would have threatened the demographic dominance of the Jewish population. In the 1970s and 1980s, a series of demographic projections showed clearly that the differential growth rates of Israel's population and the Arab Palestinian population under its administrative control would result in a declining Jewish proportion and would entail the risk of losing a Jewish majority in a little over a generation (Friedlander and Goldscheider 1974, 1979, 1984). Ironically, some of the most nationalistic among the Israeli Jewish population argue for the incorporation of the Palestinian population. If they were successful, the demographic result would be the emergence of an Arab Palestinian demographic majority. Hence, the more extreme among the Israeli nationalists instead argued for the incorporation of the administered land within the state without integrating its Palestinian population.

These early demographic scenarios were not designed to project what would happen but what would be the demographic consequences if there were no policies to deal with the future of these areas. Indeed, the alternatives to returning control over the administered territories to the Palestinians ranged from the development of a quasi-colonial relationship between Israel and the Palestinian population under its administration (which in part occurred) to the evacuation of the Arab population, to be replaced by Israeli residents (which has occurred only marginally). The notion of a combined Israeli-Palestinian state shared between Jewish and Arab Palestinian populations was not acceptable to either side of the conflict. Such a state would require a radical transformation of the institutions, values, and symbols that mark Israel as a Jewish state.

The size of the Arab population of these territories is somewhat in dispute, since there are different estimates depending on how Palestinians are defined and by which officials.[10] Some of the basic demographic patterns over the two decades beginning in 1970 show that there was a substantial growth in the population of the West Bank and Gaza, increasing to 4.4 million from fewer than 1 million in 1970, of which 2.7 million were living on the West Bank in 2010. These estimates for 2012, obtained from the Palestinian Central Bureau of Statistics, may incorporate some non-resident Palestinians and those living in territories and are not identical to the areas and populations covered by the Israel Central Bureau of Statistics at early points in time. In any case, the comparisons over time reveal a tendency toward high population-growth rates with the attendant consequences. The official birthrate of Palestinians on the West Bank has declined significantly from 47 per 1,000 in 1990 to 30 per 1,000 in 2013, as have death rates, and the potential for continuing growth is high but diminishing.

Indicators of health conditions and health infrastructure reveal the poorer and disadvantaged economic conditions of Arab Palestinians in the administered areas, relative to Israeli society as a whole and to the Arab Israeli population. Here again significant improvements have been documented over the last decades. A major problem remains the significantly high unemployment rates of Arab Palestinians and the absence of opportunities. (Crude estimates of unemployment rates among Palestinians on the West Bank are 17% for males and 25% for women in 2013).

The administration of these territories by Israel involves political control and the presence or involvement of government agencies such as health, education, agricultural regulation, and administrative justice. This administration implies that economic decisions are more likely to serve the interests of the Israeli economy and that investments in local control are minimal. Local Palestinian residents have not been part of the political process that has shaped these economic policies. Domestic needs and local economic development have been secondary to the needs of the Israeli government, including the recruitment of labor to work in Israel and the flow of Israeli goods into the territories. Thus, agricultural developments in the West Bank have been realigned to produce crops that are not competitive with the Israeli agricultural markets, and prices have been regulated.

Control is exercised by Israel over water drawn from the West Bank into Israel. Israel has also controlled some land areas in the West Bank for Jewish settlers, introduced Israeli firms to set up industry in the areas through financial incentives, and established export connections to Jordan and other Arab countries through the West Bank. At the same time, the territories have become markets for Israeli goods. Thus, two decades ago the argument was made that "Israeli policies have blatantly steered the territories toward a state of dependency on Israel. . . . The economies of the West Bank [and Gaza] still lack indigenous and financial institutions necessary for setting up development programs and channeling savings and investments into various economic sectors" (Gharaibeh 1985, 137). Again this assessment continues to characterize Palestinians even as there are indications that it is slowly changing in the twenty-first century.

The changing occupational patterns of Arab men in these territories are revealing. A significant proportion of Palestinians had been working in the state of Israel, commuting on a daily basis. In 1992, 38% of the employed males living in the West Bank and Gaza were working in the construction industry, and three-fourths of Arab Palestinians commuting to Israel were working in the construction industry.[11] Data show the decrease in the number and the proportion of Jews in the construction industry as the number of Arabs from the administered territories in that industry increased. When we look at the employers, the evidence identifies the Jewish role in construction in particular and in the stratification picture in general. Although the number of Jews in construction declined and the number of Arabs from the territories increased significantly, the proportion of employers remained overwhelmingly Jewish. About 80% of the employers in 1975 were Jewish, as were 76% in 1987. These patterns of employment changed in the years 2000 and 2001, as less daily commuting to the state of Israel was permitted and violence between Israelis and Palestinians on the West Bank and in Gaza became daily occurrences. The Palestinian workers from the territories were replaced by temporary guest workers from a wide range of countries.

A final socioeconomic and cultural indicator of the Palestinian population in the West Bank and Gaza relates to the dramatic increase in the level of formal education between the 1970s and the 1990s. In 1970, about half of the population had no formal education; 65% of the women had none. By the early 1990s, the proportion with no education declined to 20% overall and to about 30% of the women. The educational level is rapidly changing among the younger generation. In 1992, for example, over 90% of the Palestinian teenage boys and girls had some formal education, and about 70% of those ages 15 to 17 had some high school education.[12] Whether these education levels will be translated into commensurate jobs remains the challenge of the next decades. By the beginning of the twenty-first century, the local economic infrastructure and development had improved but not yet kept pace with the new educational levels.

Clearly, the political control exercised by Israel over these territories has resulted in an economic dependency, as reflected by the occupational and industrial characteristics of the Palestinians as well as by indicators of the balance of trade and economic flows between Israel and the administered territories. The identity of the Israeli Arab population has been influenced, sharpened, and challenged in a variety of ways by the links between Israel and the Arab Palestinians in the territories. First and foremost, Arab Israelis became linked to Arab Palestinians in the West Bank and in their national aspirations. The links have heightened their sensitivities to the value of ethnic networks and their own national origins and have confronted them with the choice between identifying as Arab Israelis or as displaced Palestinians. The connections between Arab Israelis and Arab Palestinians after 1967 have also sharpened the distinctiveness of the former as Israeli citizens. Arab Israelis are caught in the middle. They are beneficiaries of the system created to control and protect them as a minority and as citizens of the state of Israel, and yet they are viewed as disloyal Palestinians by their Arab-Palestinian cousins. Although Arab Israelis identify as Palestinians in some contexts, they have been living as citizens in Israel for generations. Although lacking the structural opportunities to integrate residentially and regionally with Jewish Israelis, they are nevertheless a minority with rights and entitlements as citizens of the state. Their identity may be challenged and conflicted, but they do not always identify fully with the aspirations of the Palestinians in the territories (Smooha 1991; Smooha and Hanf 1992; Smooha 2012). Even though Arab Israelis live and work and go to school in Israel and have access to the goods and welfare of Israeli society, they are connected ethnically to Palestinians. The linkages between Israel and the territories since 1967 have reinforced and legitimated the minority status of its Arab Israeli population.

Previously I noted the role of over 350,000 Jewish Israeli settlers in the territories, their Zionist nationalistic aspirations, and the dilemma they face in the emergence of Palestinian autonomy there (chapter 5). Almost all Jews living in these areas view themselves as Israelis living under Israeli auspices. They are committed to the legitimate rights of Israeli Jews to live in these areas for nationalist, security, and religious reasons. The majority are concentrated in a few select areas that are located around Jerusalem and that are within easy access to Tel Aviv. These areas are most likely to be retained as Israeli areas for at least another generation. There are other settlements that are more scattered and isolated and cannot sustain themselves as dormitory suburbs without support from the Israeli government. These are the least likely to remain under Israeli control in the next period of time and are not likely to expand in Jewish population. The Jewish population in these territories administered by Israel is segregated ethnically and religiously from the Palestinian population. The presence of the settler population in areas of the West Bank has been a serious obstacle for the independence/autonomy of Palestinians living there as has the broader administration of their lives by the Israeli government.

When (and if) Peace Arrives

Some Israelis view giving up land as a violation of a fundamental ideological principle; others are more willing to consider trading territory for a process that would lead to peace. Argument in favor of Palestinian control over land occupied by Israel for over four decades is countered by arguments over who has the "right" to the land (divine or political) and by the Israeli concern that terrorism and uncontrollable conflict, not peaceful neighborly relations, will result from greater Palestinian autonomy and statehood. Fear and distrust have often been replaced by hatred and by Israeli suppression of Palestinian self-determination. This may be slowly changing in the West Bank but certainly not in Gaza, but it is a long process that requires unfolding and has been frozen since the second intifada, uprising, of the Palestinian population beginning in 2000. Increasing cohorts of Palestinians have been raised in a context of Israeli control of the West Bank, and increasing numbers of Israeli Jews have grown up living in Israeli settlements on the West Bank. How these young cohorts will negotiate their futures together has become the major challenge of the twenty-first century.

The first decade and a half of the twenty-first century has witnessed sharply increased violence between Gaza and Israel. Attempts at a peaceful resolution of the Palestinian-Israeli conflict have been remarkably unsuccessful. Rockets launched from Gaza toward Israeli population centers and forays from Israel to population centers in Gaza have become routine and costly in human lives, property, economic growth, and trust between neighbors. Proposals by international players and by the governments directly involved have not led to a new set of resolutions or paths to peace. As of 2014, the conflict between Palestinians and Israelis has moved to higher levels and greater destruction. Violence has bred anger, increasing mistrust, and intransigence on all sides.

Starting in the 1990s, the world's international situation had altered, particularly with the collapse of the Soviet regime and its diminished influence in the Middle East, with the changing role of the Persian Gulf states, and with the increasing ethnic-national identity of the Palestinians. Israelis and Palestinians had been talking to one another, yet terrorism continued. Syria and Israel had been more open to negotiating control over the Golan Heights, but the regime in Syria in the first decade of the twenty-first century has faced bloody internal conflicts. Russia was overwhelmed with its own national and regional economic problems and was less involved in power politics with the United States. It is clear that Israel will give up territory (how much and when is not clear) and that the Palestinians will have increasing control over their own autonomous political unit in the West Bank. What will characterize the developing institutions and infrastructure in Gaza after the intense fighting between Israel and Hamas in 2013–2014 is an open question. The hope is that there will be a gradual end to the Israeli military presence in the West Bank and diminished control over local Palestinian institutions (health, education, welfare, and economic). The optimistic indicators point to processes that will result in new relationships between Israelis and Palestinians. That is the hopeful long-term scenario. But, as in the past, these policy developments toward a peaceful resolution of the Palestinian-Israeli conflict have been placed in serious jeopardy by terrorism and mistrust, by actions and reactions, by armed struggle and resistance and by the presence of 350,000 Israelis on territory claimed by Palestinians and by extremism on both sides of the conflict. The alternative scenario of one state for two peoples, with unequal political and social control and with a large but permanently disenfranchised Palestinian minority continues to be the direct challenge to the relationship between demography and democracy. And the continuation of the status quo is certainly not a solution for improving the quality of life of Israelis or Palestinians. The embedded conflict in Gaza does not appear to have any obvious and acceptable solution.

In the late 1930s and 1940s, when faced with a somewhat similar dilemma, the Jewish government in Palestine, under the leadership of Ben-Gurion, opted for people over land and accepted the idea of the partition of the land of Israel. It was a decision reached not without considerable pain and internal conflict. Faced with a similar choice, the leadership in Israel at the beginning of the twenty-first century is far from reaching similar conclusions. The costs of continuing with occupation and violence are high, as is the cost of controlling millions of Palestinian Arab residents. The toll on the quality of life in Israel and in the administered territories is high, and it remains more difficult to justify the continuation of the status quo. The dependency of both populations on other nations and on outside support is too great for either side to follow only its own ideological imperatives. The cost in human life and hatred between neighbors is substantial and not easily measurable. A pessimistic scenario of the future of Palestinian-Israeli relationships is the continuation of the status quo.

Ethnicity and Nationalism
Are Ethnic Groups Transitional?

To review the impact of Jewish and Palestinian diasporas on Israeli society, in general, and on ethnic divisions in Israel, in particular, I turn to one of the key questions raised in the beginning of this excursion into understanding Israel's changing society: What is the relationship between nation-building and ethnic/religious stratification, and what are the implications for broader issues of inequality? Specifically, what are the contexts in Israel that exacerbate the ethnic division of labor, and when do these forms of ethnic stratification and inequality diminish? How has ethnic stratification in Israel changed in the context of the external developments in the Jewish and Palestinian diasporas? In the process of understanding these issues, we shall deal with the broader question of the conflict between ethnic pluralism and nationalism in the formation of new states.

The analysis has identified some of the major ethnic divisions in Israeli society, those that divide Jews from each other and those that separate Israeli Jews from Israeli Arabs. I have documented the spheres of convergences and divergences among these groups and the basic differences in community institutions that have emerged to reinforce ethnic inequalities. I have shown how the divisions between Jews and Arabs are different from the internal divisions among Jews, although they share some basic similarities. What can one infer from this understanding of the sources of these differences about the relative permanence of these divisions and whether Jewish and Arab ethnicity in Israel is transitional? We have documented ethnic convergences in some processes (e.g., fertility, family, and mortality) and continued ethnic distinctiveness in others (e.g., residential concentration and socioeconomic measures). Have these patterns resulted in the declining significance of ethnicity and of ethnic communities? If ethnic communities are continuous features of Israel's emerging pluralism, how is national integration affected? In short, does ethnic continuity conflict with national Israeli integration? If ethnic divisions among Jews have diminished, have religious divisions substituted for ethnic divisions?

It is clear that the earlier entry into Israel's society of European immigrants and their socioeconomic and demographic backgrounds facilitated their relatively successful socioeconomic mobility and their access to power, resources, and opportunity. European immigrants could take advantage of their connections to the European-dominated society and economy that they found established as the state was developing. Burdened by larger families, higher mortality and morbidity, and fewer resources than Jews from Western societies, Asian and African immigrants arrived later in Israel, with a higher level of dependency on sociopolitical institutions. They came from less-developed societies, with fewer urban skills and less-powerful economic networks, and they were therefore less able to compete with European-origin groups in Israel. The timing of immigration and the sociocultural differences between groups reinforced these structural background factors that divided Israeli Jews.

The differential timing of immigration and the changing ethnic composition of immigrant streams created the contexts of residential concentration among Jews. Ethnic residential patterns, more so than the legacy of social and cultural origins, shape what ethnicity continues to mean in the process of nation-building in Israel. Residential concentration forged from political and economic considerations has become the key process marking off Israeli-born Jews from each other as it has been the demographic foundation of the continuing Jewish-Arab distinctiveness.

New Israeli patterns have emerged among Jews that are neither fully "Western" nor "Middle Eastern." Although ethnic cultural differences remain salient and distance from the immigrant generation continues to be an important factor in understanding social change, the structural features in Israel—particularly residential segregation and its implication for access to opportunity—are critical in retaining ethnic distinctiveness. Ethnic residential concentration is linked to educational opportunities and, in turn, to jobs; it is likely to relate to intraethnic marriages and a reinforced sense of ethnic self-identity, pride, and culture, connecting ethnic origins and families into networks of relationships. These patterns are almost totally separate between Jews and Arabs and characterize significant segments of third-generation Jews when examined by the two broad Jewish ethnic categories: Western and Middle Eastern. The convergence among Jews of different ethnic origins is reinforced among those with similar socioeconomic characteristics. The critical factors in ethnic differences are socioeconomic. And economic differences have widened in recent years, and social inequality has increased.

In the review of the political and demographic contexts of Israeli society, it has become clear that some ethnic demographic differences diminish in importance and that ethnic convergences occur over time. Ethnic convergences seem to result when differences are primarily the result of the background of immigrants and are largely the legacy of the past. Thus, for example, differences in family size and structure among ethnic groups have diminished with each passing generation, as mortality differences disappeared among the foreign-born first generation. In contrast, ethnic communities remain salient when the sources of ethnic differences are embedded in the society of destination as a result of the timing of immigration and the ethnic and economic selectivity of immigrant streams or because of emerging residential segregation, occupational concentration, or economic niches that flow from political and economic considerations. These structural features are, in turn, legitimated by cultural expressions and values.

Ethnic residential concentration among Jews and between Jews and Arabs reinforces the overlap of ethnicity and socioeconomic factors through the impact of locational factors on access to educational and economic opportunities. Together, residential and socioeconomic concentrations shape the continuing salience of ethnic distinctiveness in Israel. When groups are integrated residentially, ethnic differences become marginal in their social, economic, and political importance; where residential segregation in Israel has persisted, it has become the primary engine of ethnic persistence and inequality. Although ethnic segregation is associated at times with poverty and lower socioeconomic status, it also implies supportive and family networks that shape the lives of many Israelis. Local institutions serve as further bases for ethnic continuity. These include ethnic family networks, economic networks that are ethnically based, and some local institutions—synagogues, community centers, political interests, health clinics, and leisure-time and cultural activities (sports and music, for example)—that are concentrated among particular

ethnic groups. Jewish ethnic continuities persist despite government policies and ideological orientations to deny the salience of ethnicity.

How have the new forms of religious conflict influenced Jewish ethnic
continuities? This question has become more sharply focused as the divisions between the religious and the secular have sharpened. It seems that
for the religious whose patterns of institutional developments have been
segregative ethnically (note the chief rabbis and the segregated yeshivot
and synagogues by ethnic origin), the ethnic divisions have remained salient. In the communities as well the ethnic divisions appear to be continuous (Western origins in the kibbutzim and Middle Eastern origins in
the moshavim and in the development towns, and mostly Western origin
in the new settlements on the West Bank). The more religious (*datim* and
haredim) tend to be of Western origin, while the half of the population that
is secular is more likely to be of mixed ethnic origin or where ethnic origin
is less divisive. On the other hand, there is a strong secular Jewish identity
among Russian immigrants and their children and an increasing Sephardic secular culture among the second and third generation of Middle Eastern origins.

The Arab-Jewish distinction is driven by these same processes of economic concentration, residential segregation, and institutional separate-
ness. It also reflects the political legacy of the broader Arab-Israeli conflict,
the role of Palestinians in their quest for national identity, and the importance of Jewishness in the political shape of Israeli society and its symbols. The ethnic identity of Arab Israelis can never be fully Israeli as long
as being Israeli involves a clear and unmistakable Jewish cultural component, Jewish historical constructions, and dominant Jewish symbols.[13] The
economic integration of Israeli Arabs makes their distinctiveness sharper
and their powerlessness obvious and does not increase their social integration. Conferring political rights and welfare entitlements cannot erase
the effects of their Palestinian identity and their minority status in Israel.
The Arab citizens of Israel are likely to struggle with the conflicts of their
identity for another generation and with their unequal access to opportunities as citizens of the state. These struggles will be further tested by the
conflict relationships between Israel and Palestinians outside Israel.

These arguments suggest that convergences among ethnic groups in
some aspects of social life do not necessarily provide clues about total ethnic assimilation. Increasing similarities in family structure or educational

levels among Jews from different ethnic origins are an inadequate basis for concluding that assimilation is proceeding to eliminate ethnic communities. Ethnic communities have been redefined away from specific countries of origin toward an amalgamation of broader ethnic groups that represent new forms of ethnic differentiation. The diminished significance of Polish, Romanian, Algerian, and Tunisian ethnicity, for example, does not preclude a recombination into new ethnic categories that are specific to Israel's society and have importance as "European" and "Asian/African" Israeli communities. New ethnic divisions mark Jews off from each other and have ethnic significance only in the context of Israeli society. The conspicuous social-structural differences among Jews negate the "melting pot" response to the economic and demographic integration of ethnic populations. The resultant ethnic divisions do not imply that individuals do not move between ethnic groups or into a third ethnically neutral Israeli group. The fluidity of boundaries does not imply their absence. Ethnicity may continue to be a characteristic of populations, although it may not be an ascribed feature of each person's identity.

By the standards of ethnic assimilation, in Israel and in other pluralistic societies, the Arab Israeli distinctiveness is embedded in the social and demographic structure of the society, its values, and its political culture (C. Goldscheider 1991). Jewish and Arab residential segregation in Israel and the resultant distinctiveness and disadvantage of Israeli Arabs are unlikely to be resolved without major internal changes in the society, its institutions, values, and political system. Barring such fundamental changes in the Jewish state of Israel, the residential segregation of Arab Israelis will continue, and the consequences for socioeconomic inequalities will persist. Only local control over institutions and the development of local opportunities for socioeconomic mobility in Arab Israeli communities can reduce their disadvantaged status. How Israeli Arabs will be linked to autonomous Palestinian areas and Arab states remains unclear (see Smooha 2012 for a thoughtful analysis).

I have presented some initial answers to questions about the consequences of social and demographic changes for ethnic and religious communities in the context of nation-building in Israel. My orientation is to emphasize ethnic networks and ethnic institutions in the context of residential concentration as critical conditions wherein ethnic communities retain their salience and shape ethnic assimilation. Clearly, and for different reasons, neither the Jewish diaspora nor the Palestinian diaspora is about to join the state of Israel and Israeli society. At the end of the first decade of the twenty-first century, it is unquestionable that the relationships between external and internal developments in Israel among its diverse groups, whatever their particular nuance, will be different from those of the past.

NOTES

1. The area under Israel's administrative control included the West Bank and its population, since Gaza and Jericho came under Palestinian administration in summer 1994. The territory under Israel's administration encompassed several million Arab Palestinian residents at the end of 2013. The ongoing peace process between Israel and the Palestinians is likely to result in further administrative, political, and demographic changes over the next several years; Israel's administration of Palestinians is significantly different in 2013 than it was a decade or two earlier. The peace treaties and economic relations with Egypt and Jordan and the changing relationships with Syria will also alter Israel's regional development. For a review of the Arab-Israel conflict, see C. Goldscheider 2001b. The escalating conflict between Israel and Gaza in the first decade or so of the twenty-first century has diminished the possibility of peaceful processes.

2. There are broader areas of international relations and foreign policy between Israel and various industrialized nations in Europe and America, as well as between Third World countries and Israel. There is also an extensive literature on the Israel-Arab conflict, the Palestinian question, and the relationship of Israel to neighboring Arab states—Jordan, Egypt, Syria, and Lebanon—and other states in the region. These issues and their vast literatures address themes that extend beyond the purview of this book. I present a modest and narrow view of these issues that focuses on the major themes I have emphasized throughout.

3. A revealing illustration of how important (ideologically and nationally) Jewish communities outside Israel are to the state is the annual inclusion of data in the official *Statistical Abstract of Israel* on the "Jewish Population in the World and in Israel." These statistical data begin with the Jewish population of the world in 1882 and continue until the latest year. They include estimates of Jewish population size in the world and the percentage of Jews living in Israel. I know of no other country's statistical yearbook that includes historical and comparative materials that would parallel this statistical table. See, for example, the *Statistical Abstract of Israel*, 2013, table 2.11.

4. In the United States, the category "Jewish," therefore, includes those who define themselves as Jewish and are defined by others as Jewish. It is a voluntary

status in most Western countries. In some countries, the designation "Jewish" may be more formally noted on personal documents and, more often than not, has been the basis of discrimination and distinctiveness. Jews in Israel are automatically entitled to citizenship and are provided with a formal document indicating Jewishness by religion and nationality. Until the large number of Russians arrived, there were only marginal cases in Israel, mostly among antireligionists, involving requests to be declared Jewish by nationality (and not by religion). A small number of Jews claim that they are Jewish by religion but not by nationality (e.g., some antinational, ultraorthodox residents). But for the overwhelming majority of Israeli Jews, the difference between religious and national definitions of Jewishness is a distinction without significance.

5. I use the United States as an example to simplify the discussion. Although there are some obvious differences, there are also major similarities. For a comparative view, see C. Goldscheider and Zuckerman 1984.

6. Data on the marriage and ethnic continuity of the children and grandchildren of those currently intermarried, as they grow up and have families of their own, are not available. The need to study generational transmission of ethnicity among the intermarried was also noted in connection with interethnic marriages in Israel (see chapter 10).

7. For a very different view of issues of unity and diversity, drawing from a theological (and an Orthodox Judaic) view, see Sacks 1993. A thoroughly pessimistic view is presented by historian and Zionist David Vital (1990). I disagree with Sacks regarding the centrality of his conception of Judaism in what ought to be the "oneness" of the Jewish people. Vital misunderstands the transformation among American Jews and their power as an ethnic community and exaggerates the importance of secular nationalism in Jewish peoplehood.

8. The religious leadership of Jewish communities outside Israel has much more in common and is more likely to interact with the secular-political leadership of Israel than with the formal representatives of the religious establishment. Although some American Jewish young adults (and their parents) would place Hasidic or ultraorthodox Jews lower in their preference ranking for a "potential" spouse than non-Jews, ultraorthodox Jews are not likely to think of Conservative or Reform Jews as Jewish at all. In the view of ultraorthodox Jews in Israel, a Reform rabbi is not only not a rabbi but questionable as a Jew, and certainly not an acceptable "match" for a spouse. A Reform rabbi who is female is too exotic a creature for ultraorthodox Jews to think about!

9. As "administered territories" these areas could be negotiated about and exchanged; they were political entities under political control of the victor in a military battle. No long-term possession or control was implied, since there was a clear

recognition that control was "administrative," not ideological. In sharp contrast, "Judea, Samaria, and Gaza" are biblical names, reflecting the historic Judaic connection of these areas that were recaptured and repossessed after a long hiatus. The control is political and firmly anchored in history, religion, and legitimacy. The concept "administered territories" implies that the territory of others is administered; territory that is named by its Hebrew-Judaic origins is part of the gift of God to the Jewish people. Therefore, the switch in emphasis after 1977 was more than a name change of these parcels of land.

10. I use the official estimates of the Israeli Central Bureau of Statistics. Whether the de jure or the de facto population is counted becomes one basis for the different estimates. For alternatives, see Abu-Lughod 1983, Peretz 1986, Roy 1986, and population estimates published annually by the Central Bureau of Statistics. A different set of estimates is reviewed and presented by the Palestinian Bureau of Statistics. See its website (PCBS.org) and the website of Central Bureau of Statistics of Israel (CBS.gov.il) for the latest statistical information.

11. See the data in *Statistical Abstract of Israel*, 1993, table 27.22.

12. Ibid, table 27.41.

13. Arab Israelis cannot seriously relate to the Israel "national" anthem, which refers to the 2,000-year longing for Jewish statehood for the Jewish people "To be a free people in our land, the land of Zion, Jerusalem." National events and their symbols are infused with Judaic, religious distinctiveness (e.g., national-religious holidays such as Passover and Israeli Independence Day) and Jewish historical meaning (e.g., the Holocaust) and are annual reminders of the national cohesion of Israeli Jews and distinctive status of Arab Israelis.

Appendix
Data Sources and Reliability

For much of the evidence that I organize, review, and analyze in the book I have relied on the excellent statistical materials presented in yearbooks of the Central Bureau of Statistics of Israel (CBS) referred to as the *Statistical Abstract of Israel*. These yearly abstracts are available through the website of the CBS (www.cbs.gov .il). Often, these contain data in tabular form and charts that extend over time and among the diverse subpopulations of Israel. Usually these include ethnic/national-origin groups among Israeli Jews and religious divisions among the Arab population (Moslem, Christian, and Druze). They are based on census materials (the latest is the census of 2008 in Israel) and surveys that are conducted by the CBS. These data are the most reliable and thorough statistical materials that are available on Israel's demography and population, vital statistics, immigration, households and families, health, welfare, education, various aspects of the economy, government, and business.

In addition, there are annual labor-force surveys and surveys of special topics that are statistically organized. The Labor Force Survey is a major survey conducted regularly by the Central Bureau of Statistics among households. The survey follows the development of the labor force in Israel, its size and characteristics, as well as the extent of unemployment and other trends. These survey data contain detailed information on labor-force characteristics, age, years of schooling, type of school last attended, data on immigrants of 1990 and after. The Labor Force Survey is also a source of data on living conditions, mobility in employment, and many other topics. It is conducted on a sample of the Israeli population; quarterly data appear in the "Labour Force Surveys Quarterly" on the CBS website. As of 2012 the survey is conducted monthly.

The limitations of these data and estimates of their accuracy accompany my discussions of the data in various chapters and are presented in the publications themselves. When I refer to special research studies or summarize the conclusions of others, I cite the source and have placed the reference in the bibliography at the back of the volume. When citing statistical findings, I have without exception used the latest *Statistical Abstract of Israel*—2014 or 2013. For historical data I have relied on two previous collections of statistical data: Dov Friedlander and Calvin Goldscheider, *The Population of Israel* (New York: Columbia University Press, 1979), and Calvin Goldscheider, *Israel's Changing Society: Population, Ethnicity and*

Development (Boulder, CO: Westview Press, 2nd revised edition, 2002). One survey of special importance cited and discussed in chapter 6 is the 2009 survey conducted by the Central Bureau of Statistics on religiosity in Israel. Research by Dov Friedlander on educational inequalities and by Barbara Okun on family and fertility (both at the Hebrew University in Jerusalem) cited in several chapters also deserves special mention.

I have kept the detailed tabular materials and the charts to a minimum in this book so as not to distract the reader from the major points of the review and analysis. The few tables and charts that I have included are based on the statistical materials of the Central Bureau of Statistics of Israel.

Bibliography

Abu-Lughod, Janet. 1983. "The Demographic Consequences of the Occupation," in N. Aruru, ed., *Occupation: Israel over Palestine*. Belmont, MA: Arab-American Graduates.

Agassi, Judith. 1993. "Theories of Gender Inequality: Lessons from the Israeli Kibbutz," in Yael Azmon and Dafna Izraeli, eds., *Women in Israel*. New Brunswick, NJ: Transaction Publishers.

Alba, Richard. 1990. *Ethnic Identity: The Transformation of White America*. New Haven, CT: Yale University Press.

Alba, Richard, and Victor Nee. 2005. *Remaking the American Mainstream: Assimilation and Contemporary Immigration*. Cambridge, MA: Harvard University Press.

Al Haj, Majid. 1985. "Ethnic Relations in an Arab Town in Israel," chapter 6 in Alex Weingrod, ed., *Studies in Israeli Ethnicity*. New York: Gordon and Breach.

————. 1987. *Social Change and Family Processes: Arab Communities in Shefar A'm*. Boulder, CO: Westview Press.

————. 1992. "Soviet Immigration as Viewed by Jews and Arabs: Divided Attitudes in a Divided Country," in Calvin Goldscheider, ed., *Population and Social Change in Israel*. Boulder, CO: Westview Press.

————. 1995. *Education Empowerment and Control: The Case of the Arabs in Israel*. Albany: State University of New York Press.

Al Haj, Majid, and Elazar Leshem. 2000. *Immigrants from the Former Soviet Union in Israel: Ten Years Later*. Haifa: The Center for Multiculturalism and Educational Research.

Al Haj, Majid, and Henry Rosenfeld. 1990. *Arab Local Government in Israel*. Boulder, CO: Westview Press.

Alonso, William. 1987. "Introduction: Population North and South," in *Population in an Interacting World*. Cambridge, MA: Harvard University Press.

Amir, S. 1986. "Educational Structure and Wage Differentials in the Labor Force in the 1970's," chapter 6 in Yoram Ben-Porath, ed., *The Israeli Economy*. Cambridge, MA: Harvard University Press.

Anson, Jon. 1992. "Mortality, Ethnicity, and Standard of Living: A Minority Group Effect?" in Calvin Goldscheider, ed., *Population and Social Change in Israel*. Boulder, CO: Westview Press.

Anson, Jon, and Ofra Anson. 2001. "Death Rests a While: Holy Day and Sabbath Effects on Jewish Mortality in Israel." *Social Science and Medicine* 52:83–97.

Aran, Gideon. 1990. "From Religious Zionism to Zionist Religion: The Roots of Gush Emunim," in Calvin Goldscheider and Jacob Neusner, eds., *Social Foundations of Judaism*. Englewood Cliffs, NJ: Prentice-Hall.

Arian, Asher. 1985. *Politics in Israel: The Second Generation*. New York: Chatham House.

Arian, Asher, and Michal Shamir. 1994. *The Elections in Israel, 1992*. Albany: State University of New York Press.

Avineri, Shlomo. 1981. *The Making of Modern Zionism: The Intellectual Origins of the Jewish State*. London: Weidenfeld and Nicholson.

Avruch, Kevin. 1981. *American Immigrants in Israel*. Chicago: University of Chicago Press.

Azmon, Yael. 1990. "Women and Politics: The Case of Israel." *Women and Politics* 10: 43–57.

Azmon, Yael, and Dafna Izraeli, eds. 1993. *Women in Israel*. New Brunswick, NJ: Transaction Publishers.

Bachi, Roberto. 1977. *Population of Israel*. Jerusalem: Institute of Contemporary Jewry, The Hebrew University.

Bar-Gal, Yoram. 1986. "Arab Penetration and Settlement in Nazareth Ilit," pp. 51–64 in Arnon Sofer, ed., *Residential and Internal Migration Patterns Among the Arabs of Israel*. Monograph series on the Middle East No.4. Haifa: University of Haifa, the Jewish-Arab Center.

Bar-Yosef, Rivka. 1971. "Absorption versus Modernization," in Rueven Kahana and S. Koppelshtein, eds., *Israeli Society, 1967–1973*. Jerusalem: Academon Press.

Bar-Yosef, Rivka, and D. Padan-Eisenstark. 1993. "Role Systems under Stress: Sex Roles in War," in Yael Azmon and Dafna Izraeli, eds., *Women in Israel*. New Brunswick, NJ: Transaction Publishers.

Ben-Artzi, Yosi, and M. Shoshani. 1986. "The Arabs of Haifa, 1972–1983: Demographic and Spatial Changes," pp. 33–50 in Arnon Sofer, ed., *Residential and Internal Migration Patterns among the Arabs of Israel*. Monograph series on the Middle East No. 4. Haifa: University of Haifa, the Jewish-Arab Center.

Ben-David, Joseph. 1970. "Ethnic Differences of Social Change?" in Shmuel N. Eisenstadt, Rivka Bar Yosef, and Chaim Adler, eds., *Integration and Development in Israel*. New York: Praeger Publishers.

Ben-Moshe, Eliahu. 1989. "Marriage Squeeze and Marriage Patterns in Israel," pp. 87–96 in Uziel O. Schmelz and Sergio Dellapergola, eds., *Papers in Jewish Demography: 1985*. Jewish Population Studies 19. Jerusalem: Institute of Contemporary Jewry, The Hebrew University.

———. 1989a. "Internal Migration Processes in Israel: Demographic, Ethnic and Social Aspects." Ph.D. diss., The Hebrew University, Jerusalem.

———. 2014. "The best that can happen is that it won't be much worse." Yediot Achronot, May 1 (Hebrew).

Ben-Porath, Yoram, ed. 1986a. *The Israeli Economy*. Cambridge, MA: Harvard University Press.

Ben-Porath, Yoram. 1986b. "Diversity in Population and in the Labor Force," in idem, *The Israeli Economy*. Cambridge, MA: Harvard University Press.

Ben-Rafael, Eliezer. 1986. "The Changing Experience, Power and Prestige of Ethnic Groups in Israel: The Case of the Moroccans," in vol. 5 of Peter Medding, ed., *Israel: State and Society, 1948–1988*. Jerusalem: Studies in Contemporary Jewry, Institute of Contemporary Jewry.

Ben-Yehuda, Nachman. 1989. "The Social Meaning of Alternative Systems: Some Exploratory Notes," pp. 152–164 in Baruch Kimmerling, ed., *The Israeli State and Society: Boundaries and Frontiers*. Albany: State University of New York Press.

Berelson, Bernard. 1979. "Foreword," in Dov Friedlander and Calvin Goldscheider, *The Population of Israel*. New York: Columbia University Press.

Berglas, Eitan. 1986. "Defense and the Economy," chapter 8 in Yoram Ben-Porath, ed., *The Israeli Economy*. Cambridge, MA: Harvard University Press.

Berler, Alexander. 1970. *New Towns in Israel*. Jerusalem: Israel Universities Press.

Bystrov, Evgenia. 2012. "The Second Demographic Transition in Israel: One for All." *Demographic Research* 27:10: 261–298.

Cohen, Erik. 1977. "The City in Zionist Ideology." *Jerusalem Quarterly* 4:126–155.

Cohen, Steve. 1983. *American Modernity and Jewish Identity*. New York: Tavistock Publishers.

Danet, Brenda. 1989. *Pulling Strings: Biculturalism in Israel Bureaucracy*. Albany: State University of New York Press.

Dashefsky, Arnold, et al. 1992. *Americans Abroad: A Comparative Study of Emigrants from the United States*. New York: Plenum Press.

Dellapergola, Sergio. 1986. "Aliya and Other Jewish Migrations: Toward an Integrated Perspective," in Uziel O. Schmelz and Gad Natan, eds., *Studies in the Population of Israel*. Jerusalem: Magnes Press.

———. 1993. "Demographic Changes in the State of Israel in the Early 1990's." Jerusalem: Center for Social Policy Research.

———. 2011. "When Scholarship Disturbs Narrative: Ian Lustig on Israel's Migration Balance." *Israel Studies Review* 26(2):1–27.

———. 2013. "Demographic Trends, National Identities and Borders in Israel and the Palestinian Territory," pp. 38–62 in András Kovács and Michael L. Miller, eds., Jewish Studies VII, 2009–2011, Jewish Studies Project, Central European University, Budapest.

Deshen, Shlomo. 1990. "The Social Foundation of Israeli Judaism," pp. 212–239 in Calvin Goldscheider and Jacob Neusner, eds., *Social Foundations of Judaism*. Englewood Cliffs, NJ: Prentice-Hall.

Deshen, Shlomo, ed. 1995. *Israeli Judaism: The Sociology of Religion in Israel*. New Brunswick, NJ: Transaction Publishers.

Doron, Abraham, and Ralph Kramer. 1991. *The Welfare State in Israel*. Boulder, CO: Westview Press.

Eisenbach, Zvi. 1986. "Family Planning among the Muslim Population of Israel," pp. 1–14 in Uziel O. Schmelz and Gad Natan, eds., *Studies in the Population of Israel*. Jerusalem: Magnes Press.

———. 1989. "Changes in the Fertility of Moslem Women in Israel in Recent Years." *HaMizrach Hahadash*, pp. 86–102.

———. 1992. "Marriage and Fertility in the Process of Integration: Intermarriage among Origin Groups in Israel," in Calvin Goldscheider, ed., *Population and Social Change in Israel*. Boulder, CO: Westview Press.

Eisenbach, Zvi, Y. Hayat, P. Tzedakah, and A. Reiss. 1989. "The Inequality of Death: Socioeconomic Differentials in Israel, 1983–1986." Paper presented at the Association of Israeli Epidemiology.

Eisenstadt, Shmuel. 1954. *The Absorption of Immigrants*. London: Routledge and Paul.

———. 1969. "The Absorption of Immigrants, the Blending of Exiles, and the Problems of the Transformation of Israeli Society," in *The Integration of Immigrants from Different Countries of Origins in Israeli Society*. Jerusalem: Magnes Press.

———. 1985. *The Transformation of Israeli Society*. Boulder, CO: Westview Press.

Etzioni-Halevi, Eva, and A. Illy. 1993. "Women in Legislatures: Israel in a Comparative Perspective," in Yael Azmon and Dafna Izraeli, eds., *Women in Israel*. New Brunswick, NJ: Transaction Publishers.

Freedman, Robert, ed. 2009. *Contemporary Israel: Domestic Politics, Foreign Policy and Security Challenges*. Boulder, CO: Westview Press.

Friedlander, Dov. 1969. "Demographic Responses and Population Change." *Demography* 6:359–382.

Friedlander, Dov, Eliahu Ben-Moshe, and Yona Schellekens. 1989. "Regional Demographic Changes in Israel." Machon Yerushalayem L'Heker Yisrael, Jerusalem.

Friedlander, Dov, Eliahu Ben-Moshe, Yona Schellekens, and Carole Feldman. 1990. "Socioeconomic Change, Demographic Processes, and Population Aging in Israel's Cities and Towns: Implications for Welfare Policies." The Jerusalem Institute for Israel Studies, Research Studies No. 37.

Friedlander, Dov, Zvi Eisenbach, Eliyahu Ben-Moshe, Lilach Lion-Elmakis, Ahmad Hleihel, Shlomit Luniavski, and Dan Ben Hur. 2002a. *Changes in the Educational Attainments in Israel since the 1950s: The Effects of Religion, Ethnicity and Family Characteristics*. Research Reports. Central Bureau of Statistics, Jerusalem.

Friedlander, Dov, Zvi Eisenbach, Eliahu Ben-Moshe, Ahmad Hleihel, , Lilach Lion-Elmakis and Dan Ben-Hur. 2002b. "Matched Census Results of Education in Israel since the Fifties: Effects of Origin and Selected Characteristics, Jews and Arabs." Working paper, The Hebrew University, Department of Population Studies, Jerusalem.

Friedlander, Dov, Zvi Eisenbach, and Calvin Goldscheider. 1979. "Modernization Patterns and Fertility Change: The Arab Populations of Israel and the Israel-Administered Territories." *Population Studies* 33:239–254.

———. 1980. "Family Size Limitation and Birth Spacing: The Fertility Transition of African and Asian Immigrants in Israel." *Population and Development Review* 6 (December): 581–593.

Friedlander, Dov, and Carole Feldman. 1993. "The Modern Shift to Below-Replacement Fertility: Has Israel's Population Joined the Process?" *Population Studies* 47:295–306.

Friedlander, Dov, and Calvin Goldscheider. 1974. "Peace and the Demographic Future of Israel." *Journal of Conflicts Resolution* 18:486–501.

———. 1978. "Immigration, Social Change and Cohort Fertility in Israel." *Population Studies* 32:299–317.

———. 1979. *The Population of Israel*. New York: Columbia University Press.

———. 1984. "Israel's Population: The Challenge of Pluralism." *Population Bulletin, Population Reference Bureau* 39(2).

Friedlander, Dov, Barbara Okun, Zvi Eisenbach, and Lilach Elmakias. 2002. "Immigration, Social Change and Assimilation in Israel: The Dynamics of Educational Attainments among Jewish Ethnic Groups." *Population Studies* 56:135–150.

Friedlander, Dov, Barbara Okun, and Calvin Goldscheider. 2014. "Ethno/religious Hierarchy in Educational Achievement and Socioeconomic Status in Israel: An Historical Perspective." Manuscript.

Gavron, Daniel. 2000. *The Kibbutz: Awakening from Utopia*. Lanham, MD: Rowan Littlefield.

Gharaibeh, Fawzi A. 1985. *The Economics of the West Bank and the Gaza Strip*. Boulder, CO: Westview Press.

Ginor, Fanny. 1979. *Socio-Economic Disparities in Israel*. New Brunswick, NJ: Transaction Press.

Gitelman, Zvi. 1995. *Immigration and Identity: The Resettlement and Impact of Soviet Immigrants on Israeli Politics and Society*. Los Angeles: Wilstein Institute of Jewish Policy Studies.

———. 2012. *Jewish Identities in Post-communist Russia and Ukraine: An Uncertain Ethnicity*. New York: Cambridge University Press.

Gitelman, Zvi, ed. 2009. *Religion or Ethnicity: Jewish Identities in Evolution*. New Brunswick, NJ: Rutgers University Press.

Glazer, Nathan, and Daniel Moynihan, eds. 1975. *Ethnicity: Theory and Experience*. Cambridge, MA: Harvard University Press.

Gold, Steven, and Bruce Phillips. 1996. "Israelis in the United States." *American Jewish Yearbook*, pp. 51–101.

Goldberg, Harvey. 1977. "Introduction: Culture and Ethnicity in the Study of Israeli Society." *Ethnic Groups* 1:163–186.

Goldscheider, Calvin. 1971. *Population, Modernization, and Social Structure*. Boston: Little, Brown and Co.

———. 1974. "The Future of American Aliya," in Marshall Sklare, ed., *The Sociology of the American Jew*. New York: Behrman House.

———. 1983. "The Demography of Asian and African Jews in Israel," in Joseph B. Maier and Chaim I. Waxman, eds., *Ethnicity, Identity, and History*. New Brunswick, NJ: Transaction Books.

———. 1986a. "Family Changes and Variation among Israeli Ethnic Groups," in Steve M. Cohen and Paula Hyman, eds., *The Jewish Family: Myths and Reality*. New York: Holmes and Meier.

———. 1986b. *Jewish Continuity and Changes: Emerging Patterns in America*. Bloomington: Indiana University Press.

———. 1990. "Israel," in William J. Serow, Charles Nam, David Sly, and Robert Weller, eds., *Handbook on International Migration*. New York: Greenwood Press.

———. 1991. "The Embeddedness of the Arab-Jewish Conflict in the State of Israel: Demographic and Sociological Perspectives," pp. 111–132 in Bernard Reich and Gershon Kieval, eds., *Israeli Politics in the 1990's*. New York: Greenwood Press.

———. 2001a. "Ethnic Categorization in Censuses: Comparative Observations from Israel, Canada, and the United States," in David Kertzer and Dominique Arel, eds., *Census and Identity*. Cambridge, MA: Cambridge University Press.

———. 2001b. *The Arab-Israeli Conflict*. Westport, CT: Greenwood Press.

———. 2002. *Israel's Changing Society: Population, Ethnicity and Development*, 2nd revised edition. Boulder, CO: Westview Press.

———. 2004. *Studying the Jewish Future*. Seattle: University of Washington Press.

——. 2006. "Religion, Family, and Fertility: What Do We Know Historically and Comparatively?" pp. 41–57 in Renzo Derosas and Frans van Poppel, eds., *Religion and the Decline of Fertility in the Western World*, The Netherlands: Springer.

Goldscheider, Calvin, ed. 1992. *Population and Social Change in Israel*. Boulder, CO: Westview Press.

——. 1995. *Population, Nation-Building, and Ethnicity*. Boulder, CO: Westview Press.

Goldscheider, Calvin, and Dov Friedlander. 1983. "Religiosity Patterns in Israel." *American Jewish Yearbook* 83:3–39.

——. 1986. "Reproductive Norms in Israel," pp. 15–35 in Uziel O. Schmelz and Gad Natan, eds., *Studies in the Population of Israel in Honor of Roberto Bachi*. Jerusalem: Magnes Press.

Goldscheider, Calvin, and Frances Kobrin. 1980. "Ethnic Continuity and the Process of Self Employment." *Ethnicity* 7:256–278.

Goldscheider, Calvin, and William Mosher. 1991. "Patterns of Contraceptive Use in the United States: The Importance of Religious Factors." *Studies in Family Planning* 22:102–115.

Goldscheider, Calvin, and Jacob Neusner, eds. 1990. *Social Foundations of Judaism*. Englewood Cliffs, NJ: Prentice-Hall.

Goldscheider, Calvin, and Alan Zuckerman. 1984. *The Transformation of the Jews*. Chicago: University of Chicago Press.

Goldscheider, Frances, Eva Bernhardt, and Trude Lappegård. 2014. "Studies of Men's Involvement in the Family." *Journal of Family Issues*.

Goldscheider, Frances, and Zara Fisher. 1989. "Household Structure and Living Alone in Israel," in Frances Goldscheider and Calvin Goldscheider, eds., *Ethnicity and the New Family Economy: Living Arrangements and Intergenerational Financial Flows*. Boulder, CO: Westview Press.

Goldscheider, Frances, and Calvin Goldscheider. 1989. *Ethnicity and the New Family Economy: Living Arrangements and Intergenerational Financial Flows*. Boulder, CO: Westview Press.

——. 1994. "Leaving and Returning Home in 20th Century America." Population Reference Bureau, vol. 48 (March).

——. 1999. *The Changing Transition to Adulthood: Leaving and Returning Home*. Thousand Oaks, CA: Sage Publications.

Goldscheider, Frances, and Linda Waite. 1991. *New Families, No Families? The Transformation of the American Home*. Berkeley: University of California Press.

Gonen, Amiram. 1985. "The Changing Ethnic Geography of Israeli Cities," in Alex Weingrod, ed., *Studies in Israeli Ethnicity*. New York: Gordon and Breach.

Gordon, Milton. 1963. *Assimilation in American Life*. New York: Oxford University Press.

Grossbard-Shechtman, Shoshana, and Shoshana Neuman. 1998. "The Extra Burden of Muslim Wives: Clues from Israeli Women's Labor Supply." *Economic Development and Cultural Change* 46:491–517.

Halevi, Nadav. 1986. "Perspectives on the Balance of Payments," in Yoram Ben-Porath, ed., *The Israeli Economy*. Cambridge, MA: Harvard University Press.

Halperin-Kaddari, Ruth. 2003. *Women in Israel: A State of Their Own*. Philadelphia: University of Pennsylvania Press.

Halpern, Ben. 1961. *The Idea of the Jewish State*. Cambridge, MA: Harvard University Press.

Hartman, Harriet. 1993. "Economic and Familial Roles of Women in Israel," in Yael Azmon and Dafna Izraeli, eds., *Women in Israel*. New Brunswick, NJ: Transaction Publishers.

Hazelton, Lesley. 1977. *Israeli Women: The Reality Behind the Myths*. New York: Simon and Schuster.

Hertzberg, Arthur. 1960. *The Zionist Idea*. New York: Meridian Books.

Hertzog, Esther, Orit Abuhav, Harvey Goldberg, and Emanuel Marx, eds. 2010. *Perspectives on Israeli Anthropology*. Detroit, MI: Wayne State University Press.

Horowitz, Dan, and Moshe Lissak. 1989. "The State of Israel at Forty," vol. 5 of Peter Medding, ed., *Israel: State and Society, 1948–1988*. Jerusalem: Studies in Contemporary Jewry, Institute of Contemporary Jewry.

Inbar, Michael, and Chaim Adler. 1977. *Ethnic Integration in Israel*. New Brunswick, NJ: Transaction Books.

Israeli Central Bureau of Statistics. 1950–. *Statistical Abstract of Israel*. Various issues.

———. 2009–2010. *Special Report on Religiosity*.

Kark, J. D., G. Shemi, Y. Friedlander, O. Martin, O. Manor, and S. H. Blonheim. 1996. "Does Religious Observance Promote Health? Mortality in Secular vs Religious Kibbutzim in Israel." *American Journal of Public Health* 86(3): 341–346.

Kellerman, Aharon. 1993. *Society and Settlement: Jewish Land of Israel in the Twentieth Century*. Albany: State University of New York Press.

Keysar, Ariela. 1990. "Demographic Processes in the Kibbutzim of Israel." Ph.D. diss., The Hebrew University, Jerusalem.

Kimmerling, Baruch, ed. 1989. *The Israeli State and Society: Boundaries and Frontiers*. Albany: State University of New York Press.

Kimmerling, Baruch, and Joel Migdal. 1993. *Palestinians: The Making of a People*. New York: Free Press.

Kirschenbaum, Avi. 1992. "Migration and Urbanization: Patterns of Population Redistribution and Urban Growth," in Calvin Goldscheider, ed., *Population and Social Change in Israel*. Boulder, CO: Westview Press.

Klaff, Vivian. 1977. "Residence and Integration in Israel: A Mosaic of Segregated Groups." *Ethnicity* 4:103–121.

Klayman, Maxwell. 1970. *The Moshav in Israel: A Case Study of Institution-Building for Agricultural Development*. New York: Praeger Publishers.

Kraus, Vered, and Robert Hodge. 1990. *Promises in the Promised Land: Mobility and Inequality*. Westport, CT: Greenwood Press.

Krausz, Ernest. 1983. *Studies on the Kibbutz*. New Brunswick, NJ: Transaction Books.

Kupinsky, Shlomo. 1992. "Jewish Fertility Patterns: Norms, Differentials, and Policy Implications," in Calvin Goldscheider, ed., *Population and Social Change in Israel*. Boulder, CO: Westview Press.

Lamdany, Ruben. 1982. *Emigration from Israel*. Discussion Paper No. 8208, The Maurice Falk Institute for Economic Research in Israel, Jerusalem.

Leichtman, Mara. 2013. "From the Cross (and Crescent) to the Cedar and Back Again: Transnational Religion and Politics among Lebanese Christians in Senegal." *Anthropological Quarterly* 86:35–36.

Leshem, Elazar, and Moshe Sicron. 1999. "The Absorption of Soviet Immigrants in Israel," pp. 448–552 in *American Jewish Yearbook, 1999*. New York: American Jewish Committee.

Levy, Shlomit, Hannah Levinsohn, and Elihu Katz. 1993. *Beliefs, Observances and Social Interaction among Israeli Jews*. Jerusalem: The Louis Guttman Institute of Applied Social Research.

Lewin-Epstein, Noah, and Moshe Semyonov. 1986. "Ethnic Group Mobility in Israel's Labor Market." *American Sociological Review* 51:342–351.

———. 1992. "Local Labor Markets, Ethnic Segregation and Income Inequality." *Social Forces* 70:1101–1119.

———. 1993. *The Arab Minority in Israel's Economy: Patterns of Ethnic Inequality*. Boulder, CO: Westview Press.

Liebman, Charles, and Steve Cohen. 1990. *Two Worlds of Judaism: The Israeli and American Experiences*. New Haven, CT: Yale University Press.

Liebman, Charles, and Eliezer Don-Yehiya. 1983. *Civil Religion in Israel*. Berkeley: University of California Press.

Lustig, Ian. 2011. "Israel's Migration Balance: Demography, Politics, and Ideology." *Israel Studies Review* 26(1): 33–65.

Mandel, Neville. 1976. *The Arabs and Zionism before World War I*. Berkeley: University of California Press.

Manor, Orly, D. Jaffe, Z. Eisenbach, and Y. Numark. 2007. "The Protective Effect of Marriage on Mortality in a Dynamic Society." *Annals of Epidemiology* 17:540–547.

Matras, Judah. 1973. "Israel's New Frontier: The Urban Periphery," in Michael Curtis and Maurice Chertoff, eds., *Israel: Social Structure and Change*. New Brunswick, NJ: Transaction Books.

———. 1985. "Intergenerational Social Mobility and Ethnic Organization in the Jewish Population of Israel," in Alex Weingrod, ed., *Studies in Israeli Ethnicity*. New York: Gordon and Breach.

———. 1986. "Demographic Trends in the Population of Israel: Implications for Changing Patterns of Dependency." Discussion paper, 127–186. Brookdale Institute of Gerontology and Adult Human Development, Jerusalem.

Matras, Judah, and Gila Noam. 1987. "Schooling and Military Service: Their Effects on Israeli Women's Attainments and Social Participation in Early Adulthood." *Israel Social Science Research* 5:29–43.

Matras, Judah, Gila Noam, and M. Bar-Haim. 1984. "Israeli-Educated Men: Transition to Adulthood." Brookdale, Jerusalem. Mimeographed.

Medding, Peter, ed. 1989. *Israel: State and Society, 1948–1988*. Jerusalem: Studies in Contemporary Jewry, Institute of Contemporary Jewry.

Mizrachi, Beverly. 2013. *Paths to Middle Class Mobility among Second Generation Moroccan Immigrant Women in Israel*. Detroit, MI: Wayne State University Press.

Moore, Dalia. 1993. "Relative Deprivation in the Labor Market," in Yael Azmon and Dafna Izraeli, eds., *Women in Israel*. New Brunswick, NJ: Transaction Publishers.

Morag-Talmon, Pnina. 1989. "The Integration Process of Eastern Jews in Israeli Society, 1948–1988," in vol. 5 of Peter Medding, ed., *Israel: State and Society, 1948–1988*. Jerusalem: Studies in Contemporary Jewry, Institute of Contemporary Jewry.

Nahmias, P. 2004. "Fertility Behavior of Recent Immigrants in Israel: A Comparative Analysis of Immigrants from Ethiopia and the Former Soviet Union." *Demographic Research* 10:83–120

Nahon, Yaacov. 1987. "Dfusei Hitrahavot Hahaskalah Umivneh Hahizdomnuit Hataasukatit: Hammemad HaAdati" (Types of Educational Expansion and the Structure of Occupational Opportunities: The Ethnic Dimension). Machon Yerushalyim L'hekar Yisrael, Research Studies No. 25, Jerusalem Institute for Israel Research.

———. 1989. "Self-Employed Workers: The Ethnic Dimension." Research Studies No. 30, Jerusalem Institute for Israel Research.

Near, Henry. 1992. *The Kibbutz Movement: A History*. Vol. 1, *Origins and Growth, 1909–1939*. The Littman Library. New York: Oxford University Press.

Neuman, Shoshana. 1991. "Occupational Segregation in Israel: The Gender-Ethnicity Interaction." Bar Ilan University, Israel.

Okun, Barbara. 1997. "Family Planning in the Jewish Population of Israel: Correlates of Withdrawal Use." *Studies in Family Planning* 28:215–227.

———. 2000. "Religiosity and Contraceptive Method Choice: The Jewish Population in Israel." *European Journal of Population* 16:109–132.

———. 2004. "Insight into Ethnic Flux: Marriage Patterns among Jews of Mixed Ancestry in Israel." *Demography* 41:173–87.

———. 2013. "Fertility and Marriage Behavior in Israel: Diversity, Change and Stability." *Demographic Research* 28:457–504.

Okun, Barbara, and Dov Friedlander. 2005. "Educational Stratification among Arabs and Jews in Israel: Historical Disadvantage, Discrimination, and Opportunity." *Population Studies* 59:163–180.

Okun, Barbara, and O. Khait-Marelly. 2008. "Demographic Behavior of Adults of Mixed Ethnic Ancestry: Jews in Israel." *Ethnic and Racial Studies* 31:1357–1380

Palestine Bureau of Statistics. 1994. "Demography of the Palestinian Population in the West Bank and Gaza Strip." *Current Status Report Series*, No. 1, Ramallah, West Bank.

Peres, Yochanan, and Ruth Katz. 1991. "The Family in Israel: Change and Continuity," in Lea Shamgar-Handelman and Rivka Bar-Yosef, eds., *Families in Israel*. Jerusalem: Academon, The Hebrew University.

Peretz, Don. 1986. *West Bank: History, Politics, Society, and Economy*. Boulder, CO: Westview Press.

Peritz, Eric. 1986. "Mortality of African Born Jews in Israel," pp. 229–242 in Uziel O. Schmelz and Gad Natan, eds., *Studies in the Population of Israel*. Jerusalem: Magnes Press.

Plaut, Steve. 2014. "The Myth of Ethnic Inequality in Israel." *Middle East Quarterly* (Summer).

Plessner, Yakir. 1994. *The Political Economy of Israel: From Ideology to Stagnation*. Albany: State University of New York Press.

Rabie, Mohamed. 1988. *The Politics of Foreign Aid: U.S. Foreign Assistance and Aid to Israel*. New York: Praeger Publishers.

Rayman, Paula. 1981. *The Kibbutz Community and Nation Building*. Princeton, NJ: Princeton University Press.

Rebhun, Uzi. 2008. "A Double Disadvantage? Immigration, Gender, and Employment Status in Israel." *European Journal of Population* 24:87–113.

———. 2010. "Immigration, Gender, and Earnings in Israel." *European Journal of Population* 26:73–97.

Rebhun, Uzi, and Lev Ari Lilach. 2010. *American Israelis: Migration, Transnationalism, and Diasporic Identity*. Leiden and Boston: Brill.

Rein, Natalie. 1979. *Daughters of Rachel: Women in Israel*. London: Penguin Books.

Remennick, Larissa, ed. 2011. *Russian Israelis: Social Mobility, Politics and Culture*. London: Routledge/Taylor & Francis.

Rosen, Sherry. 1982. "Intermarriage and the 'Blending of Exiles' in Israel." *Race and Ethnic Relations* 3:79–102.

Rosenfeld, Henry. 1968. "The Contradictions between Property, Kinship, and Power, as Reflected in the Marriage System of an Arab Village," pp. 247–260 in John Peristiany, ed., *Contributions to Mediterranean Society*. The Hague: Mouton and Co.

Roy, Sara. 1986. *The Gaza Strip Survey*. Boulder, CO: Westview Press.

Sabatello, Eitan F., and Nurith Yaffe. 1988. "Israel," pp. 263–278 in Paul Saachdev, ed., *International Handbook on Abortion*. Westport, CT: Greenwood Press.

Sacks, Jonathan. 1993. *One People? Tradition, Modernity, and Jewish Unity*. London: The Littman Library of Jewish Civilization.

Schellekens, Jona, and Jon Anson. 2007. *Israel's Destiny: Fertility and Mortality in a Divided Society*. New Brunswick, NJ: Transaction Publishers.

Schmelz, Uziel O., Sergio Dellapergola, and Uri Avner. 1990. "Ethnic Differences among Israeli Jews: A New Look." *American Jewish Yearbook* 90:3–204.

Semyonov, Moshe. 1988. "Bi-Ethnic Labor Markets, Mono-Ethnic Labor Markets, Socio-economic Inequality." *American Sociological Review* 53:256–266.

Semyonov, Moshe, and Vered Kraus. 1983. "Gender, Ethnicity and Income Inequality: The Israeli Experience." *International Journal of Comparative Sociology* 24:257–272.

Semyonov, Moshe, and Noah Lewin-Epstein. 1987. *Hewers of Wood and Drawers of Water: Non-Citizen Arabs in the Israeli Labor Market*. Ithaca, N.Y.: ILR Press.

Semyonov, Moshe, and Noah Lewin-Epstein, eds. 2004. *Stratification in Israel: Class, Ethnicity and Gender*. Somerset, NJ: Transaction Publishers.

Semyonov, Moshe, and Andrea Tyree. 1981. "Community Segregation and the Costs of Ethnic Subordination." *Social Forces* 59:649–666.

Sered, Susan. 1993. "Ritual Mortality and Gender: The Religious Lives of Oriental Jewish Women in Jerusalem," in Yael Azmon and Dafna Izraeli, eds., *Women in Israel*. New Brunswick, NJ: Transaction Publishers.

Shahar, Rena. 1991. "Attitudes towards Interethnic Marriages among Israeli Youngsters," in Lea Shamgar-Handelman and Rivka Bar-Yosef, eds., *Families in Israel*. Jerusalem: Academon, The Hebrew University.

Shamgar-Handelman, Lea, and Rivka Bar-Yosef, eds. 1991. *Families in Israel*. Jerusalem: Academon, The Hebrew University.

Shapira, Anita. 2012. *Israel: A History*. Waltham, Mass. Brandeis University Press.

Shavit, Yossi. 1984. "Tracking and Ethnicity in Israel Secondary Education." *American Sociological Review* 49:210–220.

———. 1989. "Tracking and the Educational Spirit: Arab and Jewish Educational Expansion." *Comparative Education Review* 33:216–231.

———. 1990. "Segregation Tracking and Educational Attainment of Minorities: Arabs and Oriental Jews in Israel." *American Sociological Review* 55:115–126.

———. 1993. "From Peasantry to Proletariat: Changes in the Educational Stratification of Arabs in Israel," chapter 14 in Yossi Shavit and Hans-Peter Blossfeld, eds., *Persistent Inequality: Changing Educational Attainment in Thirteen Countries*. Boulder, CO: Westview Press.

Shavit, Yossi, and Vered Kraus. 1990. "Educational Transitions in Israel: A Test of the Industrialization and Credentialism Hypotheses." *Sociology of Education* 63:133–141.

Shavit, Yossi, and Ephraim Yuchtman-Yaar. 2001. "Ethnicity, Education, and Other Determinants of Self Employment in Israel." *International Journal of Sociology* (Spring): 59–91.

Shenhav, Yehouda, and Y. Haberfeld. 1993. "Scientists in Organizations: Discrimination Processes in an Internal Labor Market," in Yael Azmon and Dafna Izraeli, eds., *Women in Israel*. New Brunswick, NJ: Transaction Publishers.

Shuval, Judith. 1992. *Social Dimensions of Health: The Israel Experience*. New York: Praeger Publishers.

Smooha, Sammy. 1978. *Israel: Pluralism or Conflict*. Los Angeles: University of California Press.

———. 1983. "The Tolerance of the Jewish Majority in Israel of the Arab Minority: Comparative Perspectives," pp. 91–107 in Aluf Hareven, ed., *Is It Really Difficult to Be an Israeli?* Jerusalem: The Van Leer Jerusalem Foundation.

———. 1987. "Jewish and Arab Ethnocentrism in Israel." *Ethnic and Racial Studies* 10:1–26.

———. 1989. *Arabs and Jews in Israel*. Vol. 1. Boulder, CO: Westview Press.

———. 1990. "Minority Status in an Ethnic Democracy: The Status of the Arab Minority in Israel." *Ethnic and Racial Studies* 13:389–413.

———. 1991. *Arabs and Jews in Israel*. Vol. 2. Boulder, CO: Westview Press.

———. 2012. *Still Playing by the Rules: Index of Arab-Jewish Relations in Israel*. Jerusalem: The Israel Democracy Institute.

Smooha, Sammy, and Theodor Hanf. 1992. "The Diverse Modes of Conflict-Regulation in Deeply Divided Societies." *International Journal of Comparative Sociology* 33:26–47.

Smooha, Sammy, and Vered Kraus. 1985. "Ethnicity as a Factor in Status Attainment in Israel." *Research in Social Stratification and Mobility* 4:51–76.

Sobel, Zvi. 1986. *Migrants from the Promised Land*. New Brunswick, NJ: Transaction Books.

Sobel, Zvi, and Benjamin Beit-Hallahmi. 1991. *Tradition, Innovation, Conflict: Jewishness and Judaism in Contemporary Israel*. Albany: State University of New York Press.

Spiegel, Nina. 2013. *Embodying Hebrew Culture Aesthetics, Athletics, and Dance in the Jewish Community of Mandate Palestine*. Detroit, MI: Wayne State University Press.

Spilerman, Seymour, and Jack Habib. 1976. "Development Towns in Israel: The Role of the Community in Creating Ethnic Disparities in Labor Force Characteristics." *American Journal of Sociology* 81:781–812.

Spiro, Melford. 1979. *Gender and Culture: Kibbutz Women Revisited*. Durham, NC: Duke University Press.

Swirski, Barbara, and Marilyn Safir, eds. 1991. *Calling the Equality Bluff: Women in Israel*. New York: Pergamon.

Talmon-Garber, Yonina. 1972. *Family and Community in the Kibbutz*. Cambridge, MA: Harvard University Press.

Toren, Nina. 1993. "The Status of Women in Academia," in Yael Azmon and Dafna Izraeli, eds., *Women in Israel*. New Brunswick, NJ: Transaction Publishers.

Troen, Ilan. 2010. "Development Towns in Israel," pp. 19–37 in Zvi Zameret, Aviva Halamish, and Ester Meir-Glitzenshteyn, eds., *Development Towns*. Jerusalem: Yad Ben-Zvi.

Vital, David. 1975. *The Origins of Zionism*. New York: Oxford University Press.

———. 1982. *Zionism: The Formative Years*. New York: Oxford University Press.

———. 1987. *Zionism: The Crucial Years*. New York: Oxford University Press.

———. 1990. *The Future of the Jew: A People at the Crossroads?* Cambridge, MA: Harvard University Press.

Waxman, Chaim. 1989. *American Aliyah: Portrait of an Innovative Migration Movement*. Detroit, MI: Wayne State University Press.

———. 1991. "The Israeli-Jewish Presence in the Territories: Historical and Cultural Roots," pp. 95–110 in Bernard Reich and Gershon Kieval, eds., *Israeli Politics in the 1990's*. New York: Greenwood Press.

Weintraub, Dov, et al. 1971. *Immigrants and Social Change: Agricultural Settlement of New Immigrants in Israel*. Manchester, UK: Manchester University Press.

Wilder, Esther. 2000. "Socioeconomic and Cultural Determinants of Abortion among Jewish Women in Israel." *European Journal of Population* 16:133–162.

Yaffe, Nurith. 1976. "On Contraception and Abortion in Israel." Department of Demography, The Hebrew University.

Yaish, Meir. 2001. "Class Structure in a Deeply Divided Society: Class and Ethnic Inequality in Israel, 1974–1991." *British Journal of Sociology* 52:409–437.

Yuchtman-Yaar, Ephraim. 1986. "Differences in Ethnic Patterns of Socioeconomic Achievement in Israel: A Neglected Aspect of Structural Inequality." *Megamot* 19:393–412.

Zureik, Elia. 1979. *The Palestinians in Israel: A Study of Internal Colonialism.* London: Routledge and Kegan Paul.

Index

abortion, 149, 150, 220, 221, 222

absorption. *See* assimilation

administered territories: as community, 105–9; conflict, 106, 107, 239–46; employment, 48, 217, 241, 242; policy, 227, 243–44; population figures, 68, 106, 239–40; settlers, 105–7, 109n4, 109–10n6, 243–44; subsidies, 92, 105, 106, 109n4; term and boundaries, 16n3, 251n1, 252–53n9

African ethnicity: education and employment, 46, 48; family size, 212–13; intermarriage, 203, 204–5; mortality gap, 186–87; population and immigration figures, 27, 28, 46, 47–48. *See also* Ethiopian immigrants; Middle Eastern ethnicity

age: kibbutzim, 100; marriage, 196–98, 218, 220; religiosity, 117, 130

agriculture: Arab women, 69, 217; early immigration, 41, 83; kibbutzim, 96, 97; moshavim, 101–3; sector, 11–12; Shfar'am, 77–78; urbanization, 85, 93; West Bank, 241

agunah status, 127

Algerian immigrants, 27, 187

Arabic, 79

Arab-Israeli conflict: administered territories, 106, 107, 239–46; family size, 222; immigration, 39–40, 49, 59, 62; Jerusalem, 87–88; land use, 77, 79, 82–84, 94–95, 108; peace,

244–46; population ratio, 62, 64–66; settlers, 243–44; Six Day War (1967), 229; as unifying factor, 54

Arabs, Israeli: as community, 75–78; diversity, 22; divorce, 199; family size, 8, 28, 63, 66, 67–69, 80, 209–10, 211, 215–19; holidays, 253n13; income, 174, 217; infant mortality, 67, 180, 181–82, 192n2, 193n4, 216; internal migration, 69–70, 77; and kibbutzim, 98–99; kinship structures, 72, 78, 81n4, 217–18, 225–26n10; life expectancy, 180, 188–89; living arrangements, 200; marriage age, 196–98; mortality, 63, 67–68, 180, 188–89, 216; otherness, 22–23, 37n3; out-migration, 7, 57, 66–67; political activity, 23, 78, 79, 243; population figures, 6, 7, 27, 28, 52, 62, 64–66, 65, 80, 94; residential concentration, 63, 69–75, 78, 93–95; urbanization, 63, 69–70, 84–85, 87, 93–95. *See also* education, Arab; employment, Arab; women, Arab

Arabs, Palestinian, 48, 239–44

Argentine immigrants, 90

Ashkelon, 90

Ashkenaic ethnicity, 21, 114, 117. *See also* Western ethnicity

Asian-African ethnicity. *See* African ethnicity; Middle Eastern ethnicity

assimilation: definition of Jewish, 231–32; family size, 224; gradual,

31, 32, 53; intermarriage, 225n7,
233–34; policy, 18, 20–21, 36;
U.S., 233; Zionism, 19, 36–37n1
Austrian immigrants, 204

bagrut, 139, *159*, 159–60, 165
Balfour Declaration (1917), 37n3
bar mitzvah, 123
Be'er Sheva, 85, *86*, 90
Ben-Gurion, David, 226n11
birthplace, 20–21
birthrate, 6, 210, 215, 240–41.
    See also family size and fertility
British Mandate era, 42–43, 64
Bulgarian immigrants, 171
burials, 123, 131

cars, 13
censuses, 37n2, 255–56
Central Bureau of Statistics, xiii, 115,
    255–56
Central district, *86*, 88, 90, 103–4
children: intermarriage, 205, 207, 233;
    out-migration, 61n4; and state, 196;
    women's employment, 141–42, 145
Christian Arabs: class, 76–77;
    education, 63, 157, 158, 160; family
    size, 63, 67, 209, 215–16; figures,
    6, 28, *65*, 94; life expectancy, 180;
    marriage, 197; mortality, 63,
    180; religiosity, 128; residential
    concentration, 93, 94; women's
    employment, 217
circumcision, 123, 131
citizenship, 109n4, 230, 231, 239–40,
    243
cohabitation, 199
colonialism, 41, 71–75, 240
communities. *See* development towns;
    kibbutzim; moshavim

commuting: Arabs, 68, 69–70, 74, 80,
    217, 242; Jews, 105, 106
Conservative Judaism, 87, 127, 232,
    238, 252n8
consumption per capita, 58
contraception, 126, 149, 150, 216, 218,
    220, 221–22
conversions, 124–25, 233
country-of-origin: differentiation,
    19, 20–21, 55; employment, 167;
    family size, 212–13; figures, 26–27,
    27; income, 173; intermarriage,
    204; mortality, 182–83; residential
    concentration, 83, 89
courts, 113, 114

datiim. *See* religiosity
Declaration of Independence, 45
defense, 14, 83–84, 106, 229–30.
    See also military service
demographic themes and patterns,
    4–10, 64
dependency, Arab: administered
    territories, 239–44; family size,
    67–69, 219; mortality rates, 67–68;
    out-migration, 66; overview, 62–63;
    population ratio, 64–66; residential
    concentration, 69–75, 78, 94–95;
    women, 63, 69, 70, 71, 219; young
    adults, 69, 70, 73
dependency, young people: Arabs,
    69, 70, 73; marriage, 198, 200, 201;
    military service, 148, 153n5
deurbanization, 83
development towns, 92, 103–5, 106,
    164, 185
dietary observations, 122
discrimination. *See* socioeconomic
    inequality
divorce, 114, 126, 127, 198–99, 225n4

domestic help, 142

dress restrictions, 113

dropout rates, 164

Druze: education, 139, 158–59, 160, 161; family size, 67; figures, 6, 28, *65*, 94; infant mortality, 180; marriage, 197–98; religiosity, 128; residential concentration, 93, 94; Shfar'am, 76–77

economic development: measures, 11–14; mortality, 177–78, 192n1; population growth, 10–14, 52; Zionism, 14–15

education: administered territories, 242; development towns, 104, 164; economic development, 11, 12–13; employment, 13, 46, 48, 140–42, 154, 155–65; ethnicity, 30, 33, 46, 48–49, 53, 54, 154, 155–65, *159*, 169; family size, 67, 68, 125, 163, 214, 216; intermarriage, 205–6; marriage age, 196, 197, 218; mortality, 187; postsecondary, 157, *159*, 159–60; religiosity, 115–16, 119, 121, 125; religious education, 111, 114, 123; residential concentration, 70–71, 73–74, 94–95, 156, 164; self-employment, 171, 172, 174; urbanization, 92–93; U.S., 237, 238; vocational, 158, 164, 168; women, 13, 135, 136, 137, 138–41, 158–59, 160, 176n5. *See also* education, Arab

education, Arab: Christians, 63, 157, 158, 160; Druze, 139, 158–59, 160, 161; family size, 67, 68, 69; increase, 13, 79, 158–61, 242; lack of jobs, 72; post-secondary, 157, *159*, 159–60; women, 68, 138–40, 158–59, 161, 216, 242

Egypt, 251n1

Egyptian immigrants, 46, 162, 204

emigration. *See* out-migration

employment: administered territories, 48, 217, 241, 242; development towns, 104; education, 13, 46, 48, 140–42, 154, 155–65; ethnicity, 30, 33, 46, 48, 53, 54, 165–70, *166*; family size, 68–69, 149, 213, 216–17; informal sector, 153n3; labor quality, 12, 48; marriage, 196; military service, 146, 147; mortality, 187; moshavim, 102; out-migration, 58; part-time, 141, 142–43, 145; prestige, 168–70; religiosity, 125; residential concentration, 63, 72–74, 94–95; sectors, 12; self-employment, 170–74; temporary workers, 48, 234; urbanization, 92–93; U.S., 237, 238; women, 135–36, 140–46, 149, 151, 213. *See also* employment, Arab

employment, Arab: administered territories, 48, 217, 241, 242; family size, 68–69, 216–17; gap, 69, 94, *166*, 167, 168; residential concentration, 63, 66, 72–74, 94–95; self-employment, 171; unemployment, 174, 241; women, 68, 69, 141, 153n3, 216–17

Ethiopian immigrants, 27, 47–48, 90, 124, 191, 214

ethnicity: abortion, 150; administered territories, 107, 109–10n6; Arab class, 75–78; categories, 18–22; development towns, 103; education, 30, 33, 46, 48–49, 53, 54, 154, 155–65, *159*, 169; employment, 30, 33, 46, 48, 53, 54, 165–70, *166*; family reinforcement, 25, 29–30, 34–36; family size, 8, 28, 52, 63, 66, 67–69, 80, 196–98, 209–21;

fluidity, 24–26, 29, 31–32, 53–56; gender inequality, 136–37, 139–40, 176n5; generational transmission, 17, 20, 25, 31, 53, 91–92, 154–55; income, 173–74; infant mortality, 67, 180, 181–82, 192n2, 193n4, 216; intermarriage, 176n5, 196, 200–208, 225nn6–7, 231–32, 233–34; kibbutzim, 97, 98–99, 100–101; living arrangements, 200; marriage, 30, 176n5, 196, 200–208, 225nn6–7, 231–32, 233–34; mortality, 63, 67–68, 178, 180–92, 192n5, 214, 216; moshavim, 101–3; networks, 34–36; overview, 17–18, 26–28; policy, 18, 20–21, 22–23, 29, 30, 35; political activity, 54, 127, 153n4, 230; population figures, 6, 7, 26–28, 27, 46–48, 65; reinforcement, 25, 29–30, 32, 33–36, 54; religiosity, 117–19, 128–32; residential concentration, 30, 54, 82–83, 89–90, 91–92, 224; self-employment, 171–74; social class as, 33–34; urbanization, 89–93; women's education, 139–40, 176n5; women's employment, 141–42, 144–45; women's military service, 147

European immigrants: advantages, 54–55; distribution, 84; intermarriage, 203–4; population figures, 27, 28; return immigration, 58; waves, 43–44, 46–47. *See also* Western ethnicity

external funds, 13–14, 41, 50, 97, 228, 229, 232

family networks: Arab, 72, 78, 81n4, 217–18, 225–26n10; ethnic identity, 25, 29–30, 34–36; kibbutzim, 97;

marriage, 196–98, 200–201, 202, 208; military service, 148, 153n5; moshavim, 101; opportunities, 29; out-migration, 58; self-employment, 170–71, 172–73; women's roles, 148, 149–50

family size and fertility: abortion, 149, 150; Arabs, 8, 28, 63, 66, 67–69, 80, 209–10, 211, 215–19; education, 67, 68, 125, 163, 214, 216; employment, 68–69, 149, 213, 216–17; ethnicity, 8, 28, 52, 63, 66, 67–69, 80, 196–98, 209–21; family formation, 194–98; as internal immigration, 224, 226n11; patterns, 209–11; policy, 209, 217–18, 219–23, 226n11; population growth, 8–9, 28, 208; rates, 6, 211, 225n8; reduction, 208–23; religiosity, 116, 125–26, 214, 215, 222; U.S., 237; women's roles, 135, 149

feminization, work, 143–46

fertility. *See* family size and fertility

Filipino immigrants, 48

foreign born. *See* native vs. foreign born

foreign workers, 48, 100, 234

France, 176n3

French immigrants, 90

Friedlander, Dov, xiii, 255–56

frontier. *See* development towns; settlers

Galilee, 104

Gaza, 105–9, 244–46, 251n1. *See also* administered territories

GDP (gross domestic product), 11, 14

gender roles and inequality: Arabs, 63, 67–68, 69, 70, 71, 73, 219; education, 136, 137, 139–40, 176n5;

employment, 135–36, 143–46, 151;
ethnicity, 136–37, 139–40, 176n5;
family influence, 148, 149–50;
family size, 67–68, 69, 209, 213,
219, 222; kibbutzim, 97–98, 150–51;
marriage and divorce, 126, 127, 196;
military service, 146–48; overview,
134–38; political activity, 148–49;
religiosity, 115–16, 117, 124–29,
131, 136
generational transmission: assimilation, 31, 32; ethnicity, 17, 20,
25, 31, 53, 91–92, 154–55; family
size, 29–30, 209; religiosity, 120;
self-employment, 172–73; young
adult dependency, 69, 70, 73
German immigrants, 43, 204
Germany, 14
golah. See Jewish diaspora
Golan Heights, 93, 245
Greek Arabs, 28
Greek immigrants, 171
gross domestic product (GDP), 11, 14

Haifa, 85, 86, 88, 90
hamula system, 78, 81n4, 217–18,
225–26n10
Handlin, Oscar, 61n2
haredim: income, 174; marriage age,
198; overview, 115–16; religiosity
survey, 115–24, 118; residential
concentration, 88, 116
health care: administered territories,
241; African immigrants, 48; distribution, 30, 70–71, 94, 178, 185–86;
family size, 220; kibbutzim, 100;
mortality, 68, 181, 183–86, 188–89,
192n5
Hebrew, 54, 79
heloniim. See religiosity

holidays, 111–12, 113, 121–23, 132n1,
253n13
Holocaust refugees, 43, 44, 46
housework, 69, 125, 135–36, 144–45
housing, 13, 92–93. See also residential
concentration

identity cards, 22–23
immigration: ethnic fluidity, 53–56;
figures, 6, 43–44, 44f; first waves, 7,
41–42, 83; ideology, 15, 38–40, 41,
50, 51, 59–60, 60–61n1; illegal, 43,
45; 1948–present, 43–51; policy, 18,
20–21, 44–45, 47, 58, 59; population
growth, 8, 10, 28, 45, 51–53; quotas,
42–43, 46, 47; remigration, 49, 50;
to U.S., 39, 42–43, 49, 50, 58, 61n2,
228–29, 238. See also out-migration
imports, 14
income: Arabs, 174, 217; development
towns, 104; education, 155, 156;
ethnicity, 173–74; religiosity,
119–20, 125; self-employment, 171;
U.S., 238; women, 142, 143–44
industry, 11–12, 30, 104, 241
inequality. See education; employment;
gender roles and inequality; mortality; residential concentration
infant death, 68, 180–81
infant mortality: Arabs, 67, 180,
181–82, 192n2, 193n4, 216; family
size, 216; Jews, 67, 180, 183; location, 185, 193n4; rates, 6–7, 179, 180
institutions: ethnic diffusion, 54, 207;
ethnic reinforcement, 30, 34, 79;
gender inequality, 136–37, 148–49;
religious influence, 113–15. See also
religious institutions
internal migration, 69–70, 77, 92–93,
100, 109n3. See also commuting

Iranian immigrants, 27, 46, 47, 171
Iraqi immigrants, 27, 46, 162, 171
Israel: boundaries, 16n3; foreign aid
    to, 14; history and overview, 1–4;
    snapshot, 6–8
Israeli Mobility Study, 158
Israel Longitudinal Mortality Study,
    187

Jericho, 239, 251n1
Jerusalem, 85–88, *86*, 90, 94, 105
Jewish diaspora: assimilation, 19;
    economic support, 13–14, 41, 50,
    97, 228, 229, 232; interdependency
    with U.S., 227–30, 231–39, 251n3
Jewishness, defining: and diaspora,
    230–39, 251–52n4, 252n8; Jewish
    ethnicities, 19–22; Law of Return
    (1950), 124; political parties, 127,
    230; religious institutions, 115,
    124–25, 230, 235, 252n8
Jordan, 86, 105, 241, 251n1
Judea. *See* administered territories

kibbutzim: as community, 96–101;
    migration, 100, 109n3; mortality,
    187–88; secularization, 111–12;
    women, 97–98, 150–51
kinship. *See* family networks
Knesset, 148–49, 231

Labor Force Survey, 255
Labor party, 98
land confiscations, 77, 79
Lau, David, 114
Law of Return (1950), 45, 124, 230
Libyan immigrants, 46, 187
life-course: community networks, 35;
    ethnicity, 24–25; religiosity, 121,
    130–31; women's employment, 141

life expectancy, 7, 179–80, 183, 188–89
Likud party, 98
living arrangements, 69, 199–200

marriage: age, 196–98, 218, 220;
    Arab-Israeli, 225n6; civil, 123,
    131; ethnic reinforcement, 30, 78;
    family size, 125; interethnic, 176n5,
    196, 200–208, 225nn6–7, 231–32,
    233–34; mortality rates, 196; over-
    view, 194–96; political parties, 127;
    religious control, 114, 125, 126
Marx, Karl, 224
masortiim. See religiosity
Middle Eastern ethnicity: abortion,
    150; administered territories,
    107, 109–10n6; development
    towns, 103; disadvantages, 54–55;
    distribution, 84; education, 46, 139,
    156–65, *159*, 176n5; employment,
    46, 141–42, *166*, 166–70, 171–74;
    family size, 210, 211, 212–13, 220;
    figures, 7, 27, 28, 43–44, 46, 47, 53;
    gender inequality, 137; income,
    173–74; intermarriage, 203–8;
    living arrangements, 200; mortality,
    182–85, 186–87; moshavim, 101–3;
    religiosity, 117–18, *118*, 123; term,
    21; urbanization, 85, 89–90; and
    U.S. Jews, 237–38; women's military
    service, 147
migration. *See* immigration; internal
    migration
military service: deaths, 181;
    employment, 146, 147; family size,
    213; kibbutzim, 98; marriage, 197;
    out-migration, 58; parental support,
    148, 153n5; pluralism, 54; religious
    influence, 113; women, 146–48
minority status, 15, 19, 23, 40, 59–60, 65

Moroccan immigrants, 27, 46, 171, 187, 204

mortality: administered territories, 241; Arabs, 63, 67–68, 180, 188–89, 216; economic development, 177–78, 192n1; ethnicity, 63, 67–68, 178, 180–92, 192n5, 214, 216; family size, 216; marriage, 196; overview and patterns, 177–82; policy, 177–78, 181, 183–85; rates, 6–7, 8–9; religiosity, 187–88; residence, 178, 185–86, 188–89; young adults, 181. *See also* infant mortality

moshavim, 101–3, 106

Moslems: class, 76–78; contraception, 216, 218; education, 139, 157, 158–59, 160, 161; family size, 67–68, 209–10, 211, 215–19; income, 217; infant mortality, 67, 180, 181–82, 192n2; living arrangements, 200; marriage age, 196–98, 218; population figures, 6, 7, 27, 28, 62, 65, 94; religiosity, 128–31, 129, 215; residential concentration, 93, 94; standard of living, 217; term, 16n1

nationalism: Arab, 43, 59; assimilation, 20, 36; British Mandate, 43; holidays, 122; immigration ideology and policy, 15, 38–40, 41, 44–45, 50, 51, 59–60, 60–61n1; kibbutzim, 96–97; secular, xii, 60, 252n7; symbols and anthem, 79, 253n13

native vs. foreign born: education, 139, 156–57, 158, 159, 160–61, 162; employment, 166, 167, 170; ethnicity as cultural, 32; figures, 7, 26, 27, 28; gender gap, 139; intermarriage, 206

natural increase, 8, 28, 52, 66

Negev, 103

networks: employment, 145, 147; ethnicity as community, 34–36; intermarriage, 207. *See also* family networks

nonfamily living, 199–200

non-Israeli Jews. *See* Jewish diaspora; United States

non-Jewish Israelis: Russian immigrants, 23, 48, 234; temporary workers, 48, 234. *See also* Arabs, Israeli

North American immigrants, 27. *See also* Western ethnicity

Northern district, 90, 93, 94, 103

observation, religious. *See* religiosity

Okun, Barbara, xiii, 206, 256

"oneness," 235–39, 252n7

one-person households, 199–200

one state solution, 240, 245

Orthodox Judaism: defining Jewishness, 115, 124–25, 230, 235, 252n8; dominance, xii, 113–14, 127, 238; gender inequality, 115–16, 126–27; intermarriages, 234; U.S. tensions, 233–35, 238, 252n8

out-migration: Arabs, 7, 57, 66–67; development towns, 104–5; ethnic reinforcement, 30; rates and reasons, 56–59, 61n4; Russian immigrants, 49, 50, 57

Palestine, 40–43, 59. *See also* administered territories; Arabs, Palestinian

Palestinian Israelis. *See* Arabs, Israeli

parents, 120, 130, 148, 153n5. *See also* family size and fertility

partition, 80

peace, 244–46

phylacteries, 122

policy: administered territories, 227, 243–44; development towns, 103; employment, 145, 170; ethnicity, 18, 20–21, 22–23, 29, 30, 35; family size, 209, 217–18, 219–23, 226n11; immigration, 18, 20–21, 44–45, 47, 59; kibbutzim, 99; mortality, 177–78, 181, 183–85; moshavim, 101–3; population distribution, 107–8; settlers, 243–44

Polish immigrants, 27, 43, 162

political activity and parties: Arabs, 23, 78, 79, 243; ethnicity, 49, 54, 127, 153n4, 230; immigration activity, 51; kibbutzim, 98; religious, 111, 116–17, 127, 230; terrorism, 229–30; women, 148–49

population: administered territories, 68, 106, 239–40; Arabs, 6, 7, 27, 28, 52, 62, 64–66, 65, 80, 94; development towns, 103–4; distribution, 9–10, 82–84, 86, 88–89, 107–8; economic development, 10–14; by ethnicity, 6, 7, 26–28, 27, 46–48, 65; increase, 8, 10, 28, 45, 51–53, 52, 66; kibbutzim, 99–100; moshavim, 102; ratio, 28, 62, 64–66, 68; snapshot, 6–8; urbanization, 9–10, 84–95, 86

postsecondary education, 157, 159, 159–60

poverty, 90, 174

prayer, 122

quotas, 42–43, 46, 47

Rabbinates. See religious institutions

Reform Judaism, 87, 127, 232, 238, 252n8

refugees, 43, 44–45, 46, 48

religion as ethnic differentiation, 22–23

religiosity: administered territories, 107; Arabs, 128–31, 129, 215; development towns, 104–5; ethnicity, 117–19, 128–32; family size, 116, 125–26, 214, 215, 222; gender and, 115–16, 117, 124–29, 131; kibbutzim, 97; marriage age, 198, 199; mortality, 187–88; political parties, 111, 116–17, 127, 230; ritual observance, 120, 121–24; survey, 115–28, 118; terms, 115–16; U.S., 133n7, 238

religious institutions: administered territories, 239; definition of Jewish, 115, 124–25, 230, 235, 252n8; ethnicity, 21; gender inequality, 126–27, 148–49; Jerusalem, 86–87; power and rise of, xii, 111, 113–15, 127, 238

religious/secular tensions: immigration, 23, 49, 56; institutional power, xii, 113–15, 127, 238; overview, xii, 112–13; survey suggestions, 123–24, 131–32; with U.S., 233–35, 238, 252n8

relocation. See internal migration

remigration, 49, 50

residential concentration: Arabs, 63, 69–75, 78, 93–95; development towns, 104; education, 70–71, 73–74, 94–95, 156, 164; employment, 63, 72–74, 94–95; ethnicity, 30, 54, 82–83, 89–90, 91–92, 224; haredim, 88, 116; health care, 70–71, 94, 185–86; mortality, 178, 185–86, 188–89; urbanization, 9, 89–95

restitution payments, 14

return immigration, 58

ritual observances, 117, 120, 121–24, 131

Romanian immigrants, 27, 48, 162

Russian and Soviet immigrants: fertility, 214; figures, 6, 27, 46–47; intermarriage, 204; Jewishness, 124; out-migration, 49, 50, 57; religiosity, 23, 48, *118*, 120, 121, 123, 234; residential concentration, 90; self-employment, 171, 172; U.S., 229, 238; waves, xi–xii, 44, 46–47, 48–50

Sabbath, 113, 122, 123

Sacks, Jonathan, 252n7

Samaria. *See* administered territories

segregation. *See* residential concentration

self-employment, 170–74

separation of religion and state, 123, 131, 238

Sephardic ethnicity, 21, 114, 117. *See also* Middle Eastern ethnicity

settlers, xii, 105–7, 109n4, 109–10n6, 241, 243–44

Shfar'am, 76–78

Sinai, 105

Six Day War (1967), 229

socialism, 96–97

socioeconomic inequality: administered territories, 239–44; among Arabs, 76–78; among immigrants, 49–50, 53–55; development towns, 104–5, 164; ethnicity theory, 33–34; family size, 67; mortality, 68, 188–89; overview, 29, 154–55; persistence, 34, 154–55. *See also* education; employment; gender roles and inequality; mortality; residential concentration

socioeconomics: administered territories, 105, 106, 107; ethnicity theory,

33–34; family size, 217–18, 222–23; *hamula* system, 72, 78; immigration policy, 20; indicators, 11 14; intermarriage, 206; kibbutzim, 97–98, 99, 100; moshavim, 102

Southern district, *86*, 88, 90, 103

Soviet Union immigrants. *See* Russian and Soviet immigrants

standard of living: Arab, 69, 71, 79, 217; economic growth, 10, 13; life expectancy, 188–89; out-migration, 58

Statistical Abstract of Israel, xiii, 251n3, 255–56

stratification. *See* socioeconomic inequality

subsidies: administered territories, 92, 105, 106, 109n4; development towns, 103, 106; employment and industry, 170; family size, 217–18; immigrants, 47, 48–49; internal migration, 92

suburbanization, 9, 87, 90

Sunnis, 28

Sweden, 9

synagogues, 113, 122

Syria, 245, 251n1

technology, xii, 135, 175

Tel Aviv, 85–88, *86*, 90, 109–10n6

temporary workers, xii, 48, 234

territories. *See* administered territories

terrorism, 229–30, 244–45

Thai immigrants, 48

total fertility rate, 211, 225n8

Tunisian immigrants, 27, 46, 187

Turkish immigrants, 204

ultraorthodox Jews. See *haredim*

unemployment, 119, 174, 241

United Kingdom immigrants, 90

United States: assistance from, 14; defining Jewishness, 231–32, 233, 251–52n4, 252n8; immigration from, 46–47, 50, 90; immigration to, 39, 42–43, 49, 50, 58, 61n2, 228–29, 238; interdependency with, 228–30, 231–39, 251n3; intermarriage, 233; parental support, 153n5; religiosity, 133n7, 238; Zionism alternative, 60, 234. *See also* Western ethnicity

urbanization: Arabs, 63, 69–70, 84–85, 87, 93–95; deurbanization, 83; ethnicity, 89–93; population, 9–10, 84–95, *86*

Vital, David, 252n7
vocational education, 158, 164, 168

water, 241
Weizmann, Chaim, 81
welfare services: African immigrants, 48; assimilation, 20; ethnic reinforcement, 30; family size, 209, 217–18, 220; mortality, 183–85; strain on, 53–54
West Bank: birth and death rates, 240–41; employment, 74; Jews, xii, 105, 109n4, 239; peace process, 244, 251n1. *See also* administered territories
Western ethnicity: abortion, 150; administered territories, 107, 109–10n6; education, 156–65, *159*; employment, *166*, 166–70, 171–74; family size, 209–11, 212–13; figures, 7, 43–44, 46–47, 53; gender inequality, 136; income, 173–74; intermarriage, 203–8; kibbutzim, 100–101; living arrangements, 200; mortality, 182–85, 186–87; religiosity, *118*, 118–19, 125; residential concentra-

tion, 89–90; term, 22; urbanization, 85; women's employment, 141–42; women's military service, 147
women: education, 13, 135, 136, 138–41, 158–59, 160, 176n5; employment, 135–36, 140–46, 149, 213; kibbutzim, 97–98, 150–51; life expectancy, 179–80, 188–89; military service, 146–48; politicians, 148–49; rabbis, 238, 252n8; religiosity, 125, 131; U.S., 237. *See also* family size and fertility; gender roles and inequality; women, Arab
women, Arab: dependency, 63, 67–68, 69, 70, 71, 73, 219; education, 68, 138–40, 158–59, 161, 216, 242; employment, 68, 69, 141, 153n3, 216–17, 241; life expectancy, 188–89; marriage, 197–98; religiosity, 131. *See also* family size and fertility

Yemenite immigrants, 27, 162, 171, 183, 204
Yiddish, 236
Yosef, Yitzhak, 114
young adults: dependency, 69, 70, 73, 198, 200, 201; living arrangements, 69; marriage, 194–96, 197, 198, 200, 201; mortality, 181

Zefat, 90
Zionism: administered territories, xii, 106, 107; assimilation, 19, 36–37n1; distribution, 82–84, 107–8; economic development, 14–15; ethnicity, 19–20; family size, 209, 220, 221, 222, 226n11; ideology, 15, 38–39, 40, 41, 50, 51, 59–60; intermarriage, 203, 225n7; kibbutzim, 96–98; moshavim, 102; nationalism, 43; secular, 111–12, 132n1